Advance Praise for

Chicken Lips, Wheeler-Dealer, and the Beady-Eyed M.B.A

An Entrepreneur's Wild Adventures on the New Silk Road

The most honest, insightful entrepreneur's memoir I've ever read. Today, it seems that everyone who undertakes a business venture is deemed an entrepreneur. Frank Farwell is one of the few who deserved and earned the title. *Chicken Lips* strips away the prevailing romantic illusions about entrepreneurship and provides an honest in-depth account of the WinterSilks story. Every businessperson or prospective entrepreneur can benefit from the lessons Farwell learned on the new Silk Road.

Bill Pinkovitz
Professor, University of Wisconsin-Extension
Former Director, Wisconsin Small Business Development Center

The reader sees here the link of the retail supply chain to China in a far more revealing story of complexity and personal risk than any Harvard Business School case. Farwell tells the gripping story of a commercial chess game in which the opposing pieces are unknown in number and in strength. He adds the story of bankers willing to buy rotten mortgages but reluctant to lend to the entrepreneur with emerging but delicate value.

John Balkcom
President Emeritus, St. John's College, Santa Fe
Former Partner, Booz Allen & Hamilton

I wish I had this book when I was teaching management and marketing and counseling small business owners. Farwell's story is based on first-hand experience and reads like a suspense novel. It covers target market, product mix, pricing, promotion, and distribution; planning, organization, and leadership; perseverance, adaptability to change, crisis management, watching the numbers, developing mentor relationships. . . . Name the issue and it is here, in a fast-paced, humorous style.

Allen Raymond
MPA, Princeton University, Politics and Economics
Former Instructor, U.S. Military Academy

As a business school professor, I can testify that we are now far better prepared to help budding entrepreneurs than when Frank started his business 30 years ago. But as a former entrepreneur, I can testify that nothing has changed. It's all there—the euphoric highs, the despairing lows, the pressures on the entrepreneur's family, and the sense of personal loss when the company is finally not yours any more. Entrepreneurs past and present everywhere will recognize themselves in Frank's story.

Patrick Turner
Affiliate Professor of Entrepreneurship
INSEAD Asia Campus

If you are considering a jump from the uncertain world of corporate employee to starting a business of your own, this book will encourage you while also serving as a cautionary tale. Farwell tells his story in a compelling and humorous fashion, taking you through the sometimes-harsh reality of entrepreneurship: people issues, personal sacrifices, international disasters, cash flow crises, evolving business processes, leadership challenges and financial intricacies. In the end, his passion for having his own business— and the desire to avoid being an employee—is the force that allows him to emerge victorious.

Dr. Deborah Streeter
Bruce F. Failing Sr. Professor of Personal Enterprise
and Small Business Management,
The Dyson School of Applied Economics and Management,
Cornell University

This book is required bedtime reading for every budding entrepreneur. At the end of a long hard day of having many things go wrong and a few things go right, it's reassuring to know that success is possible and that you are not the first to follow the often zigzagging trail a growing business follows.

David Ketchum
President, Asia Pacific, Bite Communications

CHICKEN LIPS, WHEELER-DEALER, AND THE BEADY-EYED M.B.A.

AN ENTREPRENEUR'S WILD ADVENTURES ON THE NEW SILK ROAD

CHICKEN LIPS, WHEELER-DEALER, AND THE BEADY-EYED M.B.A.

AN ENTREPRENEUR'S WILD ADVENTURES ON THE NEW SILK ROAD

Frank Farwell

Obsessed founder and former president of WinterSilks
(www.wintersilks.com)

WILEY

John Wiley & Sons (Asia) Pte. Ltd.

Other Wiley Editorial Offices

John Wiley & Sons, 111 River Street, Hoboken, NJ 07030, USA

John Wiley & Sons, The Atrium, Southern Gate, Chichester, West Sussex, P019 8SQ,
    United Kingdom

John Wiley & Sons (Canada) Ltd., 5353 Dundas Street West, Suite 400, Toronto, Ontario,
    M9B 6HB, Canada

John Wiley & Sons Australia Ltd., 42 McDougall Street, Milton, Queensland 4064, Australia

Wiley-VCH, Boschstrasse 12, D-69469 Weinheim, Germany

Library of Congress Cataloging-in-Publication Data

ISBN 978–0–470–82866–3 (Hardcover)
ISBN 978–0–470–82868–7 (ePDF)
ISBN 978–0–470–82867–0 (Mobi)
ISBN 978–0–470–82869–4 (ePub)

Typeset in 11/13pt ITC Garamond Light by MPS Limited, a Macmillan Company
Printed in Singapore by Saik Wah Press Pte. Ltd.
10 9 8 7 6 5 4 3 2 1

To Sarah

. . . and to Dick Norgord, Bob Beach, Dan Schwartz,
Rad Hastings, John Jeffery;
and in memory of Bob Barth and Smiling Dan.

Contents

PART 1

Building and Blundering

*E*ven though it's been more than 20 years, I still can't believe it's really over. Not a week goes by that I don't think of her and our journey; sometimes I awake at 3:00 A.M., sweating and trembling, with some nightmare of deadlines and mishaps from the old days.

But it must truly be done with, because on this spectacular night, looking through my tent screen at the dying campfire and watching a cold, clear sky full of stars—well, I feel real freedom. There's no other feeling like it—especially when a person is up here on the edge of the big, magical lake, in the richest cradle of boreal forest and granite-studded coast between Labrador and Alaska's Glacier Bay. I savor every minute, breathing the sweetness of cedar and balsam by the shore.

When I say "her," I am referring to my former business. It's thanks to her that I'm free and able to be up here in God's country. Now, you might think that talking about a business is a stupid thing to do when I'm unshaven and happy, just me and my canoe under the cloud-dusted cold dome of a northern night sky, where stars peep out of the clear blackness like tiny silver candies on a dark chocolate cake. And you'd be right.

Except for this: Although a business can eventually offer the time and resources to take its caretaker to a new life, close to 95 percent of business start-ups fail within the first 10 years, according to the U.S.

Small Business Administration and other research groups. The winner's circle is an elusive 5 percent.

Despite these odds, entrepreneurs keep jumping off the cliffs of job security like a bunch of intoxicated lemmings, expecting to find some new elixir in the sea below. Usually only unforgiving rocks await them at the bottom. Even so, these leaps for freedom create new businesses like nothing else. It must be the human spirit, desperate to get out.

Back in 1979, I too wanted to get out—out of the tedious routine of corporate employment, that is. I needed to cut loose emotionally, financially, the whole enchilada. I had heard about the 95-percent failure rate but, damn, I didn't want some statistician's number standing in my way. So I just ignored it.

Clueless, I too took the leap, and the adventure began. It was a rough ride in the early years; there wasn't a boneheaded blunder I didn't make. But things got figured out and, well, my family lives by the greatest lake of them all now—the giant, clear belly of God. There is hardly a better place to sail, paddle, cross-country ski, or raise a child.

As years have passed into decades, I've realized there were plenty of entrepreneurs who had gone solo, as I had, yet few of them knew how to share what they had learned. It would be a crying shame for anyone to endure the hell I went through, so I figured I'd tell my tale, share a few laughs, and maybe help others' journeys to freedom become a whole lot easier.

You be the judge.

1

Cigar Butts and Newspaper Junkies

If you had told me 30 years ago that knitted silk turtlenecks and long johns would change my life, well, I would have written you off as a lunatic and run the other way. But chance and fate are strange, powerful forces. Match them with a young, fire-in-the-belly entrepreneur, and big things can happen.

That's assuming a person is willing to quit working for someone else and go for it. To do that, you've got to be a brave clairvoyant, or just plain nuts. Me? I'd say I was the latter.

Back in the hot days of late summer 1979, I hadn't fully realized it yet, but I was a complete, utter misfit of an employee, regardless of the job or industry that proffered a paycheck. I was either mediocre or bored out of my mind. Maybe both.

But when I quit gainful employment at 28 to become an entrepreneur, all the lights on my cranial circuit boards suddenly lit up and my spirit went off like a Roman candle on a clear moonless night. New life surged into my soul along with a dream of financial, professional, and spiritual freedom that gathered steam as the months of working for myself rolled by.

The next 11 years were off-the-charts demanding, way too exhilarating, just occasionally fun, and sometimes scary as hell. But they were more fascinating and profitable than working anywhere else. I got to plumb the sweet depths of American opportunity the old-fashioned way, playing the chess game of a lifetime.

Fear was a good motivator: Soon after the launch, my wife and I started running out of our savings. Despite my newfound energy, M.B.A. coursework, and subsequent reading and studying, I realized I was just another start-up greenhorn who had paddled himself into the dangerous Class V rapids of entrepreneurship.

Unforgiving economic wilderness, no compass, little remaining food, dangerous forces all around. Not good.

This narrative relates my adventure of starting what became the WinterSilks catalog (www.wintersilks.com). The sequence of mishaps and recoveries gives a living lesson on how to, as well as how not to, go out on one's own. Its real-life lessons are mixed with the often ridiculous ha-ha's of the day-to-day struggles along the way. It's a story for our staggered and slowly recovering global economy, in which the employment landscape has become an increasingly unpredictable playing field that can viciously shed salaried and hourly workers as if they were fleas on an intolerant beast. Knowing how to create your own job is more critical than ever.

I won't hide the fact that I got my tail kicked plenty of times. But persistence and common sense are amazing, compounding energizers. As soon as I figured out how to win with the cards that were dealt, well, life changed. My little company took off like a streak of aurora borealis. We had cash flow and profits aplenty, so once-flinty bankers opened up the floodgates to credit. Great people became key employees and managers, taking various loads off my back. We made the *Inc.* 500 list in 1986, 1987, and 1988, and we were co-winner of the 1990 first-place gold medal from the *Catalog Age* American Catalog Awards, apparel division. I felt like a Mississippi riverboat king with a pocketful of fresh cigars, a growing pile of chips on the table, and a family at home that would never have to worry or go hungry again.

Quitting corporate America to work for myself turned the tables of my life, filling me with passion, purpose, and empowerment. It was a precious reawakening from the tired-eyed, workaday commuter I had become.

I took the first steps over three decades ago, in the midst of a dark recession. As the years passed, I have come to realize that few people understand start-ups—even though they're the cornerstone of job formation in every economy. So I said to myself, *hey, I should tell my story, my entrepreneur's tale*. Otherwise I'd be complicit with those lame-brained, pork-spewing big-spenders in Washington who claim *they're* the ones who create jobs. That's enough to make any self-respecting company owner pull over to the side of the road and puke.

So let me take you back to dewy-eyed Day One, where you can see for yourself how somebody like you or me can tread water through the "normal life" we are all expected to settle for, sniff out a little wisdom here and there along the way, and then break free to start the first sparks of a small business that one day can spectacularly catch fire. You never know—making the leap may give you happier work than you've ever known before. And if you hang in there, you might end up with a piece of a Kansas rainbow. Not to mention a bit of the gold that comes with it.

If you or a friend or loved one are a victim of layoffs or downsizing—or if you're still employed but unhappy, feeling lost in the maelstrom of office politics and bureaucratic decision-making—this story is for you. With a little reeducation, you can leave behind The Land of Modest Paychecks and Walking Dead. This book can start your journey.

My search for fulltime employment after college began in October 1973, in rural, east-central Vermont, and led to a seven-year foray into journalism. The first two years in Vermont provided valuable early career scars, especially for an entrepreneur. It was a template of experience without which I could never have envisioned and carried out the successes of later years.

It was the era of long sideburns and ridiculous bell-bottom pants, Vietnam, gas-guzzling behemoth cars, Nixon, Watergate, Woodward and Bernstein and their groundbreaking reporting for the *Washington Post*—and the subsequently fashionable status of newspaper reporting.

The craving for a newspaper job seized me, and I flaunted my thin resume of published college newspaper and C-grade small magazine articles around New York, Chicago, and New England, to no avail. Publishers large and small turned me down with little ceremony, as if swatting a slow-moving mosquito. Retreating to my great Aunt Hilda's cottage in Norwich, Vermont, I read the local paper, the *Valley News*, by the warmth of her fireplace. The next day, I wandered into its offices across the Connecticut River in Lebanon, New Hampshire and made a spur-of-the-moment inquiry.

"No openings," a harried secretary replied without breaking her impressive 85-word-per-minute stride on a slick new electric typewriter.

"Can I leave a resume?"

"We get tons. We'll just throw it out."

She exhaled a robust cloud of cigarette smoke and motioned toward stacks of resumes on a row of old metal file cabinets. Then she went back to her typewriter.

I turned to go, but before I reached the door a fellow with fuzzy muttonchops popped around the edge of the newsroom door, chewing on a pizza slice.

"Get down to the *Daily Eagle*," he called across the room. "Just hadda fight in the newsroom. Reporter's out of a job."

The rocket-fingered secretary slowed to 45 words per minute and repeated the news, in case I was too dense to appreciate it.

"Get thee to Claremont."

"Where's that?"

"South. Half an hour."

A break at last! I froze with excitement. *Thanks*, I mouthed to the newsroom guy.

Racing southbound on a narrow, two-lane highway, I steered with my knees while I opened the New Hampshire road map until it covered both front seats.

"Claremont," I muttered. "Why haven't I heard of Claremont?"

Twenty-four minutes later, my car sat smoldering in front of the *Daily Eagle* building. I burst inside at precisely the moment a tired-looking mustachioed man with a sour look on his face reached the bottom of the stairs from the newsroom.

"I heard you got a job opening," I blurted out.

He introduced himself as Andy, the editor-in-chief. He eyed me up and down, taking in my hopeful smile and outstretched resume. He hesitated thoughtfully, no doubt weighing the value of time and convenience. Then he said, "Walk with me to the Moody."

I noted that Claremont, a paper mill town, had aged ungraciously. It looked sad and withered, its streets lined with empty, boarded-up buildings with cracked and taped windows. The Moody Hotel, Andy's after-work watering hole, appeared to have been last remodeled about the time of the Spanish-American War. I sensed it might collapse at any moment.

While we waited for drinks, Andy scanned my meager collection of published clippings.

Time, place, and circumstance can be powerful. Two cold mugs of beer later, I had a job. On January 14, 1974, I started as a cub reporter for $120 a week.

The paper had 7,000 paid subscribers and a staff of 30-something, including a one-armed, Vietnam vet circulation manager who gazed with unrestrained animosity at the six long-haired reporters and editors who populated the newsroom. Andy, a refugee from a New York ad agency, stashed bottled beer in the photo lab's icebox where I developed film every morning.

So there it was: a broken-down town, underpaid work, and long hours—a storybook first newspaper job. After my first six months as a reporter, working 50 to 60 hours a week, Andy took me aside. "I'm raising you to $125," he said, as grandly as if he were sending me to Paris with a fat expense account. He pumped my hand enthusiastically. It felt like I had won a mini-lottery.

At the *Daily Eagle,* the technology mirrored the late stages of the Industrial Revolution. United Press International and Associated Press teletypes in the *Eagle* building tied us to the outside world, and when a story broke those teletypes came to life with a sudden, berserk thumping energy. As the teletype heads hammered out barely legible news of the day on worn-out ink ribbons, our second-floor offices with their slanted, unfinished hardwood floors and aged plaster walls shook ominously. Sometimes it felt like the Luftwaffe had come back to life and was carpet-bombing one of the poorest, most nondescript townships in the Granite State.

Before anything went to press, the *Eagle's* numerous typesetters and pressmen had to do their handwork, as well as set up the engraving machine for every photo illustration. Every day, after the managing editor—a slight, brainy, long-haired fellow—approved manuscript copy in the newsroom, the copy went into a wooden box in a dumbwaiter sort of device and was transported by a vertical clothesline pulley system to the typesetting room below the newsroom. First, the pressroom clerks keyed in every letter. The aroma of melted, lead-based metal wafted up through the copy chute, steaming the single-pane windows on winter mornings. Then typesetters inserted the resultant lines of metal type into a flat wooden printer's chase, one by one. Once the chase was packed full of type, a machine pressed a pliable, rubber-like blanket over it. The blanket was then bound to cylinders on the huge printing press in the basement. The blanket's material repelled ink, except where the lead type and photo engravings had made indentations.

One day a French-Canadian typesetter—too drunk and hung over to handle the last-moment volume of deadline-bound copy coming down the chute—sent the copy back up, growling after it: "Use eet t'morrow or trow 'er out. Nobuddy'll miss this shee-it!"

The managing editor—who stood about five foot five and weighed maybe 130 pounds dripping wet—hollered back down the chute, "It's about Nixon, hot off the wires. He got pinned to Watergate. Run the story, you son of a bitch!"

"*Nee*-xon who?" The typesetter's voice echoed back up the tunnel, followed by a deep, provocative laugh that rattled the wooden box.

The managing editor stuck his head into the tunnel. "Nixon's done for!" he shouted. "So are you unless you get off your ass and set the type!"

Andy looked up from editorial-page copy that coughed sporadically out of his manual typewriter. The publisher left his corner office and walked ceremoniously into the editorial offices. It was five minutes until our press deadline, but the French-Canadian typesetter would not be appeased. He hollered a new stream of obscenities up the chute and went home to work on his snowmobile.

A few months later, in June of 1975, the *Daily Eagle* invested in new-fangled computer-driven, photographic-based cold type and not long afterward all but two of the typesetters were laid off.

That August I left the *Daily Eagle* and took a month to ride my bicycle through the labyrinth of central Vermont's unpaved back roads and pick wild berries. I was living happily on a shoestring, but uncertain what to do next. Clearly newspapering was not going to produce riches—just long hours and miserly pay. One night in my little rented mountainside house—which I shared with arborist and professional tree climber Leo Maslan and his dog, Spike—I got a call.

"Windsor needs a newspaper," a low voice growled over the phone. "We should talk." It was Armstrong Hunter, a former clergyman, now a weekly newspaper publisher and printer in Weathersfield, 15 miles southwest of Windsor. Armstrong was in his sixties; I had heard respectful comments from regional editorial staffers about his fine character, writing and printing ability, and good head for town government.

As darkness fell the following evening, I sat in Armstrong's home, a renovated barn. It was headquarters for the *Weathersfield Weekly*, which he and his family produced.

"How would we do it?" I asked him. "What would it cost?"

Armstrong scrawled anticipated costs on a paper napkin with a fountain pen. The edges of his figures bled through the flimsy paper napkin, creating a barely recognizable blur.

Holding his half-smoked cigar in one hand, he handed me the rumpled wisp of napkin with the other. "Ink, paper, printing, wages—see, doesn't take much," he said confidently.

I squinted at the blurry figures and got the feeling divinity school had not included finance and accounting classes. But the thought of a real newspaper start-up was intriguing.

Then Armstrong baited the hook.

"I'll throw in a thousand. You do the same. We'll be partners. You do the reporting and paste-up work up in Windsor, and you can shoot page film and print here."

Here in flesh and blood was a Grade-A newspaper junkie. All he needed to expand his mini-empire was a young, energy-infested cub reporter who could work 65-hour weeks, live on a pittance, and half-balance a checkbook.

"I think we'll need more capital and manpower," I said, excited, but dumbstruck with fear.

Armstrong grimaced and waved his glowing cigar butt dismissively. Clearly administration and finance were also repugnant topics to a man of the cloth.

"You know the guy the *Eagle* hired to replace you?"

I shook my head.

"John Van Heusen," he said. "Weathersfield boy. Smart as a whip, hard worker. Tractor fell on his dad. Journalism degree, University of Vermont, full scholarship. Get him to go in with you."

I got home late that night, my head spinning with the possibilities.

John Van Heusen was a more practical fellow than I; he seemed nonplussed with my sales pitch. But when he visited Armstrong, he too fell for the allure of having his own newspaper. By the end of the week the *Daily Eagle* had lost another reporter, and the *Windsor Chronicle* was on the drawing board.

I spent seven months co-founding and co-editing the *Chronicle*, a pipsqueak of a weekly, for an even smaller paycheck than I'd last had at the *Daily Eagle*. Some weeks there were no paychecks at all, because

John and I were part-owners, having coughed up $1,000 each, and now had a growing stack of bills. (Armstrong and a well-heeled Windsor woman had also invested $1,000, so we began with $4,000 in the till.)

John and I hustled seven days a week trying to sell advertisements, write local coverage, paste up the paper, shoot it into film, opaque the resultant negatives, and then deliver it to newsstands and subscribers. Late one night before the first issue came out, I lay down for a rest on the office floor and was out cold for the night, having logged 98 hours that week. John made it three hours longer and then collapsed in a chair. Our schedules seemed like a private Olympics for workaholics.

We covered the Vermont State Prison, a drowning, main street gossip, high school sports, town selectmen meetings, regional school boards, the when and where of baked bean suppers, and pay rates for Rosie the Dog Catcher. Big stories, survival wages, miserably long hours, and few family, old friends, or support systems around. Armstrong provided a start-up mind-set and further immersion in printing and publishing. The lessons would come in handy later.

About a year later I went for an M.B.A. at Northwestern University, on the north edge of Chicago—one of the top 10 M.B.A. programs in the U.S. I lasted two semesters. As valuable and useful as an M.B.A. is, more school of any type was just not for me. So when I landed a summer job in New York at *Ski* magazine, part of the old Times-Mirror powerhouse, and then they offered me a full-time job as managing editor, I jumped at it—what a great excuse to quit school. *Ski* turned out to be good experience, but marginal pay. Two years later I migrated a few blocks west to *Yachting* magazine, then part of the Ziff-Davis empire, for much better pay and less workload. I edited feature articles and wrote some myself. Thousands of sailing aficionados would have killed for the job. But me? Well, penned up in a cement fortress, wearing an ill-fitting suit and tie, I missed the outdoors—Lake Superior, especially. The planets of professional bliss just wouldn't line up for me; I festered in malaise, not unlike entrepreneurs-in-the-making around the world.

About the only great thing that happened was meeting Sarah House, who startled me by saying yes when, on our eleventh date, I asked her to marry me. The wedding was held in a small white church in the tiny western Illinois town where she had grown up. We were feted by friends and relatives on a Mississippi riverboat and exchanged toasts at a bridal dinner in a hog barn spiffed up for the occasion. Her father had graduated from Harvard and the law school at the University of Michigan, and then returned home to a storied career in the land he loved. Unbeknownst to me, his pretty blond daughter was another cornerstone in the foundation of an entrepreneur-in-the-making.

Sarah and I enjoyed the Manhattan career scene; we commuted daily from an old house in Piermont, New York, an hour north, along the west bank of the Hudson River. But after a year of this, both of us began quietly pining for something different, maybe even a return to the Midwest.

And so, late one summer afternoon in 1979, after two years with *Yachting*, I responded to a feeling deep in my gut: I cut the cord to the Land of Modest Paychecks and Walking Dead. All it took was a short walk down the hall to my boss's corner office. Maybe it was ignorance, maybe it was the arrogance of youth, but I made the walk.

2

Over the Falls

Of course, it took a catalyst to make me take that walk.

One afternoon that summer of 1979 I uncharacteristically ignored the mounting stack of papers on my desk and fell asleep just as my boss, Tony, walked by. He was editor-in-chief of *Yachting*, the son of a famous *New Yorker* editor and had a plethora of magazine articles and a few books to his credit. He was once a competitive wrestler, but his compact body had softened; there was gray in his thinning mat of red hair.

As he peered into my office, I think he heard me begin to snore. I must have sensed his presence eventually, and my head jerked to attention. I wiped the gathering drool from my mouth, sat up straight, and sputtered some ridiculous excuse. Tony stood there for a moment, his eyes wide with disappointment and fury, then walked away.

As his footsteps padded down the linoleum-tiled hall and the secretaries outside my office door tittered with new-gossip delight, I realized it was time to get out. My employer had taken a risk two years before and given me a good job, decent salary, responsibility, even a window overlooking Manhattan's Sixth Avenue and 43rd Street six stories below. I had performed reasonably, but had no passion for my work—and never quite enough income to keep from worrying about money. I felt like a furnace with only its pilot light on, trying to heat an entire house. I wondered how many in the vast midtown lunchtime crowds below felt the same. If my informal poll of friends and associates was any indication, the answer was: *most*.

Everyone, it seemed, wanted challenge, fulfillment, an ability to control their own career destiny, and immunity to layoffs.

I figured going solo might be the answer. So, a year after marrying Sarah, I marched into Tony's office, looked him in the eye, and blurted it out.

"I'm leaving to start my own company."

A touch of amusement sparkled in Tony's tired blue eyes. He told me, as gently as he could, that he'd seen others with qualifications far better than mine set out on their own, and all had failed or not amounted to much.

I just stared straight ahead.

Tony continued looking at me as if I had said I'd jump naked off the Brooklyn Bridge at lunch hour. He was probably thinking: *Why would a comfortably salaried employee quit a good job to start a company, when small business statistics clearly predict that a start-up's failure is all but assured?*

I shuffled my feet nervously as the seconds of silence stretched out to an agonizing half minute, then more. Tony waved a hand toward the window and lower Park Avenue, many stories below. "It's cold out there," he finally said.

I was suddenly aware that he thought I would fail. He was dampening my dream right at the outset. A slow-growing fear took shape deep in my gut, as well as a need to prove him wrong.

"I've thought about it for a while," I said. "I've got a new project going."

He slowly shook his head and forced another uncomfortable pause, giving me a last chance to retract the lameness of my statement. Finally, he shrugged and stuck out his hand.

"Well then, good luck."

The quitting part was done. I *could* go over the falls in a barrel, just like I wanted.

Late that afternoon, waiting in Grand Central Station for a train home, I thought *My God, what have I done?*

Three weeks later the editorial staff chatted through a customary goodbye luncheon. I think they were more interested in the company-financed lunch than in saying goodbye to me. Then I pushed through the revolving doors at 2 Park Avenue for the last time, giddy with a final paycheck and two weeks of accrued vacation pay in my coat pocket.

For a few precious hours I bobbed on a floating, excited feeling. I had cut my mooring lines and set myself adrift. I was free. Or so I thought.

Back home with Sarah that night, I called my Calvinist, Depression-era father in Chicago, and I could hear his dismay; his voice cracked over the telephone. "You need to finish an M.B.A. first."

My mother? Her voice rang with excitement. "It sounds like a great adventure!"

She didn't know what Dad knew. And had I known about the black abyss of small-business failures that would come before I, or anyone, reached the success envisioned, I might have given up my dream right then and crawled back to Tony, tears in my eyes, pleading for my boring old job and steady paycheck.

The truth is, I didn't want to know about the abyss. Nor did Sarah, who that summer had traded her New York job with clothier Yves St. Laurent for a local one, sans commute, and was happy with the way things were, with a shy, nine-to-five staff editor for a husband. She supported my decision mostly out of newlywed loyalty. Maybe she sensed that my heart was slowly breaking, seeing dreams of living by the inland sea pushed back to an unattainable far horizon. That's why I needed to make The Walk. And the embarrassment of falling asleep was the push I needed to make it.

It didn't seem to matter that I had no business plan and little experience, just a lame-brained idea that would make any grizzled entrepreneur spit out his dentures in a spasm of laughter. I thought leaving my job and starting a company would be as easy as hopping onto a Second Avenue bus. Surely success and happiness would follow . . . wouldn't it? I was just a 28-year-old kid disguised in a coat and tie, optimistic and dewy-eyed.

It was a good thing neither Sarah nor I knew what was to come.

I had told Tony the truth: I did have a new project going. I was pursuing an idea for a business—the revised edition of a cookbook that had already been through 20 printings.

My paternal grandmother, Edith Foster Farwell, had gone into a depression not long after the end of World War II when, having recently lost a child to suicide, she lost another child who had just given birth to my cousin. Neither my father nor my grandfather would ever speak of this period, but I do know from quiet local gossip that her depression lasted a year or so and ended only after a friend introduced her to gardening. It turned out she loved working with the soil, and it brought her fully back to life.

She cofounded the Chicago Botanic Garden and cultivated extensive vegetable, herb, and fruit gardens in her backyard, along with beehives, a chicken coop and an apple orchard. For two decades she ground her own wheat to make bread, produced organic apple cider, and delivered raw honey to her two surviving children's families. On Sundays she fed her offspring a legendary, mostly homegrown luncheon. Streams of visitors came from around Chicago to see her gardens and marvel at the miracle of it all. When *Time* ran an article on medicinal and culinary herbs in the mid-1970s, my grandmother was one of the few people quoted.

During the 1960s she wrote a cookbook, *Have Fun with Herbs*, and was disappointed when it was rejected by several big-city publishers. She self-published it with the help of her son-in-law, a sales executive with a printing company in Chicago.

The book turned out to have legs—in fact, it went through the aforementioned 20 printings before her death in 1977, two years before I quit my New York job.

Why start a risky, unproven business when you can pick up one that's already got a head of steam? My grandmother's cookbook, reprinted so many times, was the obvious, can't-lose answer to my greenhorn businessman's dreams.

For five months before quitting my *Yachting* job I had worked every spare moment polishing up and enlarging the book. On daily train rides between Tarrytown, New York, and Grand Central Station and my day job in Manhattan, I had studiously focused on it. On weekends I had spent another eight to 10 hours. I had researched the herbal field, added more material, and prepared a new cover that I considered more pleasing to bookstores (my grandmother's book was spiral-bound, with homespun, black-and-white, antique-style illustrations).

A printing company in New Jersey asked for full payment up front; negotiations ended with $1,000 down, balance on delivery, cashier's check only.

Three weeks later, in mid-October 1979, a few days after my last day of salaried work, I backed up Sarah's old station wagon to the printing plant's loading dock. In went cartons of books; down went the springs of the weary car. It took two trips to and from the printer before the 5,000 books were stacked neatly in the basement of our house. We felt like new parents.

Three mail-order ads ran in various country-living magazines to coincide with the press date. I expected dozens of orders to pour into our mailbox daily.

But nothing happened.

"What's the count?" Sarah asked when I returned from the mailbox the fourth day after the publication date of our magazine ads.

"Not many." I saw her eyebrows rising; it was time to come clean. I hung my head. "Actually, zero," I said.

"Maybe they'll come tomorrow."

The next day, two orders arrived. "Here we go," I called out on the way back from the mailbox. Sarah met me on the front porch, and we looked at those first envelopes with wonder. Inside were checks made out to our newborn company, The White Pine Press, named after my favorite tree. People we had never met wanted our product and were sending us money; it seemed a miracle. That afternoon we packed and shipped each cookbook to its new owner as if sending a child off to school. From then on I felt excitement every time I saw the mailman. It wouldn't be long now until our anticipated avalanche of orders.

Days passed, but the order flow turned out to be rather modest: six orders of $6.95 each a few days later. Then the daily order flow collapsed to zero or two. This anemic volume twittered precariously for four weeks and then died completely. We still had 4,971 cookbooks in our basement.

A week later, on a miserably gray and rainy day, there was nothing in our mailbox but second-notice bills from the magazines' advertising offices; we owed them $3,000.

Thinking the first ads weren't big enough, I secured a good rate for a full-page, black-and-white ad in *Organic Gardening*—America's largest horticulture magazine, with two million paid subscribers, and a powerhouse for mail-order advertisers. I sketched out and oversaw production of the advertisement.

After that ad ran, results were about the same, relatively speaking, just on a larger scale. The book just wouldn't sell by mail, even with a cost-efficient full-page ad that reached a large, mail-order-oriented subscriber base.

"Death by cookbooks," Sarah said at dinner one night, trying to get a rise out of me. I fought back a smile, but a voice inside my brain said: *Quit now, or get ready for a marathon.* The ton and a half of books in our basement began to feel like an anchor whose long chain was wound permanently around my neck. At night I got clammy palms thinking about the art production, magazine advertising, and other bills due. Many nights I thrashed sleeplessly in bed, trying to figure out how to come up with more cash flow.

During lunch breaks I often wandered into the basement to gaze at the books. I tried to will them away, but the dozens of boxes of books seemed to say: *Listen, knucklehead. We're not half the book your grandmother's was. We're just another soulless paperback. Yeah, sure, we look better than Grandma's book. But we don't have its charisma. People bought her book because they liked her gardens and got to know her. You don't know beans about gardening, herbs, books, or even business. What didja expect?*

It was true. My months of work had produced a mediocre book. It had been upscaled with new material, a two-color cover, and proper binding, but the original book's homespun character had been neutered. I could sense my grandparents, side by side in their tree-shaded graves on the west shore of Lake Michigan, shaking their heads in disappointment.

As weeks crept by, our mailbox remained a lonely place. In the spring of 1980 I wondered what to do with the 4,612 cookbooks still in our basement (by then 388 had been sold and delivered to our small cadre of devoted customers, wholesale accounts, and a few sympathetic relatives who bought several copies each). I checked on the books every night before bed, feeling a sense of hopelessness. I needed to convert this inventory to cash, soon. How? Why weren't customers banging on our front door to buy them? If only a torrent of orders would pour into our mailbox, we could ship all the books, cash an armful of checks, and pay off back debts.

Wishful thinking. The stacks of cookbooks just stared back at me day after day.

"*What's he going to do now?*" I heard my aunt whisper to my father at a family gathering that Christmas.

"If it doesn't work out by springtime, he can finish his M.B.A. in a year and still get a good job," my father said.

I had drifted away from other projects before, but this time would be different.

"Things will work out, won't they?" I asked Sarah.

She cleared her throat. "If we find something to sell that can produce steady revenue and profits . . ."

We were both silent. Time slowed to an uncomfortable crawl. It always stings to find out what a numbskull you really are.

3

Searching for
The Product

"Look, all you need is positive cash flow—more revenue coming in than expenses going out," my friend Rad Hastings patiently explained over the phone one night. "Get that and you can grow a business."

I remained silent on my end; I was depressed by the difficulty of this start-up. Rad, on the other hand, had been a star M.B.A. student at Northwestern and was now a fast-rising banker in Chicago. He knew he was dealing with an English major, not a CPA.

"Just think of a cigar box filling with cash at a hot dog stand on 42nd Street," he went on. "Say you start the day with $10 in change. The hot dogs and soda cost you $25. You end the day with $100. *Bingo!* Sixty-five bucks of positive cash flow."

OK, now it sounded easy. Until I looked at our bank balance and stack of overdue bills.

We needed to find The Product—a thing or service around which a company could be built—before we ran out of the funds we had saved and could borrow. As it was, only a tiny revenue stream from mail-order and wholesale orders trickled into our mailbox.

For us, 40 bucks was a good day–about as much as a sharp panhandler could hustle in three hours' work on Seventh Avenue. We also had Sarah's part-time income from her outside job, about $70 a month in dividends from a stock portfolio my father had built for me over 30 years of careful saving, and about $120 a month from Sarah's share of her family's farm profits. Our mortgage was $314.04

monthly; we had no kids. We were uncertain that being out of the workplace during these key career-building years was worthwhile; friends in New York and other cities were getting promotions and raises while we teetered on oblivion. I wondered how utterly stupid I would look in five or 10 years.

We used gasoline credit cards to pay for fuel and car repairs, gambling that the business would soon be more secure and allow us to pay off these debts. I used one credit card for a home improvement loan; the credit analysts' computers still thought Sarah and I were solvent DINKS—Dual Income, No Kids—with respectable jobs in Manhattan, a decent combined income, and a manageable mortgage. In the spring of 1980, the computer at a major New York bank spat out a check for $5,000, at 12 percent interest. I used the loan's proceeds to pay off advertising costs. If things changed for the better, we'd look smart; if things went sour, it would be another story.

Several New York business acquaintances, with high-profile Ivy League M.B.A.s and years of finance and marketing experience at major corporations, went into business for themselves that year. They started off confident, full of grand intentions, and talked down to me and my failing home-based cookbook business.

When I asked one of them what his product was, he replied disdainfully: "We'll be vertically integrating a specialty packaging company we recently bought in Pennsylvania."

"How did you finance the purchase?" I asked.

"Private equity," he sniffed, tiring of my sophomoric inquiries.

As the seasons passed, all of those cocky financiers remained marginal, then failed. When I asked one of them what had happened, he replied smoothly:

"Our bankers didn't understand the financing needs of our enterprise."

I bit my tongue and smiled inwardly. I also felt a bit of a boost. We, after all, were still in business—debts, unsold herb books, and all. The arrogant Ivy League M.B.A.s, on the other hand, were not. They had spent a good chunk of their own money and a fortune of someone else's and had nothing to show for it—other than a few near-bankrupt companies that had to be unloaded for a song to an opportunity buyer. The overconfident M.B.A.s seemed startled that starting and running a small business could be so difficult, demanding skills that their years of higher education and corporate experience did not prepare them for.

I didn't have their corporate business experience or private equity financial cushion. But I had remained focused on staying financially alive and searching for a winning product—before the curtain of reality came down.

Occasional checks in our mailbox helped keep our little company's pulse beating. Thankfully, we were a cash business; customers paid when orders were placed. This was no accident. On numerous evenings after the library closed, my roommates and I had knocked down a few cold beers at the Summit Hill Tavern, next to our alma mater Trinity College, in Hartford, Connecticut. Watching the proprietor handle transactions superbly demonstrated the attributes of a cash business versus a credit business better than any lost-in-theory business school professor could. After graduating from Trinity in 1973 with a flimsy English degree, I paid attention to businesses I saw around me in real life; this was a good teacher.

These observations of real-life proceedings helped Sarah and me opt for a consumer (as opposed to wholesale) mail-order business, in which transactions are prepaid by check or credit card, thus saving infinite energy and emotional and financial costs by not having to collect on monies owed. With a consumer mail-order business, we would simply ship goods to people who paid up front. Now we just needed to find a product that would draw enough customers. I wondered if we could hang in there until then. We desperately needed that spark to light the company's fuse.

"We'll find it," Sarah assured me one night. She was still brimming with hope for the future. I felt lucky to be her partner. I also knew that if her hard-working grandfather, L. B. House—a Depression-era farmer and businessman—were around, he might whack me with the flat side of a shovel and tell me to get a real job.

Maybe he was right. I wondered if I had wasted my education by going out on my own. I missed my steady paycheck.

June 1980. Still 4,536 lonely cookbooks stacked in our basement with no place to go. I figured the easiest way to grow revenues was to market a collection of herbal-related books. Greater diversity would surely draw customers, right?

I worked for six months that spring and summer, six days a week, 10 hours a day, and produced a small book catalog. To line up our offerings, Sarah and I had pored over publishers' booklists and ordered a few copies each of the nearly 200 titles of herb-related books on every aspect of herbal medicine, herbal cooking, and nutrition. Sarah continued as shipping coordinator, chief proofreader, and general sounding board when she wasn't working her administrative assistant's job. Tragically, during this time, her father was crippled by a fast-growing brain tumor and died weeks later. The bedrock of her life was shaken. But for me, lost in deadlines and distracted with worry, his death seemed unreal until I attended the funeral. Sarah began to visit west-central Illinois more often; it became a nourishing tonic that re-anchored her and gave solace I was too distracted to provide. In her adult life's first moment of dire need, I had failed her.

By September we went to press with the *Herbal Library*. The print run was 28,000 catalogs, 25,000 going to names rented from a list broker in New Jersey and the balance mailed to lists compiled from garden clubs, as well as the few hundred buyers of our cookbook. I had devoured direct-mail textbooks and even convinced a business magazine editor to assign me to cover a direct-mail conference, where I met and interviewed industry experts. After the seminar, I phoned one of the old-timers and arranged an interview at his New York office.

It turned out to be a musty, sixteenth-floor Lower East Side office that hadn't been redecorated since the early 1950s. The fellow was elderly, but still looked plenty tough. Tough-as-Nails, who I guessed was in his eighties, was a thin, bony man in a gray wool suit. From a penniless start at age 12, he had become a big success in New York City's direct-mail businesses. He was a library stack of textbooks rolled into one durable, street-smart human being. As I posed questions, Tough-as-Nails' answers came back like three-quarter-inch steel nuts rocketed from a slingshot. I wrote as fast as I could.

"Stick to basics," he told me, "or you and your company'll go to hell in a hand basket fast."

At the end I posed one last query: "What was the most important thing that started your career in this industry?"

Tough-as-Nails wrinkled his brow as if there was too much to tell. How could a rookie like me possibly appreciate what he had to say? I sensed his mind crunching data down to a sound bite a journalist wouldn't screw up. In the background an elevator rumbled; a fire engine shrieked outside. Finally he parceled out this morsel:

"Keep costs down and watch the numbers. Learn what they're saying."

He rose to walk me to the door. I stood hesitantly, not wanting the interview to end. Tough-as-Nails briefly gripped my outstretched hand. His words sank deep into my memory.

On the one hand, Tough-as-Nails' self-made, no-money-for-education success story in the gray, cement canyons of New York. On the other, Northwestern's M.B.A. program, taught by professors from around the world in tree-shaded, well-endowed buildings on Chicago's prosperous north shore. These two polarities of business education were teaching the same thing: Find out what the numbers mean, then let them lead the way.

On the way home I wondered how to turn Tough-as-Nails' old-timer advice into a stream of dollars to pay our bills. The small-business magazine article I wrote about him paid a few hundred dollars. The education from the interview was beyond value.

I had hoped the first step would be to go deeper into the product line we were already in. Cement blocks supporting pine board shelves now lined our attic offices. These were stacked with the new herbal books, which I figured were idiot-proof products: they were returnable if they didn't sell.

The *Herbal Library* catalog came off the gigantic web press at a New Jersey printer, triggering a sobering invoice. Our checking account was ravaged again.

Anxious days passed. A week from the catalog's mailing date, the first order arrived. Two days later, a second. Thereafter, the order stream ranged from two to 10 orders a day. In the end, not enough income to cover catalog production and mailing costs. Once again, failure. A hollow pit reopened in my stomach.

At least the setback came on a relatively small, survivable financial scale, and provided data that would be useful if a saleable product could be found. Still, 13 months had passed since I quit my job and 18 months since beginning the project during my commuting time to and from the *Yachting* office. The security and steady paychecks of regular employment looked more and more appealing. Doubters' gossip was also rumbling in the background.

"People are talking," a friend told me. "They're saying, 'What's Farwell doing now? Besides dusting off 5,000 unsold cookbooks?'"

I sometimes thought about quitting, but when I heard what the grapevine was chatting up, I never considered it again. I resolved to live with the mess I had created.

Mid-November 1980. I often ran loops of very steep hillside streets near our house—anything to offer myself encouragement and stay sane. While running one afternoon, I was struck with an idea: *Don't let another year go by. Try catalog selling now with a different product while the Christmas selling season is still hot. Test something, test* anything, *but test it now before the year's selling window is lost.*

One mail-order veteran had told me during a phone interview, "Mid-October through late December is the time to sell gifts by catalog, the only profitable season for catalog retailers—except for garden and other seasonal product lines. After the fall and holiday catalog-shopping period, a catalog company has to hang on until selling season comes around the next year." Even year-round outdoor recreation and clothing catalogs, I learned, struggle to be profitable in spring and summer.

I climbed the back stairs to our attic office and pulled together files of some new products from trade shows and herb farms around New England. *What the heck*, I figured. *Go for it.* For eleven hours I worked nonstop on a simple 12-page catalog, using my thirdhand 1965 IBM steel typewriter as a typesetting machine.

About two o'clock in the morning the typewriter's carbon ribbon ran out of ink. For half an hour I hunted around for a new one, unsuccessfully. So I tried rewinding the ribbon backward between two pencils, flipped it over, and used it again. Bingo! It worked.

Out came a bottle of glue and scissors to cut out black-and-white illustrations of wild herbs from one of the books in our failed minicatalog. By seven o'clock the next morning, at zero cost, I had pasteup boards with type in place for 12 pages of the *Herbal Market*, which offered a few books, soaps, shampoos, and herb teas from Switzerland, Germany, and boutique American providers. We would mail it to our house list and catalog request names.

I convinced a local printer to drop other jobs and run our 1,200 catalogs in black ink on leftover ivory-toned paper, at a discount price. He decided to gamble. Maybe we'd grow into a bigger customer.

Two days later Sarah and I hand-sorted the catalogs for bulk postage discounts on our dining room table and boxed them for mailing. We looked like the ramshackle beginnings of a cottage industry.

Four days after the *Herbal Market* mailing went out, the first order came in by telephone. The next day, several more. Over the next week dozens of orders streamed into our mailbox. The tiny circulation base of 1,100 catalogs mailed was unlikely to produce hundreds of orders. But we did get piles of them, about 120 in all. This 10-percent response rate was spectacular, considering most of the people on the list had never ordered from us under the new catalog's title. At an average order size of $35, the 120 orders produced revenue of $4,200, or $3.82 per catalog mailed. In catalog industry jargon, we pulled $3.82 a book—as much as or more than a mature catalog would pull from the best portion of its own house list. That was a big, powerful data point of a number—the breakthrough we had been looking for.

This last-minute, black-and-white catalog—thrown together in less than a day and produced and distributed for a total cost of about $500, including printing and postage—had done about 15 times better per unit than a sophisticated small catalog on which we had spent six months and more than $15,000. For the first time in our business life, one year and two months since severing the cord from salaried employment, substantial revenue had materialized in our mailbox. We could pay our bills, and there was still some left over. Only a few hundred bucks extra, but enough to give fuel to our psychological fire.

If we could perpetuate this demand on a larger scale, we could build a winning business, because the *Herbal Market*'s sales were statistically significant, as quantitative analysts like to say, and as I had been taught during two semesters at Northwestern. The same procedure could be followed on a bigger scale with hardly more risk; such is the beauty of the catalog (and eventually, Internet) direct-marketing businesses. A small success can be exploded into a large success if you follow the fundamentals.

In January and February 1981, I continued freelancing articles and photography for annual reports and magazines. Few could make a good living at this as a freelancer, but the modest revenue provided supplemental cash and bought us time before we'd have to borrow again. From the mail-order business, we had a paltry cash flow of $25,000 or so in 16 months. It was negative cash flow, but it had provided a ton of relevant experience. I figured I was getting a practical, street-level Ph.D. for half the price of an M.B.A. But the process was beginning to take a toll.

"You don't look like a recent college graduate any more," Sarah said one day.

I didn't feel like one, either.

4

Chicken Lips and Happy Linebacker

One day at lunch Sarah said, "Quit whining. Just because we don't have a hot product doesn't mean we're not still in the game."

Although our quest to find The Product hadn't turned anything up, it was easy to spot products that *didn't* sell. Slow-selling books were returned to their publishers for credit. Books that couldn't be returned became birthday and holiday gifts over the next five years. Remaining copies of the cookbook were unloaded to a closeout buyer for 10 cents on the dollar. Phase One came ignominiously to an end.

Late February 1981. With high hopes, we finalized a spring version of the previous Christmas catalog, pasted up on my light table. The catalog focused on best-selling items: gifts and gadgets in the herbal, soap, and natural food-motif line. The catalog looked more polished than the successful, albeit last-minute December one. List brokers helped select rented names.

Late March. We mailed 30,000 16-page, black-ink-on-thick-ivory-paper catalogs at a cost—including printing, postage, design, paste-up, film and list rental—of 23 cents each, or a total of $7,000 to get them into the mail. Sarah and I took a long walk along the Hudson River, readying ourselves for a new wave of orders.

Five days went by, then six. No response. I felt a familiar queasy feeling in my stomach.

A veteran mail-order entrepreneur in our new home town of Piermont, New York, had hired Sarah as a part-time administrative aide. I swallowed my pride and asked for his opinion.

"Late March, early April? Bad time to mail," he said. "Unless you're selling garden stuff. Holiday shopping's long gone, spring's way off. Customers are feeling broke getting ready to pay income taxes."

I sat with the telephone frozen to my ear. The bad dream continued.

"Miserable time to sell anything, except booze or trips to the Caribbean," he continued. There was a pause. "You didn't mail any catalogs, didya?"

"Uh, well, actually . . . yes. We had a burst at Christmas, so I figured I'd try again."

"Pretty dumb." The conversation wound down; I hung up under a cloud of embarrassment.

May 1981. My innocently bad timing was further compounded by two external disasters: attempted assassinations of first President Ronald Reagan and then the Pope. TV coverage hyped the disasters, and retail and catalog sales stopped dead in their tracks. A traditionally poor catalog selling time became a terrible one.

We scraped in enough orders to pay printing and list rental bills, but not enough to pay merchandise costs. The loss was $3,500; we were in the tank again, financially and emotionally. I learned the hard way that spring is a time to mail sale catalogs to existing customers only, for marginal cash flow, not the time for potential profits—unless you are selling swimsuits or garden seeds.

I kept freelancing, selling stories to the *New York Times*, Kiplinger's *Changing Times, Signature,* one to *Sports Illustrated* (which they never ran), and numerous smaller publications. Even so, our joint incomes were lean.

Later that year an article appeared on the front page of the *New York Times*: "Freelance Authors Average $5,000 Annual Income." Indeed, my long hours of part-time freelance writing the previous year had produced about that much.

"Five thousand a year? Who could live on that?" I muttered. Sarah came over to see the article.

"That's not exactly news," she said. The article in the *Times* quantified what we suspected: Freelance writing is an unwise way to try to make a living, unless a person either can afford it as a paying hobby or is unusually connected and talented. Fees for articles and books were the same as 10 and 15 years before, but the number of writers had more than doubled, while the cost of living was steadily rising.

"I think I've written my last article," I said.

"Are you going to get a real job?" Sarah asked.

"No, but maybe I can create a real job. Let's sell our house, put the proceeds in a certificate of deposit, borrow against it, try to live off the interest, rent a small house, and concentrate on catalog selling only."

I could see her eyes widen, so I added the kicker: "And maybe move back to the Midwest."

That got her attention. We talked late into the night.

Catalog selling had been revitalized since the era of Sears Roebuck and Montgomery Ward; it now drove a powerful new segment of the retail economy. It was the place to focus. By 1980–81, scores of fast-talking New Jersey kids with two-year community college degrees were earning salaries of $40,000 to $50,000 as list brokers—not much less than the earnings of the top echelon of Harvard M.B.A.s of that era who'd landed coveted, top-paying jobs at big-name consulting firms. Products were selling by catalog more than ever before, thanks to the recent introduction of credit cards and zip codes, more working-outside-the-home women with newfound paychecks, and the advent of personal computers and toll-free telephone numbers.

We put our house up for sale in June 1981; in late July we had an offer, for $45,000 more than we'd paid. In late July the proceeds went into a money-market account, and we started packing. Sarah was seven months pregnant.

We left New York on August 1, 1981. Two days and 950 miles later pulled into the east side of Madison, Wisconsin, and started unpacking. I set up my desk in our little house's basement between the furnace and water softener, under a maze of wires and pipes. It was fashioned from a factory-second door bought for $5; dented two-drawer metal file cabinets held up each end. The wires of a 1960 rotary telephone bought at a New York junk shop were jury-rigged through a hole in the ceiling to a wall jack on the first floor. I paid the first month's $450 rent for our 800-square-foot house and hung a wall calendar next to my desk. It said we had six weeks to get out the next catalog.

The proceeds from the sale of our New York house were deposited in a certificate of deposit at a neighborhood bank. Interest from the CD helped cover living expenses. A week later I returned to the bank.

"Remember me? I deposited $120,000 last Tuesday. What do you say about a loan?"

After a small mountain of paperwork, a glassy-eyed loan officer eventually agreed to loan us up to $120,000, but no more. Our CD was held as collateral.

I visited other banks and asked for a larger loan. It was like trying to wake a sleeping elephant by whipping him with a cancelled check. No bank would lend to our fledgling small business beyond the value of the loan's collateral—our $120,000 CD—because our tiny company had no history of profits. Bankers looked down at my loan proposal and me as if I were subterranean lowlife, indescribably stupid for having quit a perfectly decent job.

I got the feeling our chicken-lipped neighborhood loan officer would be happy to loan $500,000 to finance our new business as long as he held a certificate of deposit for $450,000, plus deeds on $200,000 of land, buildings, and inventory he could get his hands on if things went bad. He would also require a personal guarantee providing a first lien on our car, my old golf clubs, our goldfish and fly swatter (and in community property states like Wisconsin, access to all of the borrower's spouse's personal assets). That, a set of fingerprints, and maybe a pint of blood, and he would consider a loan—for an initiation fee and interest rate that would make a dog laugh.

When I heard this one day in early September 1981, I felt a sad melting inside. Here was this pitiless banker staring at me across an immaculate, dust-free desk; for a few seconds I thought it was just a bad dream. I blinked and cleared my throat, but he was still there, lips pursed like a chicken's, hoping I'd soon leave. I wondered how capitalism was supposed to get off the ground.

"Gotta be a better way," I mumbled as I walked down Winnebago Street past seedy-looking taverns, Chicken Lips' snickering refusal still fresh in my ears.

Another option was to borrow from relatives, who I figured were more naive at lending than Chicken Lips. They would listen sympathetically and probably believe all small business loans get repaid—on time, no less. Most relatives don't know the dark secret that nearly all new business start-ups fail within the first 10 years. This was why Chicken Lips had a leg up on the amateurs. If one of his loans went soft and the borrower couldn't repay, he would merely call in the loan and vacuum up company and individual assets. Doing so activated his pre-agreed right to seize the borrower's savings, certificate of deposit, business inventory, house, kids' college funds—right down to the aforementioned goldfish and fly swatter. Because the entrepreneur hadn't gotten his or her business up and running— at a large enough sales volume, with good enough profit margins, throwing off enough positive cash flow—before he or she ran out of carefully saved and borrowed money, the unfortunate borrower would be out on the street, and Chicken Lips would have done what he promised right from the start: pull the plug, with nary a yawn.

Relatives' money, although sometimes more accessible, might come at a heavier price. If I couldn't repay them, they might humiliate me for the rest of time because, unlike Chicken Lips, they wouldn't think, at the outset, to require collateral or stipulate some other recourse. If they lost their shirt, I, the borrower—relative or not—would be eternally to blame.

It was hard to choose which was the lesser evil—borrowing from a guy like Chicken Lips at a local bank, or from relatives. I'd had plenty of relatives, in-laws, and acquaintances already guffawing at me from early 1980 to 1981 as our cookbooks sat mostly unsold in our basement before the move, and I figured it could get a lot worse. So having used up our $5,000 home improvement borrowings, our savings, Sarah's $10,000 gift from her grandmother, and $28,034 I inherited from my grandmother and Aunt Hilda, I chose to borrow from a bank.

I soon found that bankers like Chicken Lips have a handy multipart form they insist borrowers sign: the Unlimited Personal Guarantee. Or, if a business has been successful and stockpiled some cash after state and federal taxes, the Limited Personal Guarantee. Once I pored through all the fine print it became the Mother Creator of All Fear. It was the bank's license to shut down my business, seize inventory, take title to a house (if we owned one), throw us out of it, and auction our stuff off, hoping to reclaim a sliver of depositors' hard-earned cash that, in hindsight, the bank had unwisely lent. And that the borrower, lamebrained knucklehead that everyone always knew he was, couldn't repay.

I had very limited assets, but Sarah's fractional interest in her ancestral family land in west-central Illinois was meaningful. By

Wisconsin's marital property law, any unpaid debts I rang up could pass through to her (and vice versa). If I was unable to repay bank loans, the bank could take over her portion of sixth-generation farms. The prospect of losing them kept me up worrying many a night.

So we'd reached a crossroads: unless I could convince a bank to loan beyond the $120,000 threshold of our CD, all our hard work would end up like a dumpster full of unwanted cookbooks.

I went to work on a polished loan proposal. When I presented it to Chicken Lips in late September 1982, he did his best to hide his contempt. If he lent me a dime beyond the value of our CD and I couldn't repay it, he would be risking his depositors' money, tainting his career, and potentially incurring collection and legal fees.

"I'll continue your credit line for the amount of your certificate of deposit," he said month after month, as if making a concession by loaning us back our own money and getting a fee and interest for doing so. We'd have to finance inventory and off-season expenses some other way. Or quit.

Soon I had a third set of projections. Chicken Lips shook his head at me again, hoping I would go away.

"We've got to see some retained earnings in the business," he said. It was as if he were asking a farmer to fatten up his herd without money for plowing, fertilizer, seed, and feed. After a few months he took a job in Iowa and I never saw him again.

Chicken Lips' understudy, Happy Linebacker, took over. He had the build of a Green Bay Packer and the contented smile of a handsome new father at his child's christening. But he too said no.

A few friends from my M.B.A. class at Northwestern came to visit that summer and slept in our "guest room"—two old beds in our basement surrounded by my desk, the furnace, water heater, bare concrete walls, and a maze of electrical wiring and piping. They were in fast-track corporate positions and went back to fancy jobs in Chicago, Boston, and New York at the end of those weekends while I toiled in my basement. One friend, ensconced in a plush office with private secretary outside, reported to another that I had traded a respectable title and office in Manhattan for a dark Wisconsin basement and now had a baby on the way.

"He's gone loony," he added.

"No," the other replied, "he's an entrepreneur."

34

5

A Chinese Clue

Let me retrace our steps a bit, to a pivotal event in September 1981. One morning I had told Sarah, "This is nuts. Too many deadlines, too little time. Long days in my dungeon-like basement office. Things have to change."

She cocked her head, hanging on to her now full-term abdomen. "Wasn't this your idea?"

She was right. I had to work my own way out of the swamp.

On my desk lay a folder containing potential new products gathered, before the move, from New York-area trade shows. I solicited printing bids and booked studio time with a Madison photographer.

It was hot. Halfway through the studio shoot, my vision started to blur and my voice slurred.

"Caaa' muh whiiv . . ." I attempted to say. The photography studio owner raced for the phone. I stumbled like a drunk looking for something to hang onto and slumped into a chair. Someone brought me a glass of water.

By the time Sarah waddled in to bring me home, I could not voice details of who I was—not my middle name or birthday—and I couldn't remember my sister's names. I stayed in bed the rest of the day. Two days later a doctor examined me and guessed at a diagnosis.

"Maybe a mild stroke, maybe not. Try to slow down," he said. In two days I felt normal again; catalog production resumed.

From that first experience with a photo shoot I learned the first of many lessons about fashion models. We were selling clothing items for the first time that fall—three British wool sweaters and three other knitted items from an importer in New York. I had vendor-provided photos for everything but the sweaters. Paying steep fees for professional fashion models seemed daunting, so the studio photographer, sensing my tightfistedness, suggested his niece.

"Only 40 bucks an hour. She'll work great as a fill-in," he said.

I looked at two newspaper advertisements for a local clothing store she had modeled for and decided she was my low-cost answer.

The next morning I was pacing the studio floor when an attractive yet quite robust young blonde arrived. She was a Norwegian-American from nearby Mt. Horeb and stood about six feet tall once out of her shoes. She looked like she could toss a bale of hay over a tractor one-handed, or whip the daylights out of me. She gave me a firm handshake and I thought to myself, *Well, it's OK*—she would be photographed alone without size or spatial references; we would shoot the sweaters one at a time.

The shots were taken, the semi-pro Mt. Horeb Honey smiled impeccably; film was developed, selected, stripped into preprint film, and plated; and in due time the catalog was printed, addressed, and mailed. When it hit customer mailboxes, over the next 10 days friends and family members started calling.

"Who is that husky, Scandinavian-looking blonde on page two?" my mother asked in a concerned tone.

"Does she play for the Green Bay Packers?" a college roommate wrote. "She looks like she'd be a pretty good middle linebacker."

"Budgets are tight," I stammered.

The sweaters did not sell well.

I cowered in my basement office, ghosting through long hours every day as the furnace kicked in 10 feet away. Our 1960 black rotary telephone linked me precariously to the outside world. When it rang, its mid-century clanging sounded like a three-alarm fire in an old movie. I half expected the Marx Brothers on the other end of the line. I needed more space to work, and ended up with 400 square feet on the first floor of a building on nearby Williamson Street, then Madison's Skid Row. The neighborhood was populated by taverns, low-rent apartments, and a tattoo parlor. Some of the local bums were well known to local merchants. Once or twice I found one of them sleeping on our front doorstep.

The inside space was long and narrow; in an 8 × 12 foot section by the front window we displayed our country and health food style items. I often spent 20 minutes trying to sell a young hippie couple $4 worth of herb tea. I wasn't so sure about this location.

Sarah drew up telephone order forms for responses from the Christmas catalog, and I built a shipping station from old lumber where we could box items for UPS. By early October 1981 we were ready to pull the trigger at the printer for the holiday catalog we had spent all summer working on. Then, around two in the morning on October 2, Sarah's water broke. A few hours later I marveled at the magic of Lisa's tiny hands.

The house was transformed into a nursery; Lisa slept in an old family crib in the second bedroom. I went to the office feeling I was missing the real show at home. Sarah continued working part-time at the office, Monday through Friday in the cold-weather months, and around-the-clock hours at home as a busy and always-on-call mom. When necessary, Lisa was in day care with a woman across the street.

After the fall catalog hit, Lisa was often in the mail-order trenches, sleeping on the shipping table. We tried to keep up a professional front on the telephone while frantically taking down orders from our small, ramshackle office. Sometimes the ringing telephone woke Lisa from a nap and she started wailing.

Our two secondhand telephones had no hold buttons, so one of us covered the receiver while the other rushed a fresh bottle to Lisa, hoping this would quiet her.

Sarah, an energetic conversationalist, occasionally struck up telephone chats with customers about babies and motherhood. A family company staffed and run by real live people with a crying baby in the background turned out to be an advantage; it was authentic, believable, and trustworthy.

We knew that really listening to what our customers had to say, even while Lisa was clamoring in the background, was key. Customers provided free, invaluable feedback. If we followed through on their critiques we could iron out wrinkles in our operation—and positive cash flow could more easily materialize.

While Lisa slept, Sarah and I processed and shipped orders and tabulated sales. Our product analysis consisted of a few sheets of accounting paper in a three-ring binder with 60 or 70 products listed in columns. Every time we sold another item we entered a check mark in its respective space. The product with the most check marks in its column at the end of the season was the winner.

Diapers were changed, phones answered, orders shipped. We incorporated in Wisconsin as the White Pine Company, Ltd. By December 10 the company's health food and general store motif catalog had enough sales data to show it was a . . . marginal failure. We had orders, but not enough to break even; we were in a cash deficit again. If only our life were as blessedly simple as Lisa's.

Our catalog's circulation of 35,000 copies mailed (at a cost of about 45 cents each, or $15,750 total, including postage and printing) was too small to cover its production expenses (models, photography, film separation, typesetting, and paste-up) and fixed operating costs (rent, telephone, insurance, and so on). Unless we were selling a hot, in-demand product on every page, there was no way it could be profitable at its small circulation.

But the same thing, done on a larger scale with better-selling products, could support us—because along with volume, per-unit printing and postage costs would come down. So too would product acquisition costs. Fixed costs like photography and color film separations could be allocated over a wider base. Add strong-selling products, crank up the volume, control costs, and deliver good service and products, and we'd have a winning game.

In between such dreams of prosperity and the reality of our lackluster sales on Williamson Street was a hazardous No Man's Land. And piles of diapers.

Our checkbook was chronically ill; the clock was ticking. Where, I wondered, would we find the magical products to deliver positive cash flow and lead us out of No Man's Land?

The answer, it turned out, lay slightly hidden, right before our eyes. If we could read the numbers . . .

Three of the products in that season's catalog were selling briskly: knitted silk long johns, silk glove liners, and a silk balaclava (a ski hood type of hat). Their discovery had been a fluke: Just before we'd packed up our household to move from New York to Madison the previous August, a sweater saleswoman I met at a New York trade show had called.

"We've got a new line of knitted silk garments. Why don't you sell them in your catalog, along with your country-store motif product line and the three wool sweaters?"

Her employer, a New York importer, contract-manufactured the knitted silk garments in China, imported them to his East Coast warehouse, and tried to sell them wholesale in the United States. The silk items hadn't caught on, so the importer was attempting to sell them to anyone who had visited their booth at trade shows, including tiny, unproven accounts like ours.

"*Silk long johns?* Are you kidding?" I had been skeptical at the trade show and was even more so when Sweater Woman tried to hook me over the phone.

Knitted silk long johns didn't fit my self-image as an outdoors-appreciative person. In the 1970s I had cross-country skied most of—and once, all of—the two-day, 100-mile Canadian Ski Marathon four times; rowed two years on a college crew, one of which won a small college national championship; and paddled canoes 1,100 miles to the edge of the Arctic Ocean with three friends in 23 days (aided by a three-mph downstream current). I wouldn't be caught dead in knitted silk long underwear.

Sweater Woman had tried to position them as masculine-acceptable. "They're great for cold weather and skiing," she'd said, "They're nature's best fiber, lightweight and nonbulky. Nothing feels like knitted silk right against your skin."

She was persuasive. And I'd needed to get off the phone, pack up my desk, and leave on schedule for Wisconsin. So after 20 minutes I'd acquiesced and placed a small order for the three items she was peddling—the knitted silk long johns, glove liners, and balaclavas. She'd promised to mail photographs of these new items to our new Wisconsin address for use in the upcoming catalog.

I had marked off the space in the catalog. It just so happened that, until she called, we'd had one empty page (out of 32) and no idea what was going to fill it.

Now, two and a half months later, while Lisa dozed on the shipping room table in Madison, these three garments were by far the catalog's best-selling items.

I discovered why one moonless night early that winter. It was −28°F, plus wind chill, as I walked home from our Williamson Street office. Feeling the cold arctic air on my face and the warmth of soft knitted silk against my skin under layers of outer clothes, I understood why these things were selling. Despite the severe cold, I felt warm and unencumbered. The knitted silk fabric was soft and comfortable, without the bulk of cotton or synthetic-fabric long johns. That single one-mile walk gave me motivation and new hope. Perhaps this was The Product.

I called Happy Linebacker the next day. "We found a hot product with promising growth," I told him. "We just need additional capital to realize the opportunity."

"Your company has no track record of earnings." As usual, his tone was unimpressed.

"Not yet. But our new product line . . ."

Happy Linebacker must have left the phone on his desk and walked away, because I could hear him talking with another customer. Three or four minutes later his phone was discreetly hung up. The resultant dial tone resonated through the wires into my brain and through my body like a low-voltage electric shock.

What Happy Linebacker refused to listen to was what could make our little company great: knitted silk garments have ideal price-to-weight and price-to-shipping-cost ratios for a mail-order company. And now they were in demand in the American mail-order marketplace. A strong, profitable niche company could be built. If I moved fast.

Apparently the few other small shops and catalogs that had purchased these garments from the New York importer and resold them to their own customers had discovered the same thing, because the importer had quickly run out. Throughout the winter of 1981–82 Sarah and I had begged the New York importer and received a slow, limited resupply, usually a week or two or three late.

It seemed the New York importer was shorting small customers like us in order to free up inventory for large clients, including the mail-order giant L.L.Bean. They figured getting their knitted silk garments into the big catalogs had a much brighter future than selling to a mom-and-pop shoebox outfit sandwiched among decrepit row houses, taverns, and comatose bums on Madison's Williamson Street.

We had nowhere else to turn, but within a week the answer wafted into our lives. It was a three-inch by three-inch, 1/100th-of-an-ounce piece of translucent, wispy paper with Chinese hand lettering on it, lying in the bottom of a sturdy cardboard box. Our importer had used the original Chinese export carton to ship us another load of knitted silk long johns. In doing their acceptance count of the import shipment, to match the count of the Chinese packing slip and bank documents against the actual count of garments received, they had forgotten to withdraw this miniature document. It was inscribed by an old-fashioned squib ink pen on rice or bamboo paper. Now the slip seemed to wink at us from the bottom of the empty carton.

I picked it up, curious, and looked it over with Sarah. We got a feeling there could be something special about it. For $40, Sarah's cousin's Chinese business partner in Quincy, Illinois, did a translation for us a few days later.

She told us the packing slip was in Mandarin and listed inventory statistics and the name and address of the Chinese government's silk exporting office in an unfamiliar province. Could we, just possibly, import from that faraway office? If so, it might change our lives.

I wrote to the designated address that night. Xiang, a new Chinese friend in Madison, translated it into Mandarin.

Dealing directly with China would not have been possible a scant decade earlier. The transition had begun in August 1971, when then President Richard Nixon authorized a secret meeting in Beijing between then Secretary of State Henry Kissinger and China's Chairman Mao Zedong. The meeting went well; Mao was surprisingly open to further talks with the United States—provided the United States ceased funding covert resistance fighters in Tibet. Kissinger agreed to these terms, and Tibet was cast adrift on its own, easy prey for the incoming tide of Chinese soldiers eager to claim that vast, geographically strategic land where most of China's fresh water originates.

Kissinger's private communications continued, and not long afterward Nixon accompanied him to meet with Chairman Mao. As far as the world then knew, this was the first reaching out by the United States to China.

Soon the Chinese government began what was, for them, a most radical experiment: it deployed scarce capital to manufacturing concerns. The experiment, the party calculated, promised two payoffs: It would occupy some of the country's enormous, growing population, which might otherwise fester without work and possibly sow political conflict. And it might garner foreign currency. With foreign currency, the Motherland of China—staggering in the wake of closed-door, financial-system implosion from the Mao era, the previous flight of capital to Taiwan, and the destructive Gang of Four years—might begin to dig out of the financial abyss in which it found itself. Some of the Communist Party senior officials had argued that the experiment of manufacturing for export to the West held a glimmer of much-needed hope.

Indeed, there were few other cards for China to play.

Communist Party hard-liners, preferring isolation and confined economic activity, eventually went along with the plan; they liked the prospect of new revenue for their military. On paper, it was a win-win position for everyone.

And so, following Nixon and Kissinger's groundbreaking diplomacy in 1972, China creaked open its long-shut door to the West and went cautiously forward. Hundreds of thousands and then millions of rural farmers began to migrate to cities to become factory workers. They marveled at the enduring, permanent feel of cement and metal buildings; the luxury of their small, Spartan government-paid housing units with roofs that usually didn't leak; and the inconceivable windfall of heating fuel rations and guaranteed wages.

To secure these comparative riches, all they had to do was show up for work, six or seven days a week. It must have been a mind-boggling sense of good fortune to people who had known centuries of periodic famines.

From the Party point of view, maybe something good would come from the radical brew of a large-scale, government-mandated, extremely cheap labor pool and a world hungry for lower prices on a wide array of finished goods. Party officials sat back as if to watch a new species of mice set loose in a vast cage full of predators.

For those who knew China's past, the commitment to trade appeared tenuous. Since China first began trading with the outside world more than 2,000 years ago, their policy "has opened and closed like a clamshell," writes Simon Worrall in the June 2009 issue of *National Geographic*. China was the first to develop gunpowder, paper, printing, and cast iron, which ". . . set China on course to become the world's leading economic power. Trade with the West steadily expanded, with Chinese seafarers taking an increasingly dominant role," writes Worrall. By 1405, China ruled the seas.

In the November 14–15, 2009 issue of the *Wall Street Journal,* Beijing-based writer Andrew Browne wrote: "The wooden ships commanded by Admiral Cheng Ho, a Chinese Ming dynasty eunuch, were among the largest vessels ever built . . . bigger by far than the ships of Christopher Columbus."

But the last expedition sailed in 1430. "You would have thought the Chinese would take the next step—explore the Atlantic and become the dominant world culture," notes Worrall. Instead, the expeditions came to a sudden halt. "Cheng Ho's adventures helped ruin Ming finances," notes Browne. "The emperors put a halt to sea trade and closed the shipbuilding industry." China burned its fleet and turned its vision inward—for the next 400 years.

It was this distrust of merchants and their foreign influences that tipped the decision scales and suppressed China's global emergence. This distrust, writes Worrall, "dated back to Confucius, who believed trade and commerce should not dictate Chinese culture and values . . . The Silk Road and the Maritime Silk Route, which had linked China to the outside world, lapsed into disuse. By the late 17th and early 18th centuries, Europe had begun to dominate world trade."

Perhaps this explains China's subtle attitude of superiority and entitlement today; they were a past global champion who walked away from the mantle of victory. In the years following the 1971 meetings, they wanted it back.

Within three weeks of mailing my first inquiry, we received an air-mail reply. Xiang translated it into English. "The Chinese are anxious to do business with you," he said.

"Boy, they must be desperate."

Was buying from the dark recesses of China beyond our reach? I was just a small-time business rookie. But in a way, so was China. The combination was perfect.

I called the Hong Kong Trade Development office in Chicago for a list of English-speaking, Chinese-native, import-export agents. With a list in hand, I wrote a form letter and mailed a copy to each of them, outlining our silk garment needs and listing the address of the factory's silk exporting office. Five of the agents in Hong Kong immediately wrote back.

It took four to five days for an airmail letter to reach Hong Kong from Madison, and another five to six days for the reply. Assuming a two-day turnaround in the Hong Kong office, I had an answer within 14 days or less, all for the price of a half-ounce air mail stamp—then 42 cents. For under $10 we had taken our first tentative steps on the modern Silk Road.

I pressed the senders of three of the more coherent replies a little further with another letter. One of the three agents immediately sent back a second reply and asked if I had a telex number. For $35 a month I leased access to a telex in Chicago and confirmed the number to him two hours later.

One acquaintance in Hong Kong volunteered to check up on the agent. We learned he was a middle-aged Chinese fellow working with his wife and teenage children out of his cramped, well-kept living room in a lower-middle-class section of Hong Kong. He seemed reliable and honest. He was a hungry entrepreneur with a family to support, just like me.

Off went our first imported-goods order by airmail to this Hong Kong agent, all $10,000 of it (worth about $40,000 at the prevailing U.S. retail prices, for a 75-percent gross profit margin). The Hong Kong agent hand-delivered our purchase order to the factory's sales office in China via a two-day trip from Hong Kong. I opened a letter of credit to the Hong Kong agent at a Milwaukee bank that served as a correspondent to Happy Linebacker's neighborhood bank. The letter of credit was backed by our certificate of deposit, still representing the proceeds from the sale of our house.

The Hong Kong fellow, using our letter of credit as collateral, opened a smaller letter of credit at his Hong Kong bank to cover his cost for the goods. His bank sent this second letter of credit to the factory office's bank in China. The deal was set. We had a promising mail-order product and, perhaps, a high-volume, low-cost source for it. The future was looking better.

What we did not know was that China at that time was agonizingly slow to deliver and, in some government offices through which our order had to pass, somewhat nonchalant about doing business.

The winter of 1981–82 played out. Our Christmas season produced modestly robust cash flow; by February it wound down to near zero. I paid the season's bills and our house rent. We managed to take off three days at Christmas to visit my family near Chicago. The daily worries of a fledgling business stayed with me through the holidays, especially because the proceeds from selling our New York house were now partially in hock.

The talk at my aunt and uncle's house on Christmas Eve centered on our extended Calvinist-oriented family and the various careers within it. Doing anything out of the ordinary was frowned on— at least if you were male. So I faced curious skepticism and little encouragement. I lingered on the fringes self-consciously, having little to show for 30 months of hard work, and perhaps embarrassed by our wreck of a car in their driveway. Two years before I'd had an impressive title at a well-recognized publication. Now all that was forgotten and I could barely afford my own business card.

I overheard another hushed conversation between my aunt and my father.

"How's Frank doing?"

"I'd say . . . struggling," my father replied with obvious regret, not knowing I was within earshot. "I think he might fold and come back to Chicago."

Fuming quietly, I resolved to harness the doubt around me to fuel a fire burning within. Survival, regardless of the obstacles, became my mind-set.

Seagull in the Desert

"Do you think we can pull this off?" I asked Sarah on the drive back from Chicago two days later, with Lisa sleeping in the back seat. Sarah turned to me with a smile that said, *Of course. Don't ask more dumb questions.* I admired her upbeat attitude, but I had my doubts.

A rare few moments of silence passed; we turned west in Milwaukee toward Madison. "We might make it," I mumbled. Peripherally, I saw Sarah's head nod. She was probably thinking, *This guy wasn't much of a risk when he was a magazine employee. But now . . .*

A few days later came the full, frozen force of January 1982. That winter's catalog was mailed in late December and received by prospective customers the first week of January. Its overall sales were also less than break-even, but orders continued to stream in for the three knitted silk items. I wondered if those might succeed in the high-cost, high-risk—but potentially high-reward—arena of magazine display advertising, the method Lands' End was using to build its mailing list and brand awareness.

When we'd lived in suburban New York, Sarah had ended up working part-time as administrative assistant for a direct-mail pro who wrote and sold home-improvement books—the same fellow who told me what a bonehead mistake I'd made to mail spring catalogs. This fellow, Old Pro, had set up his own ad agency at zero cost to save 15 percent off published magazine advertising rates. Demand for his products was elusive, but he eked out a living working from his home, where he wrote, produced, advertised, and sold home-improvement books from his dining room table. If he'd had a hot product, things might have been very different.

Old Pro was hard-nosed; no one had done him any favors. One day I got up the nerve to call him.

After some brief quasi-pleasantries, I asked, "Should I try space advertising?"

Old Pro liked Sarah, her jokes, and the good work she had done at his office. But he didn't know me well and probably resented the advantages I had had early in life—a hard-working, sometimes high-earning father at a Chicago stock brokerage and investment banking firm who'd put four kids through college. Old Pro was reluctant to share his wisdom.

"That depends," he answered in a semi-growl. He was a lifelong smoker, and his voice sounded like a diesel exhaust pipe lined with years of soot. I think he was hesitant to give free advice to a squirming rookie who hadn't yet served enough time in the trenches. The way he saw it, some unknown kid pitching in the Mexican winter league had stumbled onto the secret to throwing a perfect fastball and slider, one after the other, but needed a special pair of eyeglasses to see home plate. Why should *he* help the lucky S.O.B.?

"Depends on what?" I asked in a carefully neutral voice.

"On whether you got the right product. And the balls to run with it."

I was about to probe for detail, but Old Pro preempted me.

"You figure it out. How's Sarah and Lisa?"

"They're good, thanks," I said, trying to hide my disappointment. I'd hoped he might be a mail-order godfather to me, because he had the experience and I had a hot product. But he probably didn't believe I had the staying power to make something of it. He stalled the conversation and left me to fend for myself.

Outside, raindrops smeared the dust on shop windows along Williamson Street. Our little company would go nowhere unless we could leap to China and back.

That night at dinner, Sarah encouraged me to follow up on Old Pro's secrets. The next morning I typed our "agency" name, White Pine Associates, on a piece of paper and reproduced it on our relic of a photocopier. Adding first-class stamps and plain #10 envelopes, we were in the advertising agency business for under five bucks. I was now the ad agency representing The White Pine Company, Ltd., and eligible for 15 percent off published magazine advertising rates. A $1,000 advertisement would now cost $850, before volume and cash discounts and other negotiations, making break-even points for each ad easier to attain. With our old copier spewing toxic fumes throughout the office, I looked at our new advertising agency letterhead. Maybe we'd get to the next level. Just maybe.

I called the *Wall Street Journal.* When I explained my product and fledgling company, I could hear the ad rep trying to choke back guffaws. But he sent a rate card and credit application.

I filled it out, roughed an ad for an art production team to produce, and then sent in the ad film and a check. Conveniently, Jack and Bill Jerred's art production offices were a few blocks away in the Hooper Construction Building. The Jerred brothers, then the best art technicians in Madison, produced the ads in their shoebox office, following my copy and layout. I placed the ads through our new in-house agency. By going directly to the source, avoiding an ad agency, we'd also bypassed production costs of several thousand dollars per ad. I paid $300 or so per ad production unit and another $300 for conversion into film. Once my check cleared at the *Wall Street Journal,* our ad ran.

When I came into the office from an errand one morning a few days after the ads hit, Sarah held up a handful of orders.

"Do we have enough stuff to fill these?"

I stopped dead in my tracks. Lisa chirped from her baby carrier, parked on the shipping table. Sarah and I pored over the orders and filled out response tracking sheets.

"When we get good ad placement, the *Wall Street Journal* is great," Sarah said, following my eyes on the accounting sheet filled with pencil entries. "If the weather gets really cold when we have page two or three placement, it could be a knockout."

Indeed, when our ads ran on those pages, they sometimes pulled several times their cost. Because only 35 cents of every sales dollar was needed to pay for the cost of the product, shipping, and customs duty, leaving 65 cents of gross profit to cover the cost of the ad and a share of fixed expenses such as rent and utilities, our per-product profit margin was at least 65 percent—so many of those early advertisements could deliver a heck of a profit. And it was still January.

"There's some winter left. Let's go for it," I said.

"O . . . K . . ." In Sarah's drawn-out reply, I heard loyalty along with fear and uncertainty.

I ran more ads in the Southwest and Midwest regional editions of the *Wall Street Journal* and sometimes, when cold weather swept the country, in the national edition. As a daily, the *Wall Street Journal* has short advance closing deadlines, so we could run ads until the first week of warm temperatures in late February or early March.

The financial risk and business demands of increased advertising were new challenges. Sarah wanted to stand with me, but she also wanted time for a here-and-now life for our expanding family. I didn't blame her. Still, I was betting that the statistical confidence level would hold up with a bigger investment on the line. I plunged forward, thinking of the next season as well. I ordered quantities of knitted silk long johns, silk turtlenecks, silk glove liners, and silk balaclavas from the importer in New York and from our import agent in Hong Kong.

Once daylight stayed longer and temperatures warmed, the selling season was over. Until holiday shopping fever started up again in October, it was a matter of hanging on.

That spring of 1982 coughed up a few small wholesale orders, which brought in extra cash. We also liquidated slower-selling items. If we could pay the rent and phone bill in those summer months, and a little to ourselves, we were still in business.

The temperature soared to the 90s that summer as I ordered large quantities of knitted silk garments. It was hard to imagine there would be a demand. We were in a netherworld between planning for a larger scale and the painful cash-starved reality of the here and now. I tried to convince myself I was not totally, gone-'round-the-bend crazy.

We looked at a larger, more professional-looking space across town in the Hooper Construction Building. After pacing the empty three-room office suite on several visits, we signed a lease for $285 per month. We made it through the summer, although there were at least 60 days between April and September 15th when sales were absolutely zero. A big day of summer orders was $50.

The new office was a mile from our rented house and just past Happy Linebacker's neighborhood bank, which had a night deposit drawer on a brick wall in a side alley. I drove in at the end of a long day's work, made our deposit with all the care of a father handing an infant back to its mother, and listened to the envelope make its way down the chute into the bowels of the bank. On summer evenings, when there was anything to deposit, the envelope took many seconds as it tentatively fluttered its way to the bottom of the deposit chute, tapping the metal sides as it descended. On winter days, a thick, heavier envelope plunged into the abyss of the chute and reached the bottom with an authoritative, satisfying thud.

In between telexes to our buying agent in Hong Kong—who traveled into China every three weeks to oversee production, packing, and shipment—we produced the upcoming catalog and display space ads for newspapers and magazines, contracted for ad film for the magazines' printer, tracked inbound progress of import orders, deciphered mailing list response, and made list rental orders to match upcoming press runs. At home I tried to forget the worries of coaxing a small business toward elusive profitability.

Some nights before dinner I carried Lisa on my shoulders to a nearby park and savored her laughter and delight as we walked along the shore of Lake Monona. At dinner one night in August, with Lisa happily catapulting food onto the floor from her high chair, Sarah and I came up with a name for our new product line: "WinterSilks—The Ultimate Winter Warmth." It was 93°F outside.

To that point, we'd made mistakes on a small, survivable scale. Now it was a matter of sticking to basics and running the marathon of a lifetime.

Most days after work I jogged for 45 minutes or so to release tension and temporarily displace my fear. When a bus passed one dark October night on Oakridge Street I chased it for several minutes, darting in and out of shadows between streetlamps like some nocturnal, running madman. Sprinting, I made it an even race for a block or so. I sensed an inner self emerging, away from the public scrutiny of corporate employment. The furnace within me was now lit.

One day that fall Sarah held Lisa on our front steps and marveled at late October color on trees lining our street. Her blond hair was long and pure, and rich color filled her cheeks; with Lisa in her arms she looked to be at the zenith of life. It seemed a shame to leave that bucolic scene, but I had deadlines, so I set out on foot for our office. For weeks afterward the memory of that lovely, fleeting scene haunted me. I realized that an increasingly complex little business had obligated me to withdraw from the simpler life that every family, in the end, so yearns for. Now I was 31, close to broke, working long hours alone, six days a week, in an empty three-room office suite.

I felt as stranded as a lone seagull in the desert.

7

The Trouble with Miss Wisconsin

Baraboo, Wisconsin. About 8:00 A.M. one morning early that fall, a sleek red sports car pulled up, driven by a tanned and fit male model, fresh from a morning workout at his Milwaukee gym. Next to him was a former Miss Wisconsin, whom I had also hired. One look at her and I realized I had screwed up again. It looked like a replay of the Mt. Horeb Honey debacle, though on a more robust scale.

A phone call to model agencies in Milwaukee had triggered a small avalanche of model portfolios in our mailbox. I selected an experienced 34-year-old and an accompanying male without interviewing them in person. The rate was $500 a day each, in 1982 dollars, which was half of Chicago rates and a third of New York's. The woman's portfolio showed her fully clothed in winter street clothes, eveningwear, and sportswear. She had a sophisticated look I hoped would appeal to our customers, who would say to themselves: "Wow! She looks great in that knitted silk turtleneck, and she's not *that* much younger than I am . . ."

The female model's biography had mentioned that she was a former Miss Wisconsin, but I had missed the cue. Then again, how could I have known what she'd look like in our knitted silk long johns she would be modeling? Should I have asked her to come to my office, close the door, strip down, and model long underwear for me? With an infant at home, a fragile young business, borrowed money, and too little time to sleep, I didn't need to look for trouble. So I'd signed a contract with her agent, dropped it in the mail, and given directions to the photography studio. Despite my scars from the Mt. Horeb Honey experience, I was not ready to shell out for New York talent.

The photo shoot was held at a two-story barn converted into a studio, on a steaming hot day. Temperatures hit the mid-80s by noon and kept rising. The barn had no air conditioning.

Photographing clothing indoors requires, besides the photographer and lighting technician, a hair stylist and someone to pin and drape clothing. And I had read in a trade magazine that if you get good shots in less than 60 minutes and two rolls of film per garment, you're being admirably efficient. So our photo team set out to shoot two or three rolls of $2\frac{1}{4} \times 2\frac{1}{4}$ color transparency film per garment in about an hour, and seven sets and 21 rolls of film in an eight-hour day.

I had learned the hard way that catalog production schedules are complex and unforgiving. There's no room for surprises; changes are tricky and expensive. A missed deadline in June can cause a missed press date in late September. That results in a mailing too late to sell in the peak holiday shopping season, and lost cash flow that can never be recovered.

Knowing this, and now seeing the former Miss Wisconsin in person, and envisioning our long underwear on one of the 10 most voluptuous women west of the Hudson River, my mind scrambled for a solution. But all I could come up with was pulling a waitress from a nearby tavern. That seemed more risky that going ahead with the striking woman who now stood before me.

Meanwhile, the studio waited and the meter ran. So I took a deep breath and signaled the go-ahead, hoping none of our customers would care that this mega-curvy woman was about to be squeezed by some magic shoehorn into WinterSilks' turtlenecks and long johns.

My prayers went unanswered. As our model strutted through the barn-like studio to the dressing room, whispers filled the air, reaching every one of the two dozen men—photographers and film and lighting technicians—busy with various jobs in other parts of the building.

Miss Wisconsin emerged 20 minutes later in her silk long johns and a thin, knitted silk turtleneck to an audible chorus of near-orgasmic, testosterone-induced groans.

Soon eight or nine hyperventilating technicians—eight times more than the necessary number—materialized to help light our garment shots for the remainder of the day. Perhaps Miss Wisconsin's very shapeliness explained why she hadn't been called up to the big leagues of the Seventh Avenue fashion world—a world strictly for females with the contours of a wire coat hanger.

As the minutes ticked by under the hot studio lights, the perspiring male employees at the studio acted like they had won the lottery. Here they toiled, day after day, lighting and photographing machine tool bearings, dairy industry milking machines, cheese, hot dogs, sausage, and other inanimate items for Wisconsin businesses. Then one day a bona fide centerfold waltzes out of the dressing room in her winter skivvies.

Some of the studio crew must have telephoned their fishing buddies, because within half an hour the place was nearly packed. Work stopped on other photography jobs; guys came out of the film lab, quit working on their trucks in the parking lot, and even skipped lunch—a rarity in the well-nourished Badger State.

The model was a pro, smiling bravely and completing all the required shots. The film and lighting crews watched her every move.

At home two days later, Sarah was reviewing the film, squinting through a German loupe at the transparencies arrayed on our light table.

"God, Frank—look at the tits on this woman!" she called out. "Where, exactly, did you find her?"

"Uhh, I think it was Milwaukee," I mumbled, sinking down in my chair.

It was too late to reshoot the sets; our press date was coming up fast. Film had to go immediately to a color separation house for 10 days of scheduled prep work. Besides, I had a good sum invested in Miss Wisconsin. So I proceeded with print preparation, still hoping Miss Wisconsin's profile wouldn't be that big a deal. I hoped that customers would approve.

While we waited for our press date, Sarah and I learned that Miss Wisconsin's appearance in the catalog had an immediate downside: it cost an extra $400 to have the color separation lab smooth over some too-explicit anatomical details from the final press film.

"Just fixing her nipples costs almost as much as our rent!" Sarah steamed as she wrote out a check later that month. I cringed like a shy 13-year-old caught reading girlie magazines at the supermarket.

Two weeks after the mailing that fall, letters started arriving from mature customers across the country, apparently written minutes after the catalog hit their mailboxes.

"I like your products immensely, but I do think you could use better taste in selecting some of your product representatives," one diplomatic lady from upstate New York wrote.

A customer from Florida wrote: "I am 65 years old, my husband is retired, and this type of thing is somewhat upsetting in our household. It's too much for his pacemaker."

The letters from distraught customers stung like a swarm of hornets. By the end of the season a small stack of them had accumulated. Our featuring the former Miss Wisconsin had unintentionally taunted them, as if to say, "Your youth is gone forever, honey. You're all washed up. But look at *me* . . ."

Each letter also stood for hundreds of other customers who felt the same but didn't take the time to let us know. They hammered home a lesson: you've got to prescreen your models in person. By not doing so, I had taken a foolish risk that had backfired. I had alienated our customers—the very people I was trying to please.

At least the good old boys at the studio had something to talk about during ice fishing season. Several asked to be put on our mailing list.

I didn't oblige.

After the Miss Wisconsin and the Too-Titty-Turtlenecks debacle, my strategy was to use a casting agent in Chicago who handled model selection and photography for many of the major national stores and catalogs. Her comments on who was used most often tipped me off on model casting market research done by companies who could better afford it than I.

Hiring models became one of the few areas in which I was happy to pay through the nose—$1,000 to $1,500 per seven-hour day, in mid-1980s dollars—for a top model's studio time.

We eventually discovered that skin tones came through better on film exposed outdoors, when early morning and late afternoon light brought out better garment colors than could be duplicated in a studio. So after a few years of expensive and time-consuming studio shots in Chicago, we switched garment photography to Colorado. Turtlenecks, sweaters, scarves, hats, and the rest of the outdoor line were photographed in pure high-altitude dawn and dusk natural light against spectacular blue Rocky Mountain sky and log cabin backgrounds. As the seasons rolled by, these photo shoots became a favorite trip for our marketing manager and art director. Snowball fights at 7,000 feet in July became a company tradition.

But I'm getting ahead of myself. Back in the days of Miss Wisconsin, plenty more gaffes were still to come.

The Wisdom of Soapstone

Back at the office, it was time to face up to shelves of the previous seasons' unsold inventory. I had to either hide the stuff from Sarah or figure out a way to unload it for a smattering of cash.

"How about a yard sale?" Sarah asked.

"Too embarrassing," I said. "Let's unload this stuff by catalog."

The unsold inventory from the 1981–1982 holiday catalog consisted of books, herbal teas, cookbooks and cooking items, cotton canvas shirts, bronze sundials, children's stuffed animals, herbal toiletry, bed and bath items, the odd wool sweater, and solar roof deicers and other energy-saving products—a conglomeration that documented my pre-WinterSilks, Hail Mary effort to find a hot product.

Items that we couldn't sell in sale catalogs that summer were used at home or given away later as gifts. This process of burning off pre-WinterSilks excess inventory took time and taught deep lessons: Buy very carefully, and don't fall in love with your inventory. Just *sell* it. Move it out the door quickly so you'll have cash to cover merchandise costs, bank loans, and operating expenses. If necessary, take a humbling loss now, rather than a devastating loss later.

The unsold inventory reminded me why it's important to find an evergreen product line comprising items that can be sold year after year. Once that's accomplished, a merchant can study the best sellers and then carefully add similar new ones.

Me? Before finding an evergreen product line, I had spent scarce capital on untested inventory that, it turned out, wouldn't sell. Fortunately, the wasted capital was on a small enough scale to be survivable and had taught us lessons no business school could teach.

By the end of 1982 all of the pre-WinterSilks, early-era inventory was sold, given away, or forgotten—except for two sets of soapstone boot- and bed-warmers purchased from a mom-and-pop company in the quarry region of central Vermont. These were heavy, ugly little items, 1¼ inches wide, 6 inches long, and ¾ inch thick, with the smooth, gray, powdery-soft surface soapstone is known for and a hole drilled in one end for a carrying loop. In colonial days the warmers were heated on wood stoves and inserted into wet boots or frigid beds. Soapstone retains its heat for hours and made the harsh transition from stove and fireside living to sodden boots or a chilly bed a little more bearable.

Our hand-scribed ledger sheets showed that we sold exactly one set of small soapstone boot warmers (item #0101), and three pairs of large soapstone boot warmers (item #0102), and no soapstone bed warmers (#0103) at all from October 1981 through June 1982. In comparison, in 1981–82 rosemary shampoo (item #9517, from Weleda of Switzerland) sold 43 bottles, an energy-saving teapot set (item #0602) sold 31 sets, and silk glove liners sold 72 pairs. If the numbers could do the talking, each of the products had a story to tell. I divided the number of individual items sold by the total catalogs mailed during that selling period (70,000 catalogs from two separate mailings of 35,000) and arrived at a per-item sales index of .000014285 for the soapstone boot warmers and .0010285 for the silk glove liners. The unwanted soapstone bed warmers thus scored .0000000 and remained orphaned on our warehouse shelves.

At wholesale, the soapstone boot- and bed-warmers cost $6 a pair. To extract some value from the capital laid out for their acquisition, I used them as paperweights to held down telexes from Canada, Korea, Hong Kong, and China; payroll summaries from our accounting department; merchandise reports from various computer systems; bills to approve to dozens of different suppliers; resumes from job seekers; stacks of telephone messages; pictures my daughter painted; art layouts of upcoming catalog pages; and communications with our bank. They symbolized my naïveté during the early years. If ever I started to feel smart, those boot warmers were a harsh reminder. I cringed a little every time I saw them, and maybe that was a good thing.

The soft talc surfaces of the soapstone became chipped around the edges over the years, at about the same pace that my hair started to gray, thin, and fall out. We endured and aged together, companions in our journey. Their unpretentiousness reminded me that business at its most successful level—despite trends, fads, and distractions—is *simple.*

For us humans, that's what makes it so hard.

So it was that The White Pine Company catalog, successor to the *Herbal Market* and the *Herbal Library* catalogs, with its helter-skelter selection of country store products, died a natural death in 1982. The beginnings of the WinterSilks catalog, with one focused product line of knitted silk clothing items, grew from the ashes. The White Pine Company, Ltd., was kept as our corporate name, and WinterSilks was registered as our trademark and doing-business-as (DBA) operating name.

With a brand name like WinterSilks, we needed cold weather. Sarah and I prayed for frigid temperatures the way a sweaty farmer prays for rain.

Christmas of 1982 delivered our wish: frigid temperatures and robust selling. Better yet, January of 1983 stayed cold and added legs to the peak season. And in mid-February temperatures dropped to −20°F for several days, with wind chill that brought −70°F to some parts of Wisconsin. In northwestern Minnesota, wind chill hit −100°F. Demand for WinterSilks, "The Ultimate Winter Warmth," exploded. Even in Texas.

"I want my WinterSilks *tomorrow,*" a woman in Dallas stated firmly when she called in her order the next morning. She was horrified to find an inch of snow in her driveway.

People like her called from all over the United States and Canada, responding to our ads in the *New Yorker,* the *Wall Street Journal,* and elsewhere, crying out for WinterSilks by Federal Express or UPS Next Day Air.

Orders streamed in just as they had the past season, but on a larger scale. We hired six employees and rented the two-room office suite next door as a shipping room. Sarah juggled caring for Lisa and showing the new staff how to process charge slips by hand and tally magazine ad and catalog orders in pencil on our traditional eight-column green accounting sheets. We had clear sailing ahead until competition sprang up or new problems arose.

Because our marginal breakeven point (a calculation that included only project costs and excluded fixed expenses, because they were already committed) was sales of 1.6 times the cost of an ad, we could expand profitably as long as response statistics held steady. In 1982–1983, revenue from these display space ads was often 2.0, 3.0, and sometimes 7.0 times the cost. A well-placed ad that cost $10,000 would—in that window of opportunity when our product was rarely offered in other catalogs—return $20,000 to $70,000 of gross revenue. The production and film cost per magazine was $300 ($1,500 for creating, typesetting, and converting the ad to film, divided by the five different publications we'd use them in). The *Wall Street Journal,* with its daily circulation of two million, was the most powerful outlet.

After the *Journal,* our next early-stage barnburner was the *New Yorker.* Our first black-and-white ad ran there on September 13, 1982, taking up a modest half column. Thanks to the combination of a strong demand for knitted silk long johns and a top-quality magazine with readers who like to shop by mail, that little ad kept our telephones ringing many times a day for three weeks. Within another year I was buying full-page ads in the *New Yorker,* and those ads continued to pull strongly and deliver profits—until the weather warmed up.

Deadlines for magazine ads were three months prior to issue date; this made betting on the weather a slippery prospect. To counteract the risk, I studied sales data from late winter 1982 ads and learned what copy, pricing, position placement, and presentation—and weather conditions—worked best. With that information I accelerated the size and frequency of advertisements for January and early- to mid-February 1983.

We coded catalog mailing lists and magazine ads, and I calculated printing and production costs down to a tenth of a cent. What-if scenarios were run on ledger sheets with a pencil—at about the same time that early personal computer spreadsheets were coming to market. Response rates and decimal points spun in my brain like tiny minnows caught at the base of a waterfall.

We funneled a steady stream of boxes into the neighborhood UPS truck until snowmelt in early March 1983. By the end of the winter we had enough extra cash to pay off debt and cover a month or two of summer expenses. We were gaining a foothold.

But that foothold was being chipped away by our growing number of employees, who relied on me for their rent or mortgage, car payments, groceries—and happiness. Many had the insane illusion that I knew what I was doing and thus could give them sound advice in other parts of their lives. Some had no concept that cash had to be earned before their paychecks would clear. Some complained about everything and were just a pain.

A scary combination. Especially because I depended for product on the then-ambivalent-to-business Chinese—who, ironically, were helping create these new jobs in Wisconsin. The vision of gaining independence by working for myself was gone, replaced by the incessant need to support not just my young family, but the raft of people on our payroll.

Despite the obligations, this was beginning to be fun. WinterSilks had survived another year and, amidst my fears, I was beginning to find some enjoyment in the journey.

The feeling lasted about a week.

9

HR Blunders

Sales dwindled as winter wore itself out and once-pristine snow melted to late-March gray puddles. The glory days of our seasonal business were done for the year, and now there were too many employees. Summer cash flow couldn't support everyone—or anyone, really—on our newly enlarged payroll. Some had to go now, and more later.

A seasoned outsider might have asked himself, "How will the human resources department handle this?" I, however, knew nothing of human resource management and was about to learn the hard way: I had never thought to explain to new hires back in October that working for WinterSilks would be a seasonal occupation. This was an unforgivable communication gap.

The order-processing war room housed a half-dozen energetic young people. One was a very quiet, industrious 22-year-old woman with short dark hair, thick, sturdy glasses, and a serious expression. She needed the job and had performed well. But she also seemed to be the slowest. So the law of the capitalist jungle steered me to her desk. There was no warning, group meeting, or prior explanation. I think I was as inept at HR as anyone on the planet, because I merely walked to The Victim's desk and asked her to step into my office.

I was too preoccupied with importing obstacles and deadlines to offer polite pleasantries or even compliment The Victim on a job well done. Instead, about 30 seconds after she was seated, I got to the point.

"Sales are off, and I have to let you go," I said in a flat, insensitive voice.

She gasped and stammered, "Why?"

"I don't have enough cash flow to support all these jobs. I need to lay you off. Just for the summer."

Her eyes widened. She burst into tears. I sat back, shocked by the power of my incompetence.

The Victim fled my office. She had been identified as the weakest in the pack and thrown to the wolves.

I heard sobbing and worried voices from the next room. Someone looked into my office with a dagger-like expression. I sat stone still, unable to address the stack of telexes on my desk. The sobbing intensified. There was a sound of tissues being violently ripped from a cardboard carton.

A few minutes later The Victim headed for the ladies' room. I could hear deep, dry-heaving sobs going down the hallway.

Ten minutes later The Victim emerged, a tear-soaked shell of her former self. Another employee walked her to her car. I never saw her again.

The young woman who had accompanied The Victim to the parking lot passed by my door a few minutes later.

"Look what you've done!" she snarled.

I shrank in my chair. So this is what it felt like to fire someone.

The way The Victim saw it, despite all her commendable efforts over five busy months, she hadn't been good enough. The truth of the matter was, *I* hadn't been good enough. I had just cut the most reliable, dedicated person on the team. (In years to come I would realize that I would not only hire The Victim again, but would hire her *first*.)

But for now it was too late; the damage had been done. Never again would I hire someone for customer service or order processing without explaining that we were a seasonal business—a venture that, for self-protection, had to shrink down to a shell of a business as soon as the snow melted.

There was a painful quiet around the office for a while as the remaining staff wondered who would be next. I shut my door and focused on the next project: developing enough other, similar knitted silk products to fill an entire catalog, which in turn could be sent to millions of upscale American households. Without other silk products, I knew our handful of fast-selling winter garments and accessories did not have enough inertial force to sustain the business long-term.

I also realized that the timing of our mail-order venture was fortunate. The proliferation of computers, zip codes, credit cards, 800 numbers, and more women in the workplace with too little time to drive to the mall had laid the groundwork for rapid mail-order expansion. I figured this opportunity would remain ripe and lightly contested for a finite window of time.

Third-class postal rates were constantly rising, so I focused on selling our best products in magazine and newspaper ads to make hay while the sunshine lasted. These magazine ads were the sprint events of mail-order selling. The marathon, selling by catalog, would come later when we developed more products.

At the end of the summer I rushed paste-ups of the catalog and magazine ads to a film house, which worked six days a week until color separations were completed. Then film was shipped to magazine publishers and our catalog printer to make closing deadlines. As issues went to press, autumn leaves were turning, cold weather was near, and another selling season was a press run away.

Gauging products to sell in magazine ads or catalogs depended on past sales statistics. To an English major like me, this was a sea of Greek. Thankfully, the statistics-oriented courses at Northwestern had conditioned me to appreciate and interpret the trend lines of data.

When Dr. Balachandran had begun speaking the first day of my statistics class, Robb Knuepfer, on my left, and on his way to a joint law and M.B.A. degree, had looked sideways at Rad Hastings and me with alarm. Neither Robb nor I had taken a math class since junior year in high school. I saw his jaw go slack, then his head fell forward on his desk with a loud thud. The class laughed at the gesture with commiserating understanding.

Nonetheless, Dr. Balachandran's course taught an enduring lesson: *Find out what your statistics are saying: Faster, slower, too high, too low, too much, too little, reversing direction—what was the real story?*

Our 1981–1982 total circulation of 70,000 catalogs was miniscule in the catalog industry, but statistically viable, with only a moderate level of variance. What we did on a small scale in the first two seasons could be cranked up a whole bunch year by year, with little extra risk—if all fundamentals were monitored along the way.

The numbers of our past were an inertial force that waited to be released.

Calculations constantly went on in my head. I scribbled on available pieces of paper at meals, meetings, church, weddings, and funerals: the cost per catalog mailed, divided by the average per-product gross margin, equaled the break-even point expressed as sales per catalog mailed. God-awful boring stuff. But wait a minute—*I was beginning to like it.*

The crusty old man in New York had told me to follow the numbers, and now I was finding that, seen from the right angle, numbers could indeed steer me on a course I hadn't thought of before. If, for example, one of our catalogs had a 100,000 circulation and sales of $100,000 attributed by source code analysis to it, then it delivered $1 in revenue for each catalog mailed. If that catalog's press run of 100,000 copies required a total of $50,000 to prepare, print, and get into the USPS delivery stream, then it cost $.50/piece in the mail. If the average per-product gross margin was .50 (50 percent) for all the items in the catalog, then with the $.50 cost per piece in the mail divided by the .50 average per-product gross margin, the break-even point would be $1.00/catalog mailed, or $100,000 gross revenue attributed to that catalog. If that catalog pulled $100,000, then all the time, effort, and financial risk to produce it resulted in zero profit, zero loss.

But if the cost per piece in the mail could be lowered to $.45, and the average per-product gross margin increased to .61 (61 percent), then the break-even point would be $.45/.61 = $.74/catalog mailed, or $74,000 for this stanza of 100,000 catalogs (a larger quantity is usually printed at once for per-unit price efficiency, and then mailed in smaller groups, or stanzas, three or four weeks apart). If this mailing continued to pull $1.00/catalog mailed, or $100,000 for the entire mailing, then the difference between sales of $100,000 and the newly established break-even point of $74,000 delivered a gross profit of $26,000. Five stanzas of 100,000 catalogs mailed over a six-week period, each with the same cost, response, and margin criteria, would deliver a total gross profit of $130,000. If attributable fixed and variable overhead costs were $30,000 for this period, then this catalog stanza would deliver a $100,000 net profit and be well worth all the effort.

Minimize costs, maximize gross profit margins and sales—as well as product quality and accurate, quick, friendly service—and life in the catalog business could be very good indeed. But get sloppy with internal accounting and record keeping, and rapid, debilitating losses will blindside the perpetrator. Good data was everything.

Our first catalog devoted only to knitted silk and winter warmth clothing items was mailed in fall 1983. Just 16 pages, it was too skinny to hold customer interest for long. It went into the mail in early October and pulled orders in an undistinguished but decent manner. Knitted silk items sold well, despite the excessively ravishing Miss Wisconsin, but flannel shirts and synthetic, athletic-oriented thermal wear flopped. It was a limping start.

While that little 16-page color catalog did the best it could in the scant 100,000 or so mailboxes it reached that fall, the magazine ad campaign blasted ahead. When very cold weather was forecast, I bought the national edition of the *Journal* and prayed for page 2 or 3 placement. If we got it, and temperatures stayed cold, our selling fuse was lit. What had been sales of about $50,000 in 1981 grew to $250,000 in 1982 and $750,000 in 1983. Now the challenge was dealing with growth.

The challenge for Sarah was more kids. Theodore was born June 20, 1983. To no one's surprise, Sarah was a natural mother and handled newborn Ted and 20-month-old Lisa with comfortable finesse. She preferred the challenges and laughs of children to the stresses, unknowns, and stern looks of business, and I didn't blame her. But I couldn't get onto her train, nor she onto mine.

As I saw the innocent eyes and merry smiles of my small children, I often wanted to go back to a regular job and be home at 5:30 P.M. But . . . no way. WinterSilks had lifted off from the runway of trial and error and taken flight; obligations had increased steadily, month by month. We had borrowed to finance inventory and needed more working capital to grease the wheels of growth. A growing line of dominos was irrevocably linked. It was too late to turn back.

PART 2

Emergence, Growth, and Profits

We can't go back in time, but we surely can go back to a place. For me, freedom is about returning to the places where I spent the happiest days of my youth . . . .

At dusk the next day my canoe coasts into the shelter of a deep, narrow cove. A calf moose ambles out of the woods, a hundred feet away, and stands knee-deep in the shallows eating plants off the bottom. Then she sees me and freezes. A minute later a large bull moose with a huge set of antlers thunders out of the woods, notices me, and starts walking closer. I strip things out of the canoe to lighten the load, grab a paddle, and get ready to make a fast exit. The moose stops 70 feet away, perhaps realizing I'm not interested in his lady friend.

Later that evening, I doze off as the campfire dies. In the morning, a caribou with an elegant silver mane struts down to drink from the clear, shallow bay. He stays a few moments, 200 feet away, and then ambles off through the bush. I'm an imposter in his world. A while later I set off, paddling into a cold headwind, staying close to shore. Rain begins, and the sky turns the lake from clear blue and green to silver gray. Soon I reach a river that thunders out of a crevice in the granite hills and cascades down three staircase waterfalls, the last of which plunges 30 feet into the lake with a deafening roar. I paddle up close so my bow almost touches the torrent and sit for a moment, feeling the water thundering all around me.

A two-mile crossing the next morning, and then I stop to bob in diminishing swells, looking up at a lighthouse perched high on top of the western end of a rocky island. Through the 1970s, before the stations were solar-automated, light keepers from the Canadian Coast Guard lived here April to November and might not see anybody for weeks at a time. If you showed up in a leaky wood canoe, bristle-cheeked, smelling of campfire smoke and badly in need of a bath, you were just about a prodigal son returning home, and welcomed with a feast. Now the lighthouse is deserted, automated, and sterile.

Two German hikers I saw three days back were the first and last people I've encountered on this trip; there are no other humans for 40 miles to the west, east, or north, and 150 miles to the south.

Soon it's nearly dark and I'm 30 yards off the western tip of this island. Waves break over a reef to my right. The gold and silver of the fading sunset ebb into orange and darkening charcoal gray. Night brings wind, rain, and a leaky tent.

10

The Magic
of Smiling Dan

Iwished I *could* turn back, because borrowing money in the recession of the early 1980s was so difficult. Nay-saying bankers left
me feeling scarred; they doubted our company would amount to
anything. Their refusals loomed over the company like a black thun-
dercloud billowing skyward above a hot Kansas prairie.

To convince banks or investors, I produced a funding request
booklet with our company background, revenue projections, graphs,
and supporting data. Before sending it out, I asked a new acquaintance, Bob Beach—*summa cum laude* from Dartmouth College in
economics and J.D. and M.B.A. degrees from Stanford—if he'd take
a look at it. He was a few years older than me and worked at an
investment firm in Madison. Bob's a generous man; perhaps out of
sympathy, he said yes to my request. I mailed him the booklet, and
after his review he invited me to his office.

After a few minutes of polite conversation, Bob cocked his head
slightly and pointed off to the side.

"See that trash can over there?"

I nodded.

"Do yourself a favor. Throw those projections in."

I blanched. Those projections had taken a lot of work. I was a
klutz with unwieldy new spreadsheet programs, so I had typed them
up by hand on a Stone Age word processor.

"Go ahead," he repeated. "Get rid of that junk."

I sat frozen with embarrassment and stared straight ahead. Was this a bad dream?

Bob shifted in his seat. We'd connected only a few weeks before; now he had to tell me what an unrealistic turkey I was.

After an embarrassed silence he cleared his throat. I thought I saw the slightest crack of a smile.

"Look," he said. "You've got to show investors numbers you know you can exceed. Anyone with a six-pack and spreadsheet program can come up with wild projections like these. No way you'll hit these numbers for a long time, even if things go perfectly. Too many supply, operations, and personnel problems are bound to come up. So play it smart. Project low sales you can beat."

I nodded glumly, like a tethered dog taking a whipping.

Bob had given the unwelcome but priceless advice of a true friend. I stuffed the projections into my briefcase, thanked him, and drove back to my office, where I deleted the high projections and left the rows of low, easy-to-achieve ones as the new high level. Then I inputted even lower ones.

With the numbers tightened, I began the hunt for investors. I knew that venture capitalists demand a high rate of annualized return when they inject capital in return for the risk they take on with tenuous, unproven new companies.

I got the word out, and a few curious venture capital investors scheduled visits. One was a member of a wealthy family in Milwaukee, heirs to a major brewery. I asked for $220,000 in return for 25 percent of the company. Several meetings and telephone conversations ensued over a three-month period. Then the courtship stalled. They weren't ready for the deal.

A Chicago investment company considered investing $190,000. They sent a guy who looked like a well-dressed professional assassin, with a lifeless pale face and neatly slicked-back hair.

"I ran the numbers," the Numbers Nerd said with the certainty of an engineer. "We gotta have a 30-percent annual rate of return, so assuming a price-earnings multiple of 15 to one and an after-tax net profit five years after the funding of . . ."

I nodded, wondering if this would go anywhere or just be another waste of everyone's time.

". . . plugging these in, I calculated a present value by dividing the future valuation by one plus I minus the internal rate of return x N, the number of years of the loan . . ."

He could have said, ". . . and then divided by the number of hairs on the Wisconsin Badger mascot, divided by the square root of total ice cream flavors at the University of Wisconsin's Babcock Hall, and shot out of a cannon upside-down over Lake Mendota." It was the language of a loan statistics geek who lived in a disconnected, sterile, numbers-only world. He knew nothing of our product, market, customers, or employees, nor did he care to find out. I didn't want to be partners with a nerd like him. Or with anyone, come to think of it.

But I needed the dough, so I pretended to listen.

". . . so we come up with 31.6 percent of the company in return for our infusion of $190,000," the Numbers Nerd continued, with an emotionless certainty.

I opened one eye and forced an earnest, friendly expression.

"Sounds good. When do we start?"

A thin smile creased his lips. He knew he had me and could negotiate a bigger percentage in a month or so.

I would have fallen to my knees and cried like a baby if the Numbers Nerd had written a check for $190,000 that day. Alas, he did not. He was just fishing; I was naïve enough to nibble at his baited hook.

Venture capitalists like the Numbers Nerd were cautious because my little company was too tender and risky, just as Chicken Lips at the neighborhood bank had said. I had to better communicate why the product and its response statistics validated a cash infusion. I had to sell my deal.

But I was a lousy verbal salesman, especially compared to my cousin Harry—who sold boatloads of college textbooks to universities in between fishing stories. I preferred to hide in a back room and make phone calls, analyze, or write copy. Just now, though, those skills couldn't help me get a loan.

You couldn't blame the bankers or investors. They had figured out that WinterSilks was hobbled by the unfortunate combination of its tenuous supply pipeline from China, intense seasonality, and unfamiliarity with managing potential rapid growth. It was a tricky path for a lender to follow, on top of the high failure rate of new business start-ups.

Without more capital, how would we grow to earn enough profit to make all the work worthwhile? Sure, we'd probably have a good holiday selling season in a few months. But without additional credit lines and working capital, we couldn't buy additional inventory to have a bigger season the following year and increase cash flow, earnings, and company value the year after that. If we couldn't add value, the whole adventure had no reason for being. Maybe quitting was a good idea.

Not long after the Numbers Nerd left my office, fate sent me an angel. The December floodgates of the catalog and direct-mail industry were open, and all seven lights on my desk phone flashed incessantly as customers fought to get through to an order-taker. When they did, they begged for knitted silk long johns by express delivery in time for Christmas. "The Ultimate Winter Warmth" was turning out to be an ultimate holiday gift. Knitted silk turtlenecks and long johns were selling right down to the cold, gray metal of our mini-warehouse shelves, and resupplies from Asia were late. I walked a tightrope, strung tight as a drum.

Then in walked an elderly stranger with an entourage of two other men. He was six feet tall, tan, camel-hair overcoat, handsome white hair and old-fashioned glasses, confident smile like a contented lion, emanating an aura of lifetime success. One follower was an elderly Chinese man in a heavy Mongolian fur coat and matching hat; the other, a middle-aged Chinese. The elderly fellow waited near the receptionist's desk, where the pulchritudinous Major Distraction, a bright 19-year-old with a prolific social life, was solving a customer service problem. My office door, facing her desk, was partially open—just enough to let me observe the trio's arrival.

"Hi, I'm Dan, and I want to talk to the boss," he told Major Distraction, lighting up the room with a dazzling smile. "Tell him I want to buy this company."

Seeing this dapper, self-confident gentleman up close, Major Distraction ignored the phones ringing with a steady, demanding pulse on her desk and in the adjoining order-processing room. She rose slowly and, still looking at Smiling Dan and his followers, crossed the hallway and knocked on my door. She looked like her kid brother had just shot her in her well-sculpted tail end with his BB gun.

"Uh, sorry to interrupt, but there's a guy here who wants to . . . he's got two strange-looking men with him."

The visitors filed into my office. Who was this ebullient fellow with his seemingly permanent gleaming smile? I got the sense that he loved life and business and had won big at both. He stuck out his hand and got right to the point:

"Man, your ads are all over the place. I told my wife last night, 'I got to go see what's going on.'"

Now I stared with wide eyes. This guy could sell snowmobiles in the Sahara.

"I'm Dan," he continued. I took in his jeweled ring, gold cuff links, ivory-colored Egyptian cotton shirt, and dark wool suit. There was something absolutely genuine about him. I immediately wished he were my uncle.

He calmly took a seat; his elderly follower sat to his left, the middle-aged one by the door. Dan introduced the latter: Hong Kong born, educated at the University of Wisconsin, now a Madison real estate hitter. The older fellow was a big player in Hong Kong and Macau.

"They've got old China connections," Smiling Dan said. "We wanted to see if we could help you get product, maybe buy you . . ."

OK—now I got it. They wanted to be the conduit through which our Asian garment orders would flow, kicking off a stream of commissions to their Hong Kong companies.

The two Chinese men stared at me like a father and son looking curiously into a reptile display at a zoo. They had already made lots of money. I, on the other hand, was new at this game, a mere squirming rookie—albeit one recently bestowed with a hot product. We eyed each other while all the lights on my phone silently blinked. I didn't know about the Chinese guys, but I sensed there was something special about Smiling Dan.

He was a local entrepreneur; he had seen our magazine ads in the *New Yorker*, the *Wall Street Journal*, *Smithsonian*, *Natural History*, the *New York Times Magazine*, and *Christian Science Monitor*, and he was curious. So he had gathered his visiting Chinese friends and driven to the address listed in small print at the bottom of our ads. As I probed more, a storyline emerged.

"When I was a toddler my father ran off," he said without emotion. "My mother raised me and my brother on the $50 a week she earned as a secretary."

She must have been some woman. Smiling Dan and his brother worked their way through college and ended up self-made multimillionaires. Smiling Dan did it by convincing a Madison bank to loan him $5,000 in the early 1960s. He quit his job, embraced long hours, and ended up in the hotel, real estate, and media businesses. Three decades later he had a net worth well into eight figures, owned part of the Milwaukee Bucks and various radio and television stations, gave generously to charities, and at Christmas rang bells at donation centers for the Salvation Army. It sounded like I was not the first struggling entrepreneur he had reached out to.

Measured chaos continued in the rest of the offices, but in my closed-door space all was calm. Smiling Dan went on, "My friends can help you get goods out of the China. They're connected in Hong Kong and Macau and the mainland."

"I don't have time to take on new suppliers and I don't want to sell the company," I told him. "But I do need working capital. I'm looking for investors."

Dan was quiet for what I guessed was a rare moment.

"Forget about them," he replied in a cool, even tone. "Borrow more from your bank and go it alone."

"How do I survive?" I asked.

"On borrowed money."

I cocked my head in doubt.

"It's real simple," he replied. "If you can't make loan payments, you don't have a viable business."

The thought of more borrowed, instead of invested, money scared the daylights out of me—assuming I could even find any bank that would make a larger loan.

"But . . . the off season. How do I survive?"

"You'll figure it out."

I sat up straight. It was like my grandmother showing little sympathy when, as a 10-year-old, I had writhed in bed with chicken pox. She knew it wouldn't kill me.

"I want to say to hell with bankers, but I need them," I whined. "But they don't need me. So I keep looking for venture capital or a partner who could invest."

Dan's voice took on a seriousness I hadn't heard before.

"You've got to be a *samurai* and make it work the way it is. Expand marketing or change products to increase sales. Cut costs to free up cash flow. Improve quality to reduce the cost of returns and refunds. Your bank will eventually get comfortable and loan more. But avoid outside investment."

"Because . . . ?"

"Partners will drive you nuts. You gotta avoid them. Just grow sales volume and get more efficient; that'll give you more cash flow to make loan payments. As you grow, the new cash flow will pay for computers, office space, product development, and people—the things you think you need investment capital for. This way you get what you want for zero capital cost."

"I don't know if I can last that long. I need a partner with operations skills and money to invest."

"If you go with venture capital or an investment partner, they'll want a say. You could lose control. They could throw you out of your own business if things don't go well."

Smiling Dan was better than any business school lecture—informative, to the point, and fun. Listening to him was like a business case-history highlights reel. He had *done it*—started with nothing and made it big. Most of his properties, I learned a few days later, gushed surplus cash flow, and his employees liked him.

"There's another thing about debt financing," he added. "When it comes time to sell, you can own 100 percent of the company."

His two companions leaned their chairs against the far wall and pretended to be dozing, but I could tell they were studying me through their nearly closed eyelids. Was I the kind of guy who would pay his commission bills, or who would I stiff them at the end of the importing season? They knew my type—just another fool American trying to learn how to eat with chopsticks.

Smiling Dan continued, "In the early going, when it is day-to-day survival, whether you own 10, 20, or 100 percent of the company seems academic. 'What does it matter?' you ask yourself. 'We might be bust next month.' Coming up with cash to meet payroll and bills is all you think about."

"Well, you hang in there, fine-tune operations, and grow, using bootstrap financing. Eventually you turn the corner. You still own all, or nearly all—or at least majority interest—of the company's stock. Maybe you sell the business for $10 million 10 years later. If you own 20 percent of the stock, you get a check for $2 million before taxes. If you own 100 percent, the check's for $10 million. Doesn't the $8 million difference make you wish you had faced the music alone, gone with bank debt financing, and arrived at the finish line with no partners?"

Taking notes, I scribbled faster. I wished I had a tape recorder.

"Most start-up guys spend their time and energy in airports and meeting rooms, trying to raise outside capital, thinking that throwing more money at their business will fix its problems. They give up equity each time they raise another round of financing. Old problems are covered up with new cash, derived from selling the very shares in their company that could have made them rich years later. And all the time they're out trying to raise money, they lose touch with their products and services and don't know whether it has what it takes to produce positive cash flow.

"Hustling for outside cash is like taking an antidepressant for cancer. When the most recent cash infusion runs out, the problems are still there, often bigger."

I stopped my note-taking. I was beginning to see the possibilities: *Just make it to the end of the week, and the week after that. Stay independent. Make it work the way it is now.*

He shook my hand, patted me on the back, and walked out with his entourage. I clung to his business card as he headed down the hall, past Major Distraction's desk.

Smiling Dan taught me to see through the smoke of conventional thinking, to clarity. That very afternoon, I decided: *To hell with investors. I'll go solo and somehow make it work.*

11

The Silver Fox

One afternoon about three weeks after Smiling Dan's visit, I was on the phone with the New York importer, telling him his deliveries were slow and I was considering alternatives.

"So you wanna go direct, huh?" he said. "Be my guest, pal. You got no experience. Those Chinks'll eat you alive."

I gripped the phone with a sweaty hand but said nothing. He didn't know I had already gone direct.

"Besides, what kind of contacts you got over there, huh?"

As he suspected, I had no meaningful contacts. But I had decided to go direct anyway.

Sure enough, it turned out to be a dangerous theater. A week later, a key order from China went awry. Trouble started when—after a 10-month gestation period at the government-owned factory in a north-central province—our finished garments crept toward Wisconsin at an agonizingly slow pace. China was still disconnected from the mainstream world, slowly emerging from the isolation of a Communist state in which control of commerce and the masses—not capitalist-style speed and ingenuity—had been the priority. I hadn't taken this into account when I placed the order and booked the goods on our intake schedule.

Every week, our agent in Hong Kong wrote apologetic air mail letters on a manual typewriter, explaining in broken English the incremental progress on our order as he pleaded with the Chinese factory and government export office. Reading between the lines of blurry typeface on paper so featherweight it floated skyward in my office if I sneezed, I deduced that Communist Party factory and export-office

79

managers in China felt no reason to rush. I suppose the Chinese figured we Americans had government jobs, housing, paychecks, and heating allocations, just as they did. Market-driven deadlines, as the western world knew them, didn't seem to have much meaning in the People's Republic of the early and mid-1980s.

When our garments were finished and packed for export, our agent wrote, they waited for government export approval, then for transport scheduling through another government office to the nearest seaport. The first leg was sometimes by rickshaw, the second by truck to a freight train, the third by rickshaw or a rickshaw-type truck to a seaport—at which point yet another branch of government had to approve and schedule a shipping line and a specific ship and arrange a local barge to bring the goods to it. Finally, the agent explained, our order was ready to proceed. That is, when it was convenient for the Chinese.

After reading these letters I sometimes pounded my desk. How could these guys be so dense?

Once on the Pacific, our shipment seemed to stop at every port between Shanghai and Seattle. Eventually it was transported by train to Chicago, where U.S. Customs found the Chinese-prepared paperwork not in order. Painful days of waiting passed before our goods were eventually cleared and trucked to our Wisconsin offices. While Smiling Dan had laid out a blueprint to solve my financial worries, importing problems had worsened. I began to appreciate the tenuousness of buying from China, and it seemed unlikely things would ever change.

Raw fear clawed at my gut again. The situation was complicated by Sarah's decreasing availability. Ted's birth in late June 1983 had made us a family of four, and now Sarah and I had huge workloads in separate worlds.

When the Chinese shipment finally reached our mini-warehouse, it had missed the winter selling season. Instead of profiting from the delivery, we had to pay for goods we didn't need for another nine months. The quality and price were very good, but we had lost revenue and customers because of China's delays. I dug deeper into our bank line of credit; monthly interest costs rose. I cut expenses to the bone and laid off remaining employees.

A full decade after President Nixon's overtures to Red China, Chinese suppliers could scarcely produce the simplest of shoes, toys, and clothing at an acceptable quality level, and they couldn't make timely deliveries. Other than firecrackers, there wasn't a whole lot you could buy from China with complete confidence.

I wrote letters and telexed complaints, but the Chinese saw no justification for my angst. Their workers seemed to get paid whether they did a good job or not, which explained why Chinese factory managers were slow to return phone calls or telexes to our agents in Hong Kong. Our agents had to actually show up at the factory to get answers. The iron rice bowl was good for the Chinese: people were employed and going hungry less often, and they had government housing at some factories. But the iron rice bowl was hell for me.

That fall, when our second set of import agents reported to us on their visit to our Chinese suppliers, more details spilled out. The Chinese factory managers and export officials had looked at our agents from British Hong Kong as if they were from another planet. The Chinese no doubt noticed that the agents weren't starving, looked healthy, probably had money in their wallets, expensive vaccinations and modern plumbing and safe drinking water back home, and they had taken a train or airliner to China. Why all the worry? Why couldn't the agents' customer learn a little patience? *December, January, April—what's the difference?* the Chinese must have wondered. WinterSilks' customers would get their silk long johns all right, sometime after Chinese New Year this year . . . or maybe the next. But they'd get them. "No problem. Nothing to worry about. Would you like some more tea?"

Chinese factory and export office officials tended to give fictitious delivery dates for our garments, in between peaceful blank stares. They had no idea of the stress western business owners underwent with borrowed capital that had to be paid back by a specified deadline. And in this poker game, they held all the cards.

If you had told me then that China would soon become the world's fastest-growing major economy, eager to embrace a hybrid of communism, capitalism, and free-market efficiency, capable of quick deliveries of complex products and of winning and then flawlessly hosting the 2008 summer Olympics, I would have bet our profits for the year that they wouldn't. At the time, the modernization of China seemed laughably unlikely.

Perhaps China of the early and mid-1980s knew it had 95 percent of the world's silk cocoon harvest and knitted silk manufacturing capacity. Perhaps they knew that the rest, mostly in India and South Korea, was poorly organized or not price-competitive. Perhaps they knew I had no choice but to grit my teeth, stay the course, and rely on them.

Thankfully, they didn't know I couldn't get enough product, fast enough, at a decent price, from the original importers in New York.

That fall, in the 1983–1984 holiday and winter selling season, we took in paper and phone orders for three-quarters of a million dollars of knitted silk long johns, turtlenecks, and other winter clothing accessories, using magazine advertisements and a tiny catalog. The surge came on a nicely profitable level. Then we were flattened by this delivery of goods from China too late for one season and too early for the next. Some customers waited; some cancelled their orders. The late delivery was like getting a birthday card from a beautiful steady girlfriend only to read that she was dropping you.

True, the goods received too late could be sold the following fall, and we would soon be crying for more. But the pain of late delivery was hard to forget. I looked for new product sources in China, hoping for better service and delivery speed. It felt like a hopeless quest. We had a hot product line and had to grow it *now*, before competition sprang up and retail prices were driven down. The comatose pace of China's ubiquitous bureaucracy was the only thing holding us back.

I pored through trade journals for leads to promising factories in Korea, Hong Kong, Japan, other parts of China, and India; I wrote a flurry of letters. After a variety of responses, I settled on South Korea. They would serve as the stopgap supplier while we waited for China to get organized. But first we needed a resident buying agent on location to watch over production.

A Milwaukee banker referred me to a client who in turn referred me to his agent in Hong Kong. I wrote the agency's Hong Kong headquarters; they told me to contact a Mr. K in Seoul. I sent Mr. K a sample of our Chinese-made goods with a specification sheet and cover letter.

Within five weeks Mr. K. airfreighted a set of good counter samples and price quotations. Quoted delivery time was fast, but prices were 50 to 100 percent more than China's. The high prices were predictable, but a shock nonetheless. At least we could get Korean knitted silk garments on a timely basis until China learned the game of capitalism.

The Koreans were boxed into a higher cost structure, but they promised four months' delivery. The Chinese promised six or seven months but had never delivered in less than 10. At one point they shipped a year late—a total of 16 months.

I dashed out an airmail order to Mr. K's office in Seoul late in the fall, then paced nervously until their first shipment arrived four and a half months later. Demand for WinterSilks had risen since we placed the Korean order, so the few dozen silk garments Mr. K shipped to us were sold out, right down to the bare metal of our warehouse shelves, less than 60 hours from their arrival at our doorstep in April 1984.

It was time for me to visit the source.

I drove five hours to Minneapolis and spent 13 miserable hours in a coach seat to Seoul. Mr. K met me at Kimpo Airport. With his graying hair and sharp, cunning features, he looked to me like a silver fox. He stood on tiptoe holding a hand-lettered cardboard sign with my name printed in grease pencil. He bowed politely and carried my bags to a chauffeured compact car rented just for the occasion. It was a hot, muggy evening and the car had no air conditioning. I noticed part of the highway from the airport to downtown Seoul was 10 or 12 lanes wide, straight as an arrow for several miles. I inquired, and the driver and the Silver Fox conferred. Then the driver turned and yelled into the back seat, above the traffic din that roared through the half-open windows.

"Landing strip," he said, nodding with civic pride.

I stuck my head partway out the window for a better view; sure enough, if you took away the traffic, the ultra-wide, straight-as-an-arrow-for-several-miles road was perfect as an emergency runway in case of an air strike by North Korea on the airport we had just left.

As we bumped and dodged our way through fiercely competitive traffic, headed for downtown Seoul, I took a good look at the Silver Fox. He sat in the passenger seat ahead of me, puffing a cigarette in an ivory holder in the smoky semi-darkness. He was a handsome, well-manicured, thin-boned fellow in his late fifties. He looked like he had a taste for good living—if, I suspected, he could get someone else to pay for it. Not that he wasn't a generous-looking man, but I knew that capital was hard to come by in Korea.

I would come to know that the cigarette holder dangled from his lips, lit or unlit, like a permanent extension of his agile body. As he exhaled dense clouds of unfiltered smoke, it wafted around the car, buffeted by warm air rushing by the open windows. The Silver Fox seemed to have a soft, gentlemanly exterior, but I wondered if there was a hardened core he wanted to hide. It came to me that the atrocities of the Korean War were a painful memory for his generation.

This was my first international business trip, and I felt too financially constrained to stay anywhere but an $18-a-night backstreet hotel. The Silver Fox had the car stop a few blocks away because the streets that led to my hotel were too narrow and congested with vendors for cars to pass. I lugged my suitcase and briefcase the rest of the way—surely the first U.S. client his office had seen who'd chosen such a place. The Silver Fox waved as they pulled away in the streetlight-dappled darkness.

The next day in his offices he reviewed orders with me; then he took me to lunch at the nearby Chosun Hotel. We met with Mr. Kim, president of one of Korea's remaining silk manufacturing companies, and later in the afternoon I flew with Mr. Kim to the southern city of Pusan. From there it was a two-hour drive north to his factory in Jinju.

Mr. Kim spoke no English, and the Silver Fox could not come along as translator. I spoke no Korean, so we sat making polite conversation that neither of us understood. A smile now and then went a long way.

Outside Jinju, Mr. Kim took me to a traditional Korean restaurant where we sat on a polished wood floor and worked our way through dozens of spicy dishes. The quiet evening and the fresh, cool air of the surrounding countryside were a welcome relief from the noise and pollution of Seoul.

The next morning, under a bright blue sky, Mr. Kim proudly showed me his production facilities. The then-totalitarian South Korean government had chosen not to subsidize the silk industry after World War II, in favor of electronics, shipbuilding, automobiles, and other industries. So Mr. Kim had borrowed heavily to produce silk garments for the Japanese, European, and U.S. markets. It was a gutsy commitment; if lower-cost China ever got its sorry production efficiency in gear, Mr. Kim could face an unwinnable battle. However hard my modern silk road was, it was easier than his, because bouncing a check in Korea was something of a crime.

A person might stay in the slammer until a family member made good on outstanding debts.

At the end of the factory tour I boarded a bus to Pusan for a meeting with a Mr. Jung, who had also bid on knitted silk garment production. I had placed an order with him and was anxious to inspect the finished garments. His most recent letter told me to stay on the bus from Jinju until the end of the line in Pusan. There I waited at the bus terminal for half an hour, wondering what had happened to the would-be manufacturer and exporter who had seemed so enthusiastic by letter and telex.

Eventually a dark premium American sedan pulled up and a beautiful young woman stepped out and introduced herself as Mr. Jung's secretary. I looked over her shoulder and saw no Mr. Jung. The dazzling secretary saw my quizzical gaze.

"Mr. Jung busy, very busy," she explained with an uncaring smile. "He says sorry. Meet you later. Maybe tonight." She giggled and got back in the car. Ten minutes later we reached Mr. Jung's office on an upper floor of a modern multistory building. The perky secretary disappeared inside. I heard fast talking on the telephone in the other room and picked up on a sense of panicked urgency. After a few minutes, the door to that office closed and Ben Juhn appeared from another room. I was told he would be my guide and interpreter. Ben had studied at Columbia University in New York for a year and had a small business of his own—a hamburger shop in the room below the loft where he, his wife, and their small son slept. He was moonlighting as interpreter for the mysterious Mr. Jung, who was on the telephone in the other room.

Ben took me on a long walking tour through the dusty backstreets of Pusan. After five miles I guessed it was designed to tire me out and divert my mind from Mr. Jung's absence. Ben showed me clothing factories; historical monuments; and a cavernous, threestory fish market in a huge, multistory barn on the waterfront where slithering eels, octopi, and similar creatures splashed in dark tubs of sea water in dimly lit rooms. It was a scene that would have made American FDA and OSHA inspectors keel over.

After seven miles or so we ended up at a spotless *geisha* house restaurant where Mr. Jung and his secretary joined us for dinner. Each of us, excluding the secretary, was assigned a young female attendant who fed us 20-odd courses of exotic Korean dishes. Each course arrived at an interval of eight to ten minutes. I did OK through the first five courses, was slightly dizzy after nine, and almost threw up when course number 15 was served: monkey brains, I believe. Then came course number 16: "Cow eyes," Ben translated with a smirk. As distance athletes say, I bonked. I was unable to go the distance, despite my intentions to be a good and respectful guest. Worse, my knees had locked up after three hours on a hard wood floor. I don't remember how I made it back to the hotel.

The next day was hot, and Ben again attempted to walk me to exhaustion. I presumed it was still a means to keep my mind off the order I had placed with Mr. Jung months before.

Finally, at 11:50 P.M., Mr. Jung came to my hotel room with his secretary and Ben in tow. He also brought two extra young women whom he apparently hoped would stay the night with me and soothe my worries about the delayed silk garment production. To his disappointment, I waved them off.

After two beers I was able to get information translated by Ben. Mr. Jung had a long story to tell about dealing with an order for sheep from Australia—they had gotten sick on the ship and upon arrival were ordered into quarantine, but he had to pay for them anyway, whether or not they survived . . . As far as the status of *my* order, Mr. Jung was elusive. As the hands on the hotel room clock neared 1:00 A.M., Mr. Jung's cigarette smoke blurred the ceiling light, and our small sea of beer bottles sat empty, I cleared my throat and asked in an even tone: "When will my order be ready to ship?"

Ben translated, and Mr. Jung stared ahead as if I did not exist. Ravishing Secretary slipped her hand into his. Mr. Jung blew out a cloud of smoke and rattled out a command to Ben. Ben paused, looking at me with pity.

"There was a problem getting the yarn," Ben said in a quiet voice. He stared down at some blemish in the cheap carpet.

"The . . . yarn?" I said.

"Yes. The yarn." His face had a pained look. He gulped and continued: "It is in Hong Kong."

The tension and suspense I had been holding in exploded in my brain. I tightened my fists and looked away. What kind of idiot was so preoccupied he took my order and letter of credit but could not even order the yarn needed five months ago for my silk garment's production? My order was not only late, it didn't even exist. I had come to Pusan at considerable expense to inspect finished merchandise, but Mr. Jung's yarn order had been held up between China and

Hong Kong, had never been knitted into finished fabric in Pusan, and not been cut and sewn to our patterns at one of the many garment factories Ben had had taken me to on our death march. How had this soft-brained playboy stayed in business? Was there a relative in the ruling military junta setting up the family on a high-level gravy train? *Gee-sus.* First the slow-breathing Chinese who don't use calendars. Now a Korean playboy who'd thrown his out. *Why me?*

I saw Ravishing Secretary rubbing her thigh against Mr. Jung's. Bedtime. The unhappy American could wait until tomorrow. Mr. Jung stood, bowed, smiled, and headed for the door.

I high-tailed it back to Seoul the next morning and thereafter left all producer-exporter selection in Korea to Mr. K, my very own Silver Fox. I placed a fourth round of orders with him, to be made at Mr. Kim's factory. Then I headed to Kimpo Airport for the long flight home, praying Mr. Kim's silk yarns would arrive on time from China. If they did, and quality of the fabric and garments was as good as the samples, I could give the Silver Fox truckloads of business. As long as I didn't have to eat any exotic animal parts.

12

Mrs. Hollingsworth and the Choker Turtlenecks

A few weeks later, our offices nearly drowned in a sea of customer complaints. Sure, we were dealing with undercapitalized factories in Korea and language barriers in China and Hong Kong. But the percentage of finished garments that did not meet our size specifications was too high. *Way* too high.

Some of the knitted silk long johns from Korea had arrived with legs that were too long, turtlenecks that were too tight, and badly cut silk glove liners with fingers that seemed to reach half way to Chicago. One New York customer who received off-specification long johns wrote: "When the waist came up to my armpits, even my dog laughed."

As a very small importer I lacked muscle with foreign agents and factories; WinterSilks was a label on a few thousand garments a year, not yet a recognized catalog brand. Handling all the complaints was labor-intensive and expensive.

In 1984 we still operated without computers, so shipping one order created a sheaf of paperwork. Each credit card order had to be written by hand on a multipart charge slip, then swiped over our bank deposit account codes on a heavy metal card-imprinting machine that could clip the end of a finger if the user was not careful. The operations team also had to make do with old-fashioned, papers-in-file-cabinets record keeping.

The cast of employees was diverse: the wife of a Washington Redskins backup quarterback (herself an NCAA Division II 440-yard sprinter), a minister's wife, a University of Wisconsin fashion merchandising graduate, some bright undergraduate students, and a night watchman working a second job. They were clustered in suites 1 and 2 of the Hooper Construction Building, just downwind of some industrial smokestacks.

Written customer service correspondence was assigned to a well-organized but extremely shy young woman. She had a meticulously clean desk and a precise filing system, and she prided herself on answering each customer letter, and solving its accompanying problem, the day it arrived. She was a very high-quality clerk. On the telephone, though, she was as engaging as an embalmed CPA.

On the other side of the hall, in suite #3, was Tornado Jones. Tornado was in her early twenties. She stood a stocky five foot five and had long, dyed jet-black hair and quick, laser-like eyes that flashed disinterestedly from side to side. She favored daring shades of lipstick, and she had a quick, disarming smile. She was the daughter of a small-town men's clothier, and WinterSilks was her first stop after college. I figured she would last a season or two in Madison before she headed to the fast lanes of L.A. or New York. But she was becoming a shoo-in for the WinterSilks employee Hall of Fame.

I had put Tornado to work answering customer post-delivery complaints that arrived by telephone as a result of late or erroneously packed orders or off-spec merchandise. Once she'd settled in, the appearance of her office did not inspire confidence; it looked like a sticky note factory after a hit by a major twister. Papers and correspondence were strewn all over her desk, in and out of file cabinets, on shelves, taped and tacked to the wall, stuck on her chair, under her briefcase, and probably in the trunk of her car.

No matter. Tornado was a made-in-heaven match for precomputer customer service telephone challenges. A born saleswoman, psychologist, and defense lawyer combined, she had the voice and smiling manner of a caffeine-fueled Mary Poppins and a memory like an electromagnet. She enjoyed resolving customer complaints; she could make anybody happy.

If I walked by her office and saw her feet up on the desk, body leaning back as if she were nodding off, head tucked against the telephone, I knew she was hard at work solving problems and soothing irked customers. She apologized to them, sent replacement goods, and made things right. Customers forgave us, went away happy, and ordered again. Tornado did such a good job that some of our urbane customers called back, at my 800-line expense, to discuss their love lives, sick poodles, and trips to Paris.

During her tenure with WinterSilks, only one problem arose that Tornado could not handle. This came on a slow, overcast Tuesday morning in mid-November, just before the annual post-Thanksgiving rush of the holiday catalog season and just after I began importing from Korea.

Tornado banged on my office door and rushed in, uncharacteristically flushed.

"I can't handle this one," she blurted. "It's a Mrs. Hollingsworth from Texas on line six. She's mad. You gotta help."

I cleared off the day's litter of letters, bills, and telexes from various obscure buying agents around Asia and looked at the bank of lights on my telephone. Sure enough, line six was flashing ominously. If Tornado couldn't handle it, I sure didn't want to.

But the caller had insisted on talking to the boss, so I had no choice. I pushed the flashing button and picked up the receiver.

"Hello, Mrs. Hollingsworth," I said with a cheerfulness I did not feel. "What can I do for you? We want to make you a satisfied customer."

My transparent schmoozing didn't help at all. Mrs. Hollingsworth made some angry, snorting sound; she sounded out of breath. I wondered what mistake we had made.

Heavy breathing continued, then a long silence. Then something that sounded like a large dog retching.

"Hello," I continued. "Can I help you, ma'am?"

The retching sound changed subtly to a sort of cough, and then to a gagging noise. I was beginning to think this was Rad Hastings, my business school friend from Northwestern, playing a prank on me.

Finally a hoarse voice croaked in a rural longhorn drawl: "This is Missus *Haulings-wurth*, in Tehx-ass. Ah'm wearin' one of your silk turtle-naicks. Ah'm mad as an Oklahoma twist-*urr*."

I swallowed hard and my palms went clammy. "How can I be of service?"

Her voice still rasping, she said she liked our silk clothing fine enough, but wished to hell we'd get them sized right.

"Is it a bit tight, Mrs. Hollingsworth?" I asked gently.

She made a deep, muffled growl, like a rusted-out muffler on an old hill country pickup truck.

"Ah can't git this tha-ing off. Ah can't ba-reeethe. It's ch-chokin' my *whin*-pipe."

"Call 911, then send it back, Mrs. Hollingsworth," I said in the calmest voice I could muster. "We'll replace it or give you your money back."

Mrs. Smith's voice trailed off.

Oh boy, I thought, *it's the Choker Turtlenecks again*—those off-specification turtlenecks from Korea. Start-up problems are to be expected with any new product in a young company, but our problems with turtlenecks from the Silver Fox and Mr. Kim's factory were unique in both volume and description.

Woven silk—used in neckties, dress shirts, and wedding dresses, for example—has no elasticity and will conform easily to desired pattern cuts. But knitted silk is elastic, so when cut it is difficult to get exact matching pieces.

Sarah and I had measured specifications for knitted silk turtlenecks and sent them by telex to the Silver Fox in Seoul; he had prepared and delivered patterns to the factory. The factory then manufactured preproduction samples for my review prior to order placement and large-volume yarn acquisition. We sometimes received odd-looking samples; some were too wide or had long, mismatched arms. For a while it looked like we were going into business to outfit one-armed, pole-vaulting gorillas.

Eventually things smoothed out to the point where I felt confident giving the go-ahead for manufacture of volumes of turtlenecks. Apparently my go-ahead was an inconsequential formality to the factory, for production of our turtlenecks had already started. As a matter of fact, the order was already finished, packed, and headed for the docks.

When the shipment arrived a few weeks later it contained, unbeknownst to us, many off-spec turtlenecks. The silk yarn and knitted cloth quality were good, colors were vibrant and dye-lots were accurate, but the sizing and accuracy to our patterns was inconsistent.

Because our staff couldn't take apart every poly bag and check its contents on arrival, we had to rely on the accuracy of factories and spot sampling by the buying agents (who were paid 3 to 7 percent of the order value to represent an importer's interests).

The factory in Seoul had miscut many of the neck openings in the latest batch, and clearly the production boss had paid off the Silver Fox so he would let the problem pass his inspection. About 300 turtlenecks snuck into our warehouse that way, at a cost to WinterSilks of $6,000 or so, not including customer service expenses and lost sales. The total hit from that single bribe was $20,000. In 1984, to a struggling little company, that was a huge sum.

And so here was poor old Mrs. Hollingsworth, trying to keep warm on a chilly, rainy November day down in Texas, darn near choking to death. In the time I spent thinking of what the Silver Fox had done to cause this, Mrs. Hollingsworth remained silent. I thought she might have blacked out. But no, she came back to life.

"You *lissen up* young man," she drawled hoarsely. She had managed to get out of the choker turtleneck and began to tell me that one of her sons had gone to a prestigious law school and was quite capable of prosecuting me.

Some of the office staff had been listening to the call on their speakerphones. Tornado Jones now leaned against my doorframe, gazing at me with sympathy.

When Mrs. Hollingsworth reached a stopping point, I realized my only chance was to tell her the whole story, straight out. So I went for it.

I told her that in Korea the economy and silk industry was still rebuilding from long, hard years of Japanese occupation, World War II, and the Korean War. And about our agent:

"When our Korean buying representative does his quality control inspections, he rejects the goods. 'The cuts are way off and the necks are too tight,' he says.

"He tells the factory manager and workers he cannot accept the production run. The factory manager rants about picky Americans, passes the hat, and collects some cash. Counting the money, our rep says to himself, 'Well, I always wanted a flush toilet.'

"Next thing you know, the turtlenecks get loaded on a cargo ship, the factory gets paid by my bank's letter of credit, workers keep their jobs, the workers' kids don't starve and our agent, now a double agent, is happy. And so we were stuck with turtlenecks that may be a little bit too tight, but we will be happy to replace your turtleneck or refund your money. . . ."

Mrs. Hollingsworth interrupted in a sympathetic, matronly tone.

"Well now, young man. You-all got more problems than me."

She chatted amiably for a few minutes and said she would send her turtleneck back for a normal one. Then she told me about her grandchildren. She promised to buy from our next catalog.

I could feel my shirt soaked with sweat when I hung up. But a customer had been saved, as long as we found a better agent and factory. I was on the telex that night.

This deft maneuvering by the Silver Fox was not what I'd had in mind when I hired him as our buying agent for Korea. I pressed him for an explanation, and pretty soon it was clear he was at least a triple agent. It got too complicated to keep track. I just wanted our knitted silk garments made right and shipped on time.

After the choker turtlenecks episode, Tornado Jones showed me a little extra respect. And Mrs. Hollingsworth did indeed order from our next catalog.

13

Battling Seventh Avenue

When I discovered the Silver Fox working both sides of the fence, I took a deep breath and ordered directly from China again. Some time passed, and then I was found out.

The New York importers, Mr. and Mrs. Hard-Ass, were furious that one of their smallest customers had convinced their exclusive factory in China to directly ship a batch of knitted silk turtlenecks, long johns, and glove liners. The goods of course arrived in Madison late, but they were still sellable.

I pictured Old Man Hard-Ass raising hell with factory officials in Jiangsu Province. "Whuddabout th' 'sclusive rights we been payin' for?" he'd growl.

"Do not worry, you have good karma," the Chinese factory officials would reply through their captive Communist Party interpreters. Then, to each other, they probably said: "Amazing how naïve Americans are. All that education and still so stupid. We can get some real mileage out of them."

Old Man Hard-Ass took an extra trip overseas to scare the Chinese into suspending shipments to us. Sometimes New York manners, and perhaps a few American greenbacks, do come in handy. Amazingly, for the Chinese, the Hard-Asses' directive took effect: The Chinese told our agent they wouldn't ship to us anymore. Not in the United States anyway.

I ground my teeth during lunch that day, and after a half-dozen broken pencils I realized the obvious solution: Canada.

Back on the phone. I found an office services company in Winnipeg. Four phone calls, a letter, and $200 later, we had a foreign branch office.

My next order was placed with the law-abiding fellows in China, and they obligingly directed the shipment by ocean to Vancouver, then by rail to our Winnipeg affiliate. There it was forwarded to Canadian Customs, and then on to Chicago. After duty payment and U.S. Customs approval, it arrived at our warehouse. *Oh Canada!* It took 11 months, but our China supply line was alive. Phone, telex, office fees, and registration came to less than $1,200 the first year.

When the first China-Vancouver-Winnipeg-Wisconsin order arrived, the Hard-Asses heard through the grapevine where our supply was coming from. A no-name rookie from the Midwest had completed an end run on them. The Hard-Asses threatened legal action.

But Sarah and I lived in a small rented house. What were the Hard-Asses going to do—take our rusted-out, thirdhand Chevy and recently acquired rust bucket of a VW? They could have them—the weary metal hulks barely started.

When I took their call I could sense them fuming. After a few moments of shouting at me they slammed down the phone. Never before had a dial tone sounded so sweet.

Soon afterward Old Man Hard-Ass placed a reconnaissance order with us, figuring the shipping department would never know who he was. He was looking to investigate our product quality and verify its source. But Sarah's sharp eyes spotted it, and I personally packed the item in the shipping room. I knew Old Man Hard-Ass was not a tall fellow. We were sold out of the size he wanted, so I took that as an opportunity to fill his order with an XL size of silk-cotton long johns from Duofold, the veteran, highly respected American garment manufacturer.

When Old Man Hard-Ass received his order he went nuts. He couldn't inspect our product, nor could he implicate his manufacturer in China. And the long johns he received probably reached up to his chin. A week later his order arrived back on our doorstep, along with an angry letter:

"It is inconceivable that anyone, or any company, could be stupid enough to take my order for a size Medium and ship me a size

XL—in an entirely different product line! What exactly do people in the Midwest have for brains? Send me a refund, including my shipping costs, immediately."

Sarah was helpless with laughter when she handed me the letter. I loved it.

Still, there was work to do. Late every night I pounded my telex keyboard, begging one factory in Korea and two in China for quicker delivery. Our advertisements were pulling orders in nearly all of the magazines they ran in; we desperately needed inventory.

Thanksgiving was near, the peak of the catalog-selling season was upon us, and still only expensive, inconsistent quality deliveries from Korea, and better-quality, but slower deliveries from China meandered across the Pacific. It was too late to ship more goods by ocean, so I risked the high cost of airfreight from Korea.

Once the shipment left the freight terminal at Kimpo we expected it in two or three days. Four passed. Later that evening an airway bill of lading came by telex from the Silver Fox. The goods were on a plane to Tokyo, then Seattle.

The next morning, no sign of the goods. A few calls. The shipment had been bumped for two nights in Tokyo and then put back on another plane to Seattle. A day passed. Then another plane to Chicago. Another two days' siesta. The goods were eventually trucked to Milwaukee, where they got stuck at U.S. Customs for four days due to missing documents.

Finally the shipment arrived at our offices by regional carrier. The driver was a surly, unshaven union member who stood by and watched one skinny male (me) and six well-dressed females in flimsy office shoes carry huge export boxes through slush and snow into our tiny shipping room, where we desperately ripped them open to fill waiting orders.

There was no time to do acceptance counts to compare our purchase order, their packing list, and our actual acceptance count—our final count usually being a bit thinner than their list, as the fellows on the Asian loading docks and at Customs in both countries often do a little Christmas shopping of their own.

I worked to midnight for three days supervising two shifts to fill back orders. By the end of the third day every garment from those export boxes had been dropped into the UPS pipeline for waiting customers.

Credit cards are not charged until orders are shipped, so this gave us a big hit of cash flow; we upgraded to a briefcase-sized bank deposit bag. The order-line phones kept ringing, and the mailman brought stacks of fresh orders six days a week.

It was too much of a good thing; it was more than our credit-line and operational capabilities could handle. We needed more bank financing to order larger quantities of goods, further in advance. We needed to build inventories and restock faster. We simply needed product. From anywhere . . .

When Mr. and Mrs. Hard-Ass took my call, they hemmed and hawed and said there was a waiting list for their product line, due to its success with most retailers they sold to and, they deftly inferred, due to our lowly status as Midwesterners who didn't know Seventh Avenue from a corn silo.

So I offered to pay C.O.D. with a cashier's check. We were granted delivery. Prices were high, but it was a finger in the dike.

When I ordered every week or so in lots of $10,000 to $15,000 C.O.D., they started asking questions.

"That's a big order for you," the Hard-Asses' vice president of sales said with more than a tinge of curiosity. The demand for knitted silk long johns was so strong that Hard-Ass, Inc., had built a well-groomed sales force. They now had slick advertising materials and a bunch of fancy new employees with decent manners and impressive titles. I prayed we could use their inventory to keep up with our own demand until China came through.

"We'd like to work with you for the whole year's program," the vice president continued.

What he meant was, *all or nothing: if you want service, you gotta order your whole year's worth through us for a negotiated price of $12 or so a piece* (and face a three- to nine-month resupply cycle). That didn't match our mail-order mark-up needs or give me much faith about resupply timing.

I kept batting the pros and cons back and forth in my head. I knew there was no future with the Hard-Asses, even though they would offer me decent wholesale prices and very little financial risk with the inventory. If I imported for myself, I would pay $8 or so for each piece, including the garment itself, plus duty, freight, and customs broker fees—a third less than the $12 or so per piece the Hard-Asses demanded.

However, importing would require a continually expanding bank line of credit to finance placement of orders with China. If I placed our orders with the Hard-Asses, I would merely fill out their order sheets, wait for delivery the next fall, and not have to cough up payment until 30 or 60 days after their goods were received. Ordering from the Hard-Asses was thus a painless, self-financing route—one that most retail stores relied on, as they didn't want a bank holding a gun to their head.

On the other hand, the per-product profit margins were lousy, and the Hard-Asses couldn't guarantee a steady stream of inventory any better than direct importing. If we had to wait for goods, we might as well have gone direct to factories at 33 percent less cost.

The Hard-Asses' favorable trade credit was tempting, but I didn't want someone else controlling our inventory pipeline and its costs. I needed manufacturer-level pricing to minimize our break-even points and expand market share. I would learn to deal with bankers holding a gun to my head in return for lower product costs, easier-to-reach break-even points, and stronger positive cash flow. Seasonal debt from an increased line of credit would be our key to inventory and ownership independence, just as Smiling Dan had said.

And so I prayed that China would speed up deliveries. We just had to survive until then.

Actually, there were signs that such a change was in the air. By 1984 China was beginning to smell the sweet scent of capitalism—at least, their version of it. Factory managers and senior employees liked the TVs, cash, and other gifts that Hong Kong buying agents bestowed on them when deliveries were on time and quality was good. If all that loot was capitalism, then hail to free-market trade. Could deadline compliance be far behind?

I kept writing letters and sending telexes to Korea, China, and Hong Kong, searching for faster more organized product sources. I even looked into India, where there was plenty of raw silk but a disorganized and unreliable infrastructure, as well as Japan, Taiwan, Thailand, France, and Italy. I learned that anywhere but China was way too expensive, and deliveries from India were risky. Korea had to cover much of our needs for now, until China's deliveries hit their stride.

14

The Long Island Leg Breaker

We nearly made it through the season, and then another order from China arrived late—by sea. It hit our doorstep in late February 1984, just after an unseasonably warm spell had seeped across the northern United States. We might as well have been selling mittens in Mississippi on a sweltering summer day.

That late shipment left us with an additional $70,000 of untimely inventory and $70,000 of unnecessary credit line drawn at the bank, plus ocean freight and customs duty invoices. We jammed the newly arrived export cartons into a small office behind the shipping room. I put an inventory count sheet on the wall, locked the door to the small office, and hoped I would live long enough—physically, financially, and emotionally—to sell the contents of those boxes the next season.

If these export cartons had left China on time the previous summer, we would have sold most of the contents during the holiday season and made a large profit. But again the factories were late. When they did ship, they registered the goods inaccurately on accompanying export documents, causing delivery to be held up an extra week or two at Customs.

Fearing just this scenario when dealing with the China of that era, I had placed a stopgap order with the Silver Fox and had it shipped airfreight. Alas, that order was also delayed and arrived in early March 1984, closely followed by a sobering airfreight invoice.

Employees who saw it called it the Humongous Invoice, as if it were a dark giant from another land. The invoice's amount due was several times more than the value of any of their cars, or mine. They stared at it with wide eyes, grateful that, unlike me, they could go home and forget they had ever seen it.

It didn't help that by early February that year there was little snow or cold in the United States. Winter had petered out early, and demand for silk long johns vaporized.

Soon a second copy of the Humongous Invoice arrived from the Very Large Worldwide Freight Company. When I opened it and again saw the figure—$12,000—I immediately lost my appetite. Twelve thousand bucks was a lot of money. I could have bought one-and-a-half full-page ads in the *New Yorker* with it. Or office rent for 14 months. Groceries for a year. As remnant snowdrifts puddled into mud, it was hard to imagine when we would again have the cash to pay it.

After 45 days we began getting a steady stream of computer-generated overdue notices, with interest and penalties tacked onto the original sum. After 60 days I started getting phone calls from clerks in the accounts receivable department of the Very Large Worldwide Freight Company. After 70 days, a deep, rugged voice with a Long Island accent threatened every person in the office until I was put on the line. My faithful employees did not hesitate to pass the call to me so I could deal *mano a mano* with . . . the Long Island Leg Breaker.

He identified himself as a professional debt collector. "Gimme the check by the end of the week." He sounded like a hungry lion used to cornering his prey. I found myself kneeling on the floor with my elbows on my desk, begging for survival.

The Long Island Leg Breaker's message was simple: *If you don't pay soon, I'm coming out there with my chainsaw* . . .

I volunteered a payment plan of several months. "The situation of late delivery, melting snow, and a resultant lack of demand for silk long johns in February and March has made it difficult for us," I explained. "We don't have the cash right now. But we will this fall."

There was a pause at the other end of the line; then Leg Breaker's voice asked in a tone of incredulity:

"*What kinda long johns didja say?*"

"Silk."

"That's whut I t'ought ya said. Who'n Gawd's name wears silk long johns?"

I sensed an opportunity to sidetrack Leg Breaker, so I started in with my tale of woe. He quieted momentarily, muttering a slightly muffled profanity.

I imagined Leg Breaker had worked many collection accounts: printing presses, aircraft, jet engines, trucks, petroleum, computers, tires, TVs, furniture, shoes, and whatnot. But this one stumped him. I think he envisioned a hard time telling his buddies at the bar he was going to crush this deadbeat's skull out in Wisconsin because the fellow couldn't pay his airfreight bill on a few dozen export cartons of silk long johns. I think he knew his barroom friends would fall on the floor, convulsed with laughter. He'd be hooted out of the establishment. So it took him a moment to figure out how he was going to use this against me. But he couldn't think of anything, and for what I guessed was a rare time in his professional, intimidating, bill-collecting life, Leg Breaker stammered.

"M-Mistuh *Fah*-wel," he said in a gravel-pit growl, "I've nevah hoid of nobuddy dumb 'nough to try'n make a livin' sellin' silk long johns. You must be one crazy, stuu-pid guy. But I'm gonna do ya a *fay*-vah. Normally, I'd send muh boys out there with a truck to take the inventory. But I'm gonna give ya a break, jus' this once. So tell me. How much canya pay a month, huh?"

"Five hundred a month for four months through the summer, then $1,000 a month until all $12,000 plus accrued interest has been paid off," I shot back. My voice had a tone of self-confidence I did not feel.

"No fuggin' way, pal." He sounded like a nasty guard dog poked with a stick.

"Well then, how about—"

"*Shaddup.* It's my deal or I carve ya up for next Thanksgivin's dinnah."

"I suppose we might work something out."

We settled on $1,000 a month until November, then $2,000 a month until the Humongous Invoice was paid in full. There was a momentary peace, and then Leg Breaker's voice sizzled over the line again.

"Jus' dun' miss no paymunts," he snarled.

I heard the thud when he hammered his telephone receiver into its cradle. I was still kneeling by my desk. My hair was wet and disheveled with sweat and my heart was pounding. But we had a deal, an achievable, dig-your-way-out-of-a-hole deal I just might be able to manage—if we had cold weather that fall. If we did have a robust early winter, then by December 31 all of the export cartons of silk long johns could be sold and shipped to customers and the Humongous Invoice paid to the Very Large Worldwide Freight Company.

After that call with Leg Breaker, I vowed to take every delivery by ocean freight at one-eighth the cost of airfreight—preferably on American President Lines, then the best in the business. I was determined to survive my deadbeat status, emerge with four functional original limbs, and give Leg Breaker his client's dough.

A month later, in April, with the first payment sent on time, I told Leg Breaker I'd give him top priority if we expanded our wholesale business and needed help with collections. He grunted approval. Maybe he and I could be buddies after all.

A week after my conversation with Leg Breaker, I backed up a U-Haul rental truck, loaded 55 50-pound export boxes, and drove to the suburban home that Sarah and I had recently purchased in Middleton, on Madison's west side. (Bankers were quite willing to lend for house purchases, if not for imported silk garments.) The boxes were the cause of the Humongous Invoice; there was no room for them in our offices.

It was early evening, about to rain. I was determined to get those boxes safely into our house. Each box was about 27 cubic feet and reached nearly halfway up my thigh. I carried them one by one through our garage, dragged them through the family room and kitchen, and slid them down the stairs to a corner of our basement. Lisa and Ted were in their pajamas, watching with interest, not sure what was going on.

I lifted a lot of weight in the course of two hours and lost several pounds. It became a war: my will against their bulk and weight. I splashed through our rain-soaked driveway and into our garage, manhandling one carton after another. By the end it felt like I had boxed 15 rounds with some cardboard-headed monster.

The 55 boxes towered in our basement like a manmade mountain. With all costs considered, they represented an extra $110,000 owed to the bank, magazines, Leg Breaker's client, and U.S. Customs. I knew we had to hold on until the next holiday selling season before we could sell what was in those boxes and pay off debts.

In the interim I had to have enough insane faith to order more inventory for the next holiday season.

It occurred to me, as I stood dripping sweat in the basement, that it might be simpler to just declare bankruptcy and quit. We could auction off the merchandise, pay off some of the bank loan, and shut down the business. I'd be free; Sarah would be delighted. Maybe she'd have a normal husband again, and the kids a real father. What would it be like to live a simpler life, broke but happy?

Then again, we could probably sell the contents of those boxes in a few short weeks once temperatures turned cold and the holiday season neared. Our marketing history said we had a bright future. So which would it be—shut down or gear up?

If we geared up, we would do the same advertising strategy again the following year on a bigger and better-executed scale, with more profit dollars—and repeat the effort again the next year, and the year after that. If all went well, we could pay off seasonal debt and borrow to order more.

But at that moment, standing in our basement, exhausted and breathing hard, I found it hard to be optimistic. If I didn't take the option of quitting now there would be no chance later. Time, sleep, health, family, and hobbies had been jettisoned. WinterSilks had become a personal demon that consumed all aspects of my being. I was not sure whether to seek relief by walking away and selling out or to find renewed courage to fight on.

Regardless of the choice, WinterSilks would never be the same. She had metamorphosed from the innocent embryo of just a dozen months before; now she was vastly more complicated. The in-season employee count, besides Sarah and me, had grown from zero to too many, and it was difficult to communicate with and coordinate these new people. I felt the weight of their dependence on me for a job and emotional happiness. Being a boss was no fun at all.

But if I quit, I'd miss the excitement and payoff possibly soon to come. We had momentum; in many ways it was unthinkable to turn back now. Besides, our bank had its fangs deep into us. If I ended up owing them money, Sarah's family farm would not be safe.

There was also the promise of a near-term exclusive: Until L.L. Bean, Eddie Bauer, Lands' End, Orvis, and other major catalogs committed to knitted silk thermal wear, WinterSilks had little competition. The clock was ticking: I had to move fast to win customers and market share, or I'd lose the chance. The opportunity we had risked so much for was there at my feet in those plain brown export cartons.

I trudged up the basement stairs to a shower, feeling I had just stepped over a chasm of no return.

There was a stratum of confidence beneath my fear, because what we had achieved the prior season could be repeated on a broader scale. With the criteria I selected, we were using just 25 percent of profitable space advertising outlets and 5 percent of profitable direct mailing lists. We could advertise four times as much, in terms of frequency, before we used up all profitable magazine opportunities. And we could mail at least 20 times more catalogs to proven, profitable segments of already-tested mailing lists before saturating our catalog opportunity. Database analysis lists were still to come. WinterSilks had a big upside.

Even so, I hadn't fully understood until moving that mountain of boxes that when a business is started there is no turning back, no exit, no shortcuts, no soft landings, no assurances—only risks, fear, and uncertainty. There's no way out, no clear-cut victory or failure until a person sells it, shuts it down, or dies.

Weeks streamed by in a blur, like scenery flashing before a child's eyes in the back seat of the family car on a long vacation journey. Never more than a few hours to rest between selling seasons. When one ended, deadlines for the next began. What should have been a relaxing summer became a crunch of endless production cycles. I needed to analyze catalog and magazine advertisement source code response to identify profitable lists for the next season's mailing and then order merchandise to support the upcoming catalogs' planned circulation. Then we had to produce catalog and magazine advertisements against tight summer deadlines. Delivery of mailing list segments had to be followed up to ensure making the late-summer cutoff date at our vendor's mainframe computer merge/purge facilities, where duplicate names would be purged and all remaining names would be merged into three separate zip-code streams, thus minimizing postal costs. We had to rearrange our office and mini-warehouse to suit the order flow anticipated from the coming season's higher circulation. New people had to be hired and trained.

Stress caught up to me again. Sarah was away with Lisa and Ted when I was hit by chest pains. I drove myself to the hospital, went through a series of tests, and was released three hours later.

"The tests look OK," an emergency room cardiologist said, looking at a series of X-rays. "Probably just chest wall pain, when muscles contract around the heart from stress. Try to slow down."

Slowing down while owning and running a business—an unlikely combination. Make that an impossible combination. I went home and slept. The next day, at the office, I stared mindlessly out the window for a few minutes and then ordered more boxes of inventory from Korea and China. It felt like a game of roulette.

15

Grilled Squid in Backstreet Seoul

O ne morning, a week or so after moving the boxes, I found a discomforting scene at the office. Major Distraction was leaning against a wall in the hallway, looking as if someone had just died. Five other employees were staring inertly at their desks. One was crying.

"You'd better read the telex on your desk," Major Distraction said.
I pushed aside a pile of mail and found a telex from the Silver Fox:

Shocking news! Mr. Kim bankrupt.

I froze. When my mind stopped reeling I frantically sent a telex back, seeking details. Over the next few days the telex spat out cryptic replies. Slowly I pieced together the story: Mr. Kim, president of the silk cut-and-sew factory in Jinju—the only knitted silk garment outfit left in Korea—had tried to build his business without adequate financing. Yarn was hard to get from China, and shipments to customers in Japan, Italy, and the United States had been inconsistent; negative cash flow finally caught up with him. Unable to get additional financing, he was defenseless when his banker called in outstanding loans. The strong arms and quick minds of the Korean government and business aristocracy had no interest in saving their dwindling silk industry. Mr. Kim was left to face a painful financial death alone. WinterSilks was set adrift.

We had been limping through the spring of 1984 with typically diminished revenue while I scheduled inventory for the coming season. I was counting on the Silver Fox and Mr. Kim as core supplier; I had ordered using best-guess forecasting to match planned circulation increases. We had established a routine: I called in my daily messages to Korea by telephone, our telex service in Chicago keyed them and sent them clattering over the wires to the Silver Fox at evening rates. The Silver Fox and I had become comfortable with each other's shorthand. (When processing chips became faster, I bought a telex of our own—its 8-KB baud rate seemed very high tech.)

Four days after the stunning news, I arrived in Seoul. The Silver Fox looked apologetic, not so much for Mr. Kim's demise as for his country's inability to better finance small business start-ups.

It was dusk, the kind of warm, dry, spring evening when time seems suspended in a void, waiting for something apocalyptic to set it free. The Silver Fox said a rainstorm was coming; it would be cooler soon. I figured the coming apocalypse would be either WinterSilks' final demise or a last-ditch Hail Mary effort to find a new source of supply.

It was a good bet that Mr. Kim had made it worth the Silver Fox's while to hold off on informing me of the bankruptcy until I had placed big orders and backed them with an irrevocable bank letter of credit. This froze part of my credit line and gave Mr. Kim financing to draw on to stay afloat if he could ship our order before the bank's letter of credit expired. This would take time to untangle.

The next morning we met at the Silver Fox's offices in Seoul. Mr. Kim's face told the story of a desperate man. He looked scared, tired, and embarrassed that he could not deliver what had been promised. I also learned he was hiding from the law. With over $1,500,000 of debt, equivalent to several times that in the United States, Mr. Kim was in trouble, big-time.

The three of us explored all options, but there was no getting around it: Mr. Kim's silk company was bust, and sourcing our knitted silk goods from South Korea was at a dead end. The Korean silk yarn supply had diminished rapidly because Korean silk cocoon farmers could make more money growing vegetables; the Chinese, who had both a climate more conducive to growing mulberry trees and a less developed economy, could produce cocoons, silk yarn, and knitted silk fabric for much less.

But the Chinese were prohibited from directly selling their yarn to South Korea by a trade embargo, perhaps tied to memories of China's role in the Korean War (thus the need for yarn to go through Hong Kong). Because my last delivery from China had been many months late, I'd been motivated to do frequent business with the more efficient and speedy, though more expensive, South Korean suppliers. Now, without enough goods to support the anticipated sales from the catalogs, and with press time and magazine ads already reserved and committed to, I would soon be taking in money for products I couldn't ship. Once we sold through the contents of the previous season's laggard 55 cartons, and miscellaneous inventory, I would have to refund holiday orders. WinterSilks would go out of business, and Sarah and I would be bust.

As the day wore on I felt a cool bitter sickness rising from the pit of my stomach. The meeting ended, and I went back to my hotel depressed and scared. There were no plans to meet further. My life's opportunity had been rubbed out.

I did calisthenics in the hotel room until I reeked of perspiration. Then I took a cold shower, packed, and checked out of the hotel.

It was still hot and dry as I shuffled through side streets, past food stalls and narrow alleys, lugging my suitcase and briefcase. I found a $20-a-day room at a backstreet hotel, cramped but adequate. Dinner in the lobby restaurant was $5. With no production or delivery schedules to be met, I felt no short-term stress. But I drifted in an abyss of despair.

About 10 o'clock, the Silver Fox called from the hotel's lobby.

"You see, I have found you," he said in a gentle voice as I cradled the receiver to my ear. "Are you all right, Mr. Farwell?" He had scoured local hotels for hours until he found my name on the register. He had come to meet me on his own time, at night, when he could have been home. I was impressed.

A few minutes later he knocked at my flimsy door and peered into my 8×10-foot room. A bare 40-watt bulb hung crookedly from the ceiling.

"I'm worried about you. What will you do now?"

I started to choke up. He clasped his hands to his chest.

"I will try to help," he said. I was 33; he was about 25 years older. Like a caring uncle, he tried to soothe me. He knew that my kids' futures, as well as Sarah's and mine, hung in the balance. And he needed me as a customer. Despite his duplicities, in an odd way the Silver Fox was my friend. I didn't trust him on a deal-by-deal basis, but I did regard him as a good human being who was caught by forces out of his control: the huge, lucrative U.S. import market and the difficult small business environment in South Korea.

We sat in cracked green plastic chairs and talked into the night. It was a still evening, and sounds of Seoul's vendors in the alleys below, and street traffic two blocks away, drifted up to my open window. The aroma of leaded-gas exhaust mingled with that of charcoal-grilled squid.

The Silver Fox and I examined drawings of a few woven silk items that could be produced at local factories that summer to fill the catalog. Other than these handkerchiefs, neckties, and scarves, there was virtually nothing he could now have made in Korea for WinterSilks.

His unfiltered cigarette smoke hung in the stillness, filling the small room with a gray haze. Just before midnight, the Silver Fox let out a deep sigh, sat back in his chair, and blew a final cloud of smoke into the air. He extracted the stub delicately from its ivory holder and then snuffed it out on the floor with the toe of his carefully polished shoe, hard leather squeaking against polished linoleum. Outside, the late-night street noise had dropped to a murmur.

He leaned forward in his chair, hands on his knees, eyes fixed resolutely on me.

"Mr. Farwell, let me tell you something, just as a friend." He paused for a moment, cleared his throat, then said softly, as if afraid that a government spy might be listening: "*Go to the Red China.*"

I stared blankly at him, numbed with fatigue and despair. Our inability to get knitted silk out of China at a reasonable speed was the reason I was in Korea in the first place.

But now, as the Silver Fox pointed out, I had no choice. As of this week, our only source was China. Like it or not, the gauntlet had to be run. There would just have to be a way to make the China supply line work. I would place orders with China and *will* them to be shipped on time.

I stared off into space, worn down by my ongoing bad luck.

"I'll try Hong Kong," I said halfheartedly.

We walked down the bare hallway and cement stairs, past a bare-bones registration counter, and into Seoul's warm, murky night, taking our sketches of handkerchiefs, neckties, and scarves several blocks to the Chosun Hotel.

It was midnight. At the hotel's cigar stand, the Silver Fox and I waited in dejected silence while a sleepy-eyed clerk made photocopies of our product drawings.

Then I heard a familiar voice calling my name. Turning from the cigar counter, I saw Guy Heckman, a high school classmate. Grinning, he slapped me on the back; I nearly keeled over. He was a vice president at Chase Manhattan, specializing in the coal trade in Korea, Hong Kong, and Australia. He too was headed to Hong Kong. And here I was, down on my luck, eyeing failure, while Guy was on the rise in his career, living in posh hotels around Asia and backed by the resources of a huge multinational corporation.

The Silver Fox stood back politely while Guy and I chatted. Then, photocopies made, my business in Korea was finished. At half-past midnight Guy said goodnight and went up to his room in the elegant Chosun. The Silver Fox, bowing, our newly copied product sketches under one arm, shook hands with me outside the hotel.

"Good luck, Mr. Farwell."

Then he walked away, his dark-gray suit dissolving into the night's polluted murk. I waved slowly, feeling a bittersweet sadness to see him go. Then I wandered back to my lodgings through alleys eerily lit by glowing charcoal in food vendors' cooking stoves and the intermittent flashes of headlights on main streets two blocks away. The odor of grilled squid still hung in the air.

Heckman and I met up again in Hong Kong a few days later for a somber breakfast at the Hong Kong Hotel. We were an odd couple: a well-spoken fellow who had just been offered the number two position at Chase Manhattan's Hong Kong office—which came with an elaborate residence on Hong Kong Island overlooking the ocean and staffed with servants and a chauffeur—and a desperate, soon-to-be-bankrupt entrepreneur with a great demand for his product but a dead supply line.

Guy invited me on a Chinese junk his bank had chartered to entertain guests, but I was too busy running for my life, looking for traces of the modern Silk Road. We parted company at the Tsimsatsui terminal of Hong Kong's Star Ferry.

I figured WinterSilks and I were done for. It was nearly May. I needed deliveries in our warehouse by September 30, and deliveries from China usually took a year. If my bank knew my situation it would have called in my loan and run me through a meat grinder. Fortunately, many thousands of miles away in Madison, they hadn't a clue.

On the plane from Seoul to Hong Kong, I remembered a recent China connection there. It was a dim light as far as hope goes, but who knew? Maybe something could be coaxed from it. At this point, I couldn't afford to overlook any contacts.

I had been talking to an importing agent on the East Coast for several weeks. He had cold-called me after seeing our ads in the *Wall Street Journal.* I privately referred to him as Hammerhead, due to his unyielding, sometimes obnoxious style of communication and negotiation. He had ties to knitted silk factories in southern China, the vanguard of modernization. I had few other contacts in China: just a pair of Chinese brothers in Toronto who had brokered a late delivery the year before, and two small Hong Kong agents, neither of whom had the connections or horsepower to make things happen fast enough.

Once in Hong Kong, the first call I made was to Hammerhead's Hong Kong partner. By chance, not only was she in, but so too was Hammerhead, visiting from the United States. They scheduled me for the following day. They seemed eager to talk.

In the morning I took a hot, cramped elevator to one of the top floors of a building near the Star Ferry on the Kowloon side of Hong Kong. Hammerhead and his Hong Kong Chinese partner, Tiger Lady, whisked me into their spectacular showroom overlooking Hong Kong harbor. They didn't know my predicament. An assistant brought in a tray with a formal tea setting. The Potential New Client Schmooze began.

"Mr. Fah-*well*, we do good job for you," Tiger Lady said with practiced confidence and an automatic smile that revealed a predator's row of sturdy white teeth. I figured they could probably chew through steel.

"We like to do your silk," she said, holding her smile like an unsheathed weapon.

I felt like I was talking to a 1920s Chicago mob boss who was making me a special offer. I listened politely, easily playing the role of naïve Midwesterner in bustling Hong Kong. Between sips of tea,

I stole glances out the window at picturesque junks and fishing boats plying the harbor far below. Where would I be a year from now? Exiled in disgrace from Sarah's and my families for having gone bankrupt? Living in a cave in the Ozarks? Managing the night shift at a fast-food joint in Madison, having grown a beard and dyed my hair in case someone I knew walked in?

Hammerhead took over, and my reverie was jolted back to the here and now.

"Free enterprise is changing the southern region of China near Hong Kong faster than expected," Hammerhead was saying in precise English with a slight New England accent, waving one arm in a grand gesture toward the traffic-choked streets and busy harbor below.

I felt my eyebrows rise. Could it be? I soaked up his words like a large, dry sponge in the bottom of a leaky boat.

"Deliveries of knitted silk garments from a just-renovated factory in the south have made a quantum leap in production and shipment times," Hammerhead said, "from 10 to 14 months two years ago to five or six months this season."

I was a starving cat being offered a heaping plateful of fresh sardines.

"We have strong ties with this factory," he continued.

My eyes began to roll happily back in my head. May, being the fifth month, plus six months delivery, equaled November. Maybe now there was hope for WinterSilks after all. If I used the 55 cartons in my basement and delayed mailing the first salvo of catalogs by two weeks, to late October, I could cut the inventory vacuum down to the wire and possibly survive without a backorder and order cancellation debacle. And certainly without the bankruptcy that had been unavoidable up until 10 minutes ago.

Hammerhead paced the office, pointing to charts and holding up sample garments. Tiger Lady watched, her little black eyes boring into me, like a coiled snake sizing up the tastiness of its newfound and now cornered prey. She was about one-third Hammerhead's size, but I could tell from the killer instinct in her eyes that she called the shots.

I flashed an accommodating smile her way and listened as Hammerhead concluded the schmooze.

"We will visit the factories constantly, looking after your order. After garment production is finished, delivery by truck, train, ocean freighter, and train and truck again is five weeks from China to Hong

Kong, Seattle, Chicago, and Madison, if American President Lines is used. We can even get part of your first order shipped from Hong Kong in four months."

My jaw dropped. Could it be true?

Hammerhead was a bruiser of a fellow, but he sat down tentatively. Had Tiger Lady approved his performance? Would the potential new client place an order? Would this precious slice of time result in a new source of cash flow, or was this skinny American carrying a thin wallet and wasting their time?

Little did they know that they, and fate, had thrown me a life preserver. In one 45-minute visit I was theoretically saved from bankruptcy. Tiger Lady and Hammerhead did not know that I had few other contacts in Hong Kong. Only after two days of meetings and negotiations did they pry out of me that I had never even *been* to Hong Kong before. My prior importing from China, via Hong Kong, had all been done by mail and telex. By the time Hammerhead and Tiger Lady extracted this, the deal was set, prices were firm, and we had signed a binding agreement—a Hong Kong and United States contract, as opposed to the more slippery China and United States contract. Hammerhead knew he could be sued in U.S. courts if their performance was bad. It was a dream reversal.

After my order was finalized, Tiger Lady stalked around her showroom holding several new products from another Chinese factory she worked with. She smelled new-customer blood.

"We have many new things for you, Mr. Fah-*well*."

She pulled an armful of ladies' sweaters and blouses from a nearby closet. Most of them carried the Orvis label. I knew that Orvis—a distinguished company and America's oldest mail-order catalog, based in Manchester, Vermont—had said "no thanks" to errant deliveries from the Hard-Asses and instead gone directly to factories in China, using Hammerhead and Tiger Lady as United States–Hong Kong buying agents. I knew that Orvis would have negotiated exclusives on all these products.

"Aren't those Orvis products?" I asked in a quiet voice.

Tiger Woman smiled innocently. "Oh, Mr. Fah-*well*," she said in a theatrical, mock-surprised voice. "The styles we make for you will be different, just to your specifications."

I nodded slowly and offered a thin smile, wondering when our office would find time or expertise to come up with specifications for so many different unproven styles.

After a pause of 15 seconds or so, she handed me several sheets of paper with product drawings and dimensions for each piece of the garments. "Here are specifications for your garments," she said proudly.

I almost burst out laughing, but managed to bite my lip in time. Tiger Lady and Hammerhead had not only saved me from bankruptcy but also offered a plethora of new product options. Even so, I decided then and there to never waste time and legal fees to have any "exclusive" products made in Hong Kong or China.

That night I unwittingly let down my guard again. I was strolling on Kowloon's harbor-side promenade; feeling weary, I stopped for a cold drink. I ducked into a decent-looking place and sat down at the bar. Again, I was the only Caucasian.

Immediately, from behind a curtain, four or five well-sculpted young Chinese women appeared in clothing that resembled some kind of bikini after a typhoon had torn most of it away. I sensed trouble, so I stood up to leave. But another woman, about 200 pounds heavier, who probably could have played linebacker for the Green Bay Packers, appeared behind me and authoritatively pushed me back into my seat. I was a goner.

Pretty soon the half-naked girls were clamoring for drinks. Of course, a rookie tourist, overwhelmed by the spectacular show of affection, would reflexively say yes to all drink requests, thinking they would be at the usual market price. I suspected this would not be the case. A beer or soft drink in one of these establishments cost a small fortune, depending on the mood and confidence level of the owner that night.

I tried to stand up a second time and succeeded in getting three or four feet toward the door, despite several young lasses pulling me toward the bar and the hefty Gorilla Woman trying to get me in a headlock. I made it another step and felt a vise-like grip on my wrist. The guy looked like Mr. Kung Fu himself. He was only about five foot four to my six foot two, but I seemed to recognize him from some Chinese Westerns where people karate chop and kick each other until body parts end up in the next province.

At that point it seemed much smarter to just buy everybody a vastly overpriced drink and then get out of there unsmashed and/or unstabbed by whoever else was lurking in the back room. So I hung around for 25 minutes, pretending to enjoy myself while the flock of thirsty girls rang up the bar bill and feigned interest in their tired, skinny visitor. I sipped my iced soda pop and then deftly spat it back into the glass so I wouldn't ingest too much of whatever they wanted to load me with that night. I figured access to my wallet, credit cards, and passport was what they were after.

Finally I got up my nerve and asked for the bill. Those who spoke English became strangely silent and backed off. The moment of paradigm shift had arrived.

Gorilla Woman, whom I assumed was co-owner, came toward me smiling defiantly. In her outstretched hand was a most imaginative bill. I tried to divide the slew of numbers in my head by the Hong Kong-to-U.S. dollar exchange rate and came up with about $400. That seemed like a very reasonable price for escaping with my life.

While I studied the bill, I could see Mr. Kung Fu and two of his buddies milling around in the shadows by the front door, eyeing me darkly. Better not delay. I smiled approvingly at Gorilla Woman, signed the charge slip, and reclaimed my credit card. The sea of playmates parted momentarily while I made my way to the door. I thanked them for a lovely evening. Mr. Kung Fu let me out the door with a grunt. I walked quickly up the stairs to the street.

At home in Madison three days later, I cancelled my credit card and wrote a blow-by-blow narrative of the event to the vice president of our bank, which handled our credit card processing and deposits. A week later, he called.

"Can I buy you a soda?" He muffled a laugh.

"No thanks, don't touch the stuff anymore."

This time he laughed out loud. "Sorry the Gorilla Woman scared you. Tell you what: to cheer you up, I'll reverse the charges."

So $400 worth of soda was free. Our banker had a fresh story for his golf buddies. I just wished I could have seen Gorilla Woman's face when she saw the chargeback on her next credit card statement.

That fall, most of the goods from Tiger Lady and Hammerhead arrived on time. We frantically counted incoming pieces versus our packing list; the counts sometimes matched. Shortage claims were to be "consolidated at the end of the season," Hammerhead told me. A trusting Midwesterner, I took his word for it. The turnaround seemed too easy, too good to be true.

And too good to last.

16

Uncle Bob and the Sharp-Eyed Rookie

We could sell a ton more silk, but to order it from Tiger Lady and Hammerhead or anywhere else, I needed larger bank credit lines. Unfortunately, a phalanx of doubting bankers, clueless about WinterSilks' prospects, stood in my way.

While the bankers doubted, customers besieged our phones, demanding WinterSilks garments in time for the holidays. Happy Linebacker at our neighborhood bank didn't hear the ringing and turned down my loan requests with tiresome regularity. So I hit the pavement again. Several weeks went by; still no luck.

Then my father, a stock broker and investment banker in Chicago, discovered that a business friend knew the president of United Bank & Trust Company in Madison. This fellow put in a good word.

"Just listen to the kid," he said to the president. "You never know."

A week passed and then I was granted a brief meeting with Sharp-Eyed Rookie, a recently-hired assistant vice president and one of several point men for the president.

The night before our meeting, I shined my shoes to a bright gleam and memorized my speech. I figured Sharp-Eyed Rookie's job was to either snuff me out before I wasted any more of the bank's time or—risking his yet-to-be-established reputation—refer me upstairs to the president.

At 10 A.M. the next day, with my pulse steady at about 135 and my skin the color of a deceased albino lizard, I drove to downtown Madison and pumped the flesh with Sharp-Eyed Rookie. He seemed way too optimistic for a banker.

"I've done research and trial-and-error testing," I told him. "WinterSilks is special, and its products sell. I need more bank credit to import garments and finance growth. My current bank doesn't get it." I spoke solo for five minutes and answered his questions for half an hour. Then Sharp-Eyed Rookie looked into my eyes while the wheels in his head spun through what his gut was telling him.

There was a long pause. Then he said, "I'd like to have you meet the boss upstairs."

I exhaled like an April wind rushing across high country plains.

United Bank's president was available just then, and Sharp-Eyed Rookie introduced me as if I were a new right fielder from the Mexican development baseball leagues, worthy of consideration for Double-A play. I explained that I needed a revolving credit line of $450,000 plus a computer loan of $25,000, since Happy Linebacker's bank had, to that day, been willing to go to only our original house-sale $120,000 CD. If we could get $450,000 of credit and repay it by the end of February 1985, I said, borrowing on a larger and larger scale would be easier for both of us.

"We like people who make money," the president said as he shook my clammy hand after our meeting. "You do that consistently, keep the risks down, maybe we'll be your banker."

So far, so good. The bank's board of directors had favorably reviewed WinterSilks' formalized loan request, which by then was about the size and weight of a small encyclopedia. I needed a favorable opinion from just one more person: Uncle Bob, president of a $100 million-in-sales food-by-mail catalog company and a member of United Bank's board of directors. He was the go-to guy for loans to catalog and direct-mail businesses.

I imagined the board saying, "Hey Bob, check this guy out. See if he has any horse sense, or if he's just another wannabe with one of those new spreadsheets."

People who worked for Uncle Bob said he was calm and friendly, like every kid's favorite uncle, and did most of the listening. They also said he had a memory like a steel trap. So I was on edge a few days later as I drove northeast of Madison to Sun Prairie, where

Uncle Bob managed a sprawling manufacturing, marketing, and distribution facility with the owner-founder.

I sat down in his modest office and he sized me up without saying a word. Then, a quiet opener: "What makes you think you can make your company go?"

"Uh . . . we have a hot product and know how to s-sell it," I stammered.

Seeing my nervousness, he fed me easy bait.

"What colors sell best? What percentage are returned? Where does your stuff come from? What mailing lists work for you?"

I think he saw me smile when I heard the cupcake questions. Asking me this kind of stuff after five hungry years on the direct-mail warpath was like holding a match to a tank of propane.

Uncle Bob listened to my replies and then toughened the questions again. "Why do your mailing lists pull? How do you preselect your tests? What customer profiles are emerging? What makes you think China will continue selling to you—what if they decide to turn off the tap?"

I hammered out answers for another hour. Then we were done. Uncle Bob's parting words were: "Keep it up. You'll be surprised how sales and profits can grow."

I headed for the parking lot, gripping my pockmarked 1970s-era plastic briefcase like it was the last lifejacket on a sinking Filipino ferry. Was he just being polite, or did he really believe? I worried all the way home. There was no indication whether it would be thumbs up or down.

Two days later Sharp-Eyed Rookie called.

"Bob said you know the game. We'd like to be your banker."

I fell back in my chair; a smiled drifted down from the heavens and attached itself to my face.

Uncle Bob told United Bank it would be OK to loan me $450,000 in an annual revolving line of credit. This assumed collateral of our $120,000 CD and a first lien on all inventory, equipment, and office fixtures. It also assumed I would sign an unlimited personal guarantee, same as other first-time customers at the bank. It was what I needed, but it was also a fear-inducing responsibility.

And there was just one other thing—I had to come up with another $100,000 of collateral. United Bank would loan not 3.75 times the amount of collateral we were to place at their bank, but only 2.25 times. Not all that I had hoped for, but better than Chicken Lips and Happy Linebacker.

I twitched nervously all day and night, and in the morning I got on the phone to the only lifeline I had.

My father listened for a while, and then with a slightly halting voice came through with an amazing gamble of trust: He agreed to move a $100,000 CD from retirement savings at a Chicago bank and place it at United Bank & Trust as additional collateral. He would still own the CD, as long as I didn't default on the loan. If I screwed up, the bank would gobble up this piece of my father's precious retirement funds—and Sarah's and my house-proceeds CD, too.

A few days later Sharp-Eyed Rookie brought a small mountain of paperwork to our offices, and I signed. WinterSilks now had a credit facility that matched its selling opportunity. Performance, persistence, and contacts had opened the pipeline of borrowed money. (And in three years my father would get his CD back, fully intact.)

The early missteps were now recast as learning opportunities. The trick had been making them on a small scale so we could survive to fight another day. Those early failures made me realize that the less start-up money a person has, the sooner he or she will pay attention, learn the business, and become self-sustaining. The banking side of the equation was working out just the way Smiling Dan had said it would.

Having the new loan was an emotional elixir. But in the back of my mind I wondered if I was ready to be turned loose with that much money, borrowed or not. Was our product idea really solid enough? Could it drive profitability year after year? Was I the right guy to do this? Would I be better off as a schoolteacher in Saskatchewan? After all, the money had to be paid back—in less than 12 months.

The key was figuring out how secure WinterSilks' revenues were. What, or who, drove the demand for our products? I needed to quantify these fundamentals. I studied, researched, and worried my brains until they seemed to rattle like spare coins in a coffee can.

With the new bank loan in hand and February 1985 coming to a close, it was time to analyze sales data from the just-concluded season. I stared at handwritten rows of numbers on old-fashioned ledger sheets and at written notes from customers, trying to envision how a much larger company could be built, and how stable it could, or could not, become. I was looking for past data to tell our future story, just as the old-timer in Manhattan had suggested: "Find out what the numbers are saying." I needed to do that before spending a dime of the freshly borrowed money.

If I could understand the story on my accumulated accounting sheets, they could become a perpetuating force of their own; they would show that what we were doing on a small scale could truly be done on an ever-increasing scale until a good-sized, very profitable company was built—if service was friendly and fast, and quality, guarantee, and price/value were strong. Then maybe we could, with statistical confidence, create dozens of related products in an appealing catalog and build a significant American brand. Being the most profitable, and perhaps the biggest, within our niche of "The Ultimate Winter Warmth" would follow.

The Chinese were expert in cultivating young mulberry trees for their leaves, and feeding the leaves to silkworms, which in turn digested the leaves, morphed, and spun cocoons. Before these cocoons could hatch butterflies, the Chinese gathered them to soak in tubs of hot water. Their strands were then unraveled, thus producing the miracle of silk thread. (Unlike wool, cotton, or hemp, silk is the only natural fiber that is produced in its ready-to-use form. Some say that ounce for ounce, silk is stronger than steel.)

Silk threads would then be wound on skeins and twisted into multi-part yarns, ready to be washed, and then knitted or woven into fabric. The fabric would be dyed, dried, washed again, then cut and sewn into finished garments, just as the Chinese had done from the dawn of the Industrial Revolution to the eve of the Depression.

So, while the Chinese would make the product, we would create or stipulate the designs, commit to production orders, import, and *sell* them. One element was key to that level of success: we would make sure it was WinterSilks—and not one of our monster-sized competitors like L.L.Bean or Lands' End—that brought these popular silk products to all those eager customers.

"Good luck with that dream," Dan, a brainy friend in New York, told me over the phone while he studied for law school one night. "If L.L.Bean or Lands' End gets interested in these products, you might as well fold up your tent."

He was right—to sustain our products on a large scale, we needed a secret weapon, some factor or some knowledge that no large competitor had. I wrestled with this during long, dark hours in the early morning when I was supposed to be asleep.

We did have one advantage over our larger competitors: Winter-Silks was a one-product-category company, now that we had winnowed out the soapstone and other follies. We were not restrained by obligations to many seasonal product lines the way L.L.Bean and Lands' End were. When they came across a hot-selling knitted silk garment, rubber boot, fleece sweater, or wooden lawn chair, they were hesitant to risk a separate catalog of just that product type. WinterSilks, on the other hand, could; its *raison d'être* was to be a niche company.

Knowing that, I left for work that morning with a smile on my face. I called Dan and explained my reasoning. He was quiet for a moment.

"Maybe you're right," he finally replied. "If the big guys don't roll out these products, you own the playing field—until some other niche player wants to go head to head. Better move fast."

Before moving fast but first I needed more statistical clarification.

A clue came unexpectedly. That winter Howard Mead, cofounder and former publisher of *Wisconsin Trails* magazine, had occasionally joined me for a beer at rural Blackhawk Ridge after Wednesday night cross-country ski races. We both skied on the Jackrabbits, one of 12 six-man teams. After the 10-kilometer races one cold night, the owner stopped by our table. She had seen WinterSilks' ads in numerous publications and wanted to show me an actual knitted silk ladies' shirt from China, circa 1925.

Her mother had worn the shirt as a child in Minnesota, and it was still in decent condition. I studied it carefully by the light of the fire. It was better made and more intricate than anything seen from the China of the 1980s—and it was now 60 years old.

I turned the shirt over in my hands as snowflakes swirled outside and logs in the fireplace turned to glowing orange coals. After a while my thoughts started to fall into place.

Allow me to sketch the pertinent history behind the product niche we were tapping with WinterSilks:

During the early part of the twentieth century, German garment companies installed knitting machines in a few mulberry tree- and silkworm-rich locations in China and produced knitted silk fabric and finished garments for export. Those machines were assembled in China between 1900 and 1925. In the Roaring Twenties a small volume of knitted silk long johns made its way from these factories to trade shows in European and North American cities, where small retailers like ourselves discovered them and brought them into the chilly homes of northern Europe and the northern tier of the United States. They were worn by families in Vancouver, Sun Valley, Minneapolis, Buffalo, Boston, Ottawa, Oslo, Stockholm, Helsinki, Zurich, Munich, and the like.

Then the Depression, Japanese occupation, World War II, famine, Civil War, Mao, and isolation destroyed the Chinese economy and the sericulture (silk farming) industry that had been a key part of it. Production was not replicated in any other country, because no other country had large-scale sericulture.

Decades passed. Then, a few years after Nixon and Kissinger creaked open the international trade doorways to China in the 1970s, the Hard-Asses from New York—yes, those New York garment importers, whom I'd first met at a trade show in 1981, and who claimed to have *invented* knitted silk long johns—rediscovered them while poking around in China while having other garments made. After stumbling across the old forgotten German machines, Old Man Hard-Ass ordered knitted silk garments to complement his numerous other garment styles. Those knitting machines went back to work, and the Hard-Asses' first order spearheaded the *remanufacturing* of these garments for North American customers.

The Hard-Asses sold knitted silk long johns and turtlenecks primarily to outdoor apparel catalogers and outdoor retailers. These catalogers and retailers had a sports-minded, young-adult and middle-aged clientele who were buying comfortable, perspiration-wicking synthetic-fiber long johns. Knitted silk was lighter, less bulky, and softer next to the skin, but it was not the perfect match for this consumer segment, because it doesn't wick as well as some sports-specific synthetic fabrics.

Knitted silk, however, was a perfect match for our more urban consumer segment: silk doesn't retain perspiration odor the way many of the early synthetic fibers did, and knitted silk fits easily without bulkiness under men's and women's business clothes at the office in cold weather—something you can't do with synthetics. This, I guessed, was driving much of our demand, and the New York importers weren't on to it. Also, they knew the wholesale business and didn't mess around with statistics of the direct-to-the-consumer mail-order business.

So the clientele for knitted silk garments in North America was less likely to frequent the sports-motif stores and catalogs that the Hard-Asses catered to. And some of them, like the co-owner of Blackhawk Ridge, knew of knitted silk long johns long before I was a struggling catalog entrepreneur in search of a hot product. This is how a big data point lit up for me: our market was different from that of our competing importer. That was a relief.

Still, I had a recurring concern: Would our customers fuel a short-term demand or a mail-order product line that would endure? If it was going to be a short-lived game, I didn't want to borrow much. If it was going to be a potentially profitable marathon, then taking on a boatload of seasonal debt was a more comfortable matter.

I stared into the changing colors of the ski-lodge fire, lost in thought. Then I remembered that the previous season, Sarah and I had put together a questionnaire for existing customers—a one-page letter requesting a reply to a few questions on both sides of an $8\frac{1}{2}'' \times 11''$ sheet. Customers were asked to fill this out—it took less than five minutes—and return it in the provided postage-paid, return-address envelope for a $5 discount to use on a future sale.

We inserted a thousand letters and return envelopes in outgoing customer packages, and within three or four weeks had a whopping 30-percent response rate. We had tabulated the responses, but I'd been too busy to pay much attention to the results.

Now I remembered. I drove home on back roads to Madison, eager to plunge into the surveys. Arriving at the office about 11 P.M., still dressed in cross-country ski attire, I tore through our file cabinets and found the survey results, as well as copies of old customer letters. I read them until after 1 A.M.

In many of the letters customers referred to using silk long johns when they were young adults or teenagers in affluent northern-tier cities, or as young children remembered their parents enjoying them in the pre-Depression era. One customer wrote, "I've been looking for them ever since." Another commented: "Your product reminds me of my grandfather."

Three more criteria jumped off the page: The majority of that era's customers were female; household income was $50,000 or better in 1983 dollars, which at that time put them in the upper tier of mail-order lists; and average age was nearly 65, with a base range of 50 to 90. Our customers were similar to the woman at Blackhawk Ridge who showed me her mother's shirt. Many had heard of or used silk long johns before, and now our ads were offering these garments again. Some customers had waited half a century.

We were not selling a hot *new* product; we were *reintroducing* an established *old* product. No wonder it was a fast seller. Many customers were preconditioned to buy—the Hard-Asses' younger customers were not.

We had an edge. And I figured that only I knew about it.

Our niche also had a long-term guarantor—the aging factor. Once older clientele passed away, they would be replaced by the middle generation, whose skin would become more sensitive as they grew older. With the graying of America looming large and affluent on the demographic horizon, the younger, uninitiated portion of our second-tier target customers would eventually covet knitted silk's benefits. Ours was not a limited audience, but a growing, self-replacing audience. It was a direct-marketer's dream, and it was an easier target audience than I could have hoped for. It was a 60-year-old secret that now revealed itself.

Any half-sober mailing list broker could supply me with millions of rented names meeting our three criteria. All I had to do was experiment with the lists in safe ascensions of test panels to distinguish the well-maintained lists from the sloppy, poorly maintained ones, so that the unforeseen hazards of leaping from each mailing to a larger one would not increase disproportionately.

"Forget expensive, risky space ads," I mumbled to myself as the clock reached 1:15 A.M. "We have a *catalog* business to build."

Now I knew that WinterSilks would not be a flash-in-the-pan, five-year business. With careful feeding and care of products and customers, we could build her into a steadily growing enterprise. Realizing this, I stopped worrying about the dozens of export cartons that would soon be arriving, and the money that would be owed to the bank.

Back at home, tiptoeing past Lisa and Ted's cribs, I showered and was in bed by 2:30 A.M. Sleep came more easily than it had in weeks, months—or years.

17

The Delusional Printer

Understanding the 60-year-old secret gave me new confidence as winter ebbed to spring and spring to summer while we waited for goods to arrive from Tiger Lady and Hammerhead Bob. It was like every slow season—a time to prepare catalog and magazine advertisements against a phalanx of deadlines culminating in catalog press dates and magazine production deadlines. During sweltering days of August, Sarah proofread my copy about WinterSilks' "Ultimate Winter Warmth." Paste-up art boards were rushed to the film prep house, then the printer. I counted the days until positive cash flow would be produced from the holiday season harvest.

Lists were reanalyzed, ordered, monitored for delivery, and compressed into the magic of computerized magnetic tape; they were combined into continuous zip-code streams, then dumped onto magnetic tape and run through a name descrambler. The large-format magnetic tape was shipped to a printer who would zap addresses directly onto our catalogs as they came out of the printing press' bindery. Loading docks were 50 feet from the end of the bindery and addressing machines, and at the mouth of those loading docks waited semi-truck trailers from the U.S. Postal Service. It was a manufacturing process that came together like many distant-sourced creeks forming a mighty river.

At the end of that river stood the mailboxes of American consumers. Their decisions—made in five to ten seconds—would determine whether an order was to be placed or if the catalog's precious pulp would go back into the waste stream, hopefully to be recycled and run through the presses yet again, perhaps in its next life as an advertising insert for vitamin pills, garden tools, or senior citizen health insurance.

From the orchestration of this waterway, and from the timely shipping reports from American President Lines, it looked like we could have a season on the scale everyone hoped for. Perhaps we would not only survive, but also prosper—if Tiger Lady and Hammerhead Bob got their capitalist-enlightened factory friends to continue to produce on time, at the right quality level, with documents prepared accurately for shipment. So far, things were going our way. All I had to do, once pre-press film was delivered, was show up at the printer. Pre-press film had been delivered on time.

Then disaster struck.

Our color film separator from Seattle had come back east to supervise quality control on this press run, and he called with the bad news.

"Color's not coming up," he shouted above a background din of heavy machinery.

"What do you mean, 'It's not up'? You've been there nearly 24 hours!" I was at our dining room table; Lisa and Ted played nearby.

"It could be another 24 *weeks*," he replied. "If I were you I'd start making other plans."

"Whaddaya mean?"

"I mean you ought to start looking for another place to print. These clowns may never get this new press figured out."

There was a pained silence. My mouth went dry; I fumbled for words. Where would I find a printer in the midst of the printing industry's busy season? It was an unthinkable predicament.

"You serious?" No printer could be inept enough to not be able to print.

"Come see for yourself. They're running the press quarter-speed, wasting tons of your Canadian paper, and the four-color plates don't line up. They're making a mess."

If that was true, we could be close to bankruptcy again. I grabbed my briefcase, ran to the garage, and slammed the car door as the engine roared to life.

Driving an hour and a quarter to the northeast, I arrived close to midnight. Sure enough, the Aspiring Small Printer I had selected for the fall 1984 catalog couldn't get his new $4 million Italian press to work. If he couldn't print, we couldn't mail. If we couldn't mail, product couldn't sell. If product couldn't sell, we couldn't deposit cash from sales and pay back the bank for imported silk clothing financed by the bank's credit line. Nor could we make payroll; pay huge paper, list rental, and printing bills; or, for that matter, stay in business. The holiday rocket was poised, its fuse was ready to be lit, but the launch pad, a very complex printing press, was not functioning. If the now more aptly named Delusional Printer couldn't print, a whole lot of people were in a mess of trouble. Especially me. I wondered if the Long Island Leg Breaker might make a return visit.

I'd been spending 10 days each year supervising pre-press production and press-run quality of two major color catalogs and seven small two-color catalogs in various printing plants. I knew that printing was not something to mess with. You either were on time or you got financially bit, badly.

One night earlier that year I'd been checking a press run for one of WinterSilks' catalogs at a large printer in nearby Waterloo, Wisconsin. Suddenly a huge roar went up behind me. I felt the concrete floor shake—which is saying something, because the floor was over four feet thick. What was making all that noise? I turned and picked up a discarded sheet. It was the Midwest edition of *Time* magazine, many millions of copies strong. Color quality had just been OK'd by a *Time* employee and the pressroom mechanics were bringing the machinery up to full speed. Each of the 100-plus deadlines leading up to this point had been met, and now the last step of production was kicking in. It felt like a 747 taking off next door. It was awesome. It was also two o'clock in the morning.

For our own catalog later that year, several printers had bid; I'd settled on the alluring low price of the Delusional Printer. He was eager to utilize his elaborate new Italian press. Unbeknownst to me, it was still being assembled at the time they bid my catalog. In fairness, the press had looked impressive: it seemed half the length of a football field, with the complexity of a small battleship.

The good news was that I had used the best catalog color film separator in the United States to work with our fashion merchandise photos (separating them into the three core colors, plus black) to transform into production film for subsequent plating and printing. Their man was experienced enough to have given me this advance warning. He also knew that total sales of the Delusional Printer were just $4 million the previous year, and thus the Delusional Printer didn't have the capital to stand around and learn how to run the new press. They needed experimental guinea pigs, like me. By accepting his enticing bid, I had fallen into a trap.

For two days, the film technician from Seattle had dozed on a couch and waited for color to come up right on the new press. We had 32- and 16-page forms that would be printed, collated, bound, and trimmed into a 48-page catalog, at a speed that makes the Indianapolis 500 look like a go-cart track. Such is the beauty of high-volume web printing presses—*if* the pre-press setup goes smoothly.

After watching progress go sideways and a lot of paper being wasted, I bailed out, leaving the color tech rep still catnapping on the couch. Waiting for the neophyte printer would lead nowhere; I didn't want to delay an exit decision too long and miss our holiday selling season. I drove furiously back to the office and got on the phone to call each printer that had bid on the job. I asked each to find time in their press schedules. A few hemmed and hawed; none called me back.

Not being able to print a catalog on time right here in the Germanic, organized, industrial southern Wisconsin region was something I'd never expected in my worst dreams. If we couldn't get the catalog printed right then, so that it could be mailed every two weeks beginning at least in October, we would miss the entire Christmas selling season. We would have no orders (except from space ads); and we'd have a huge draw on the bank credit line to pay for arriving inventory, postage, and other unpaid bills for up-front costs.

Eventually, I remembered Barbara Warner at Krueger Printing in Milwaukee, a high-end firm. I dialed furiously and got her on the line.

"You're not going to believe this, Barbara. I stupidly passed on your bid, and now I'm getting shafted by the low-bid printer I fell for. I really, really need your help."

There was a pause. The next words from her lips would spell my execution or salvation. Painful seconds ticked by. She was a polished veteran at a high-quality, old-line Milwaukee company. Surely she wouldn't squash me and hang up the phone. Or would she?

I heard papers rustling on her desk in the background, then her voice: "What are the form configurations?"

My God, I thought, *she might be interested. Maybe, maybe . . .*

"A 32 and a 16," I shot back.

"Who did the separations?"

"The guys in Seattle."

"Oooo . . . That's good news."

Another pause. My pulse was racing.

"What kind of paper stock did you end up with?"

"Pentair coated number four, standard roll size, same weight and width as your quote, I think."

"Find out and call me back."

I rummaged through my files, got the data, and punched her number back in so hard that my phone walked across my desk to the far edge. When Barbara answered, I barked out the answers like a shipwrecked sailor giving GPS coordinates to a distant Coast Guard station before his batteries went dead.

I heard more rustling on her desk. Was she looking at their internal production calendar? I heard fingers tapping a calculator. *Please, Barbara. Please . . .*

"Call me in half an hour," she said. There was a delicate click.

I felt the finite window of the year's selling season growing smaller and smaller. I forced myself to breathe, paced around my office, and then called back. Her voice had a new clarity.

"We'll run the 32 here in Milwaukee, the 16 at our north-suburban plant. Got room Thursday, 11:00 P.M. We'll bind and mail from Milwaukee. Give me the address for picking up the plates and paper. We'll get 'em in the morning, maybe even tonight."

Yes!

I nearly slid to the floor. Krueger could use the existing plates—the four delicate blankets of soft metal that had been burned with the film's four basic colors of text and images. They would pick them up as well as the truckloads of web printing paper rolls we had inventoried at the aspiring small printer. Krueger would finish pre-press work within 48 hours, then print, bind, address, and mail nearly on time. They bet that WinterSilks would grow into a larger customer. Their competitors saw a mess; they saw opportunity.

There had been no mention of price, but I knew it would be fair. Krueger was once a small company too; in growing big, they had never lost touch with customer service.

Our catalog rolled off the presses at Krueger's two plants and was bound, trimmed, addressed, and mailed in time. I was present at each stage; no one had been trained to take my place. When the mailing was out, I returned to the office and paced. Would this catalog, and its postal and catalog production costs that were paid up front, reach ignition? I worried through several sleepless nights.

That Sunday I took Lisa and Ted to the children's zoo. The soft touch of their tiny hands made me wish I too was a child again, not an entrepreneur who had been smothered with suffocating risks. Then again, their touch also made me realize that my life beneath the wheel of deadlines was their sole source of support.

Goods continued to arrive on time from Tiger Lady and Hammerhead. The catalog's response kicked in and gathered steam. The staffed-and-waiting call center came alive; telephones rang in encouraging bursts. The post office delivered bags of orders. WinterSilks surged ahead. The Delusional Printer nearly killed us that fall, but—thanks to Krueger and Barbara Werner—WinterSilks dodged the bullet.

18

The Long Road to Almost Perfect

With the 1984–1985 season back on its feet and orders arriving in flurries, we started getting buried in paperwork again. We were accumulating a small landfill of paper records that were time-consuming to access.

"Ever thought about a computer?" Julie, our operations coordinator at the time, asked while digging through cardboard boxes of fulfilled orders. "It's either that, or hire five more people."

Computers were the Hula Hoops of the early 1980s. Everyone wanted one, and it seemed nearly everyone was manufacturing them. But they weren't really useful yet for a business of our growing scale; they were, at that stage, more of a fad.

Eventually I caved in and bought a Televideo with a pile of floppy disks. I turned it on and watched with wonder as the cursor flashed in bright green on a dark screen. The only trouble was, available software took days to set up and added more complications to day-to-day life. Julie took over and invested three weeks in trying to master the beast, but we still had no usable software. I abandoned the machine, and we continued to gut it out with paper order processing and record keeping. Maybe computers would get easier to use.

One day that year I visited a catalog company in Ohio. Lingering by their customer service department, I heard their phones ringing incessantly. Too many of their customers were apparently unhappy about their substandard products and snippy customer service. Thus the company had to spend too much on additional marketing to get customers to replace the ones they'd mistreated. I hoped we wouldn't end up like that. I wanted service my grandmother would be proud of.

The letters WinterSilks received were a bit more complimentary:

After 38 years of trying all sorts of garments for cold weather, your long johns are the only ones that have suited my husband. Many thanks.

—J.S., Paris

Thank you for the quick and accurate service. I hoped I would receive them in time for my friend's birthday. I did! Please send me a catalog of your other merchandise. I am very impressed with your company.

—J.A., New York City

I breathed a sigh of relief. Maybe we could compete with L.L.Bean after all. Someday.

Actually, those letters were from 1985 and 1986. Back in the winter of 1984 our staff fielded a gushing stream of customer complaints from our telephone- and paper-intensive inferno of office suites in the Hooper Construction building.

And these facilities—the fourth since the company began—were growing impossibly cramped. Shipments arrived frequently from vendors in Korea, Hong Kong, and China, and there was no place left to put them. We needed more space—and we needed a loading dock. Trucks with goods from U.S. Customs double-parked on the street outside and unloaded cartons of silk garments through a glass office door, held up traffic on the main thoroughfare, and created a fire hazard in the offices where we stored our goods. Eyebrows were raised in our landlord's office.

Because our address was listed in all magazine advertisements, curious local and out-of-town customers sometimes showed up.

One Saturday a gentleman from South Africa appeared, rubbing his hands together for warmth, and squinted through our unmarked glass door.

"Is this the home of . . . WinterSilks?" he asked Major Distraction at the front desk.

"Yessir, that's us," she replied proudly. He smiled triumphantly; he had indeed found us.

"I saw your ad in the *New Yorker* in Johannesburg last week," he said, holding up a tear sheet from a recent issue. "I wanted to check you out."

Our busy staff, some of whom were 18 or 19 and had barely been outside Wisconsin, gawked at this exotic visitor with his foreign accent, spectacles, three-piece suit, and winter overcoat with velvet collar. Here, in one elegant, human package, was an example of the power of advertising. From a small ad in the *New Yorker* we had drawn a customer to our doorstep from nearly the other side of the planet.

We convinced him to fill out an order form and pick up his purchase on his way back to the airport two days later. Eyeing our modest operation with amusement, he agreed.

Later that season, an affluent British man on his way from the airport to the state capitol had his taxi wait outside while he walked in. He strode right by our unmarked offices and went the length of the building.

The first people he came to were a bunch of conservative, well-dressed Madison businessmen in a conference room for Hooper Construction Company's board of directors meeting. The fellow knocked politely, entered, and declared loudly in a throaty British accent:

"Gentlemen, I'm here to buy your long johns!"

The Hooper directors were not amused. After some flustered discussion they pointed him back down the hall to our hole-in-the-wall offices.

Two years before, WinterSilks had consisted of one quiet, pale guy working solitary long hours in a bare, one-telephone, three-room office, paying $285 a month in rent. By early summer of 1984, WinterSilks occupied three office suites jammed full of ringing telephones and scampering employees.

Late one night, as I was locking up to go home, our landlord suggested, "Maybe we're not the right place for you any more." He heartily encouraged me to find WinterSilks another home.

I scoured the classifieds and signed a lease for a down-at-the-heel, 7,800-square-foot office and warehouse building in Middleton, on the west edge of Madison with cornfields to the south. It had been empty for months and looked cavernous, with a carpeted office area and two zones of warehouse space that seemed to stretch half-way to Nebraska. The building was so big that Lisa and Ted, then three and two, sometimes took a rest while walking from one end to the other. There was a loading dock, large parking lot, and room to expand. WinterSilks finally had a proper home.

Once we were settled in, one of the staff said, "Customers who have seen our ads keep coming around to see us in person. Why don't we open an outlet store?"

"Forget it," I said. "Customers like that take precious time; they're a nuisance. You can sell $60 or $70 of knitted silk garments over the phone in four or five minutes, but a walk-in customer can take up 20 or 30 minutes and end up not buying anything. Besides, we don't have any retail experience."

Other employees countered: "It's too strong a demand to ignore. And three of us have worked in retail before."

So I called Dick Norgord, a highly regarded Wisconsin catalog executive who had been suggested to me as an advisor by United Bank.

"What do you think about an outlet store in our building?" I asked.

"Great idea," Dick said without hesitation. "Your employees are absolutely right."

We added on to the building and allocated 700 square feet of the new space for an outlet store. Then we ran low-cost black-and-white ads in Madison's daily newspapers and threw a grand opening sale.

When I arrived that morning I couldn't find a place to park. Hundreds of local customers who had been receiving our catalogs swarmed in. I maneuvered through a field of customers to talk with then-store manager Ann Everson.

"How are things going?"

"Sorry, can't talk." She rushed off to handle a newly arrived cadre of sale-hungry matrons at the door.

That evening she limped into my office with the front end of a 12-foot calculator tape. In 700 square feet of space on a Saturday, with little idea of what we were doing, we'd made $11,000 in sales from a $2,000 outlay.

Our outlet store profits paid for taxes, heating, cooling, and electricity for the rest of the building and added additional cash to our checking account—all as a result of selling overstock, factory seconds, and returns inventory. Most other clothing catalogers were choking on overstocks and returns; WinterSilks was selling them for a profit.

The Sharp-Eyed Rookie called a while later to check up on his loan. "Everything OK?" he asked.

"Season hasn't kicked in yet, but shipments from China are on time and we've got this new secret weapon: an outlet store. It generates a steady trickle of cash and helps minimize debt."

"So that and the sale catalog can get you through the summer intact?"

"I think so."

The outlet store saw a steady flow of local and out-of-town catalog customers who relished driving long, inconvenient distances to pick out their purchases in person. We were happy to oblige. With each season's increased catalog circulation, more customers traveling in the Midwest detoured to come to the source. I didn't know retail from a root canal, but despite that, the store's ongoing revenue was helping us survive the cash-vacuum summer months.

We were still a struggling young company—a handful of permanent employees, an entrepreneur and his wife and two small children. We had a hot product line and got a little better at the game each year. The game was still too often a wild ride, and constantly grew more complicated and demanding, but I didn't know how to change that. From time to time the thought of a boring job working in the slow, inefficient bureaucracy of an established big company had a delicious appeal. But now, in the waning months of 1984, I had to admit that we were getting a handle on operations and off-season cash flow. I suspected we still had a long road ahead of us, but now I sensed that other innovations would help us weather inevitable setbacks and make our ascent more sure-footed and enjoyable.

PART 3

Chaos to Clarity

Dodging Bullets While Building an Organization

A strong wind pipes up and then eases at dawn, leaving a fog that envelops everything in minuscule water pellets. Cobwebs left by summer spiders are laced with droplets that glimmer like tiny diamonds. My canoe glides quietly over a garden of rocks beaming up from the bottom—5, 10, and 20 feet below—in shades of rust red, green, granite gray, white, and pink.

Rounding a small point, I surprise a loon napping just offshore. He jerks his head up and looks at me as if I were a creature from another planet—which to him I'm sure I am, in my orange life jacket, yellow rain gear, light green spray skirt stretched tightly over the canoe, and bright blue rubber packs. He paddles madly across the surface and takes off.

Nowadays, tourists come to the west edge of the park, where I began my trip, and steer their cars and vans to the government campsite. They walk a half-mile trail around some of the overlooks, look up and down the coast, and then continue back to their campers and head west toward Thunder Bay and Winnipeg, or south to Duluth. As inhabitants of a continent that was first explored and developed by canoe and foot, we've become a sorry, soft lot—all the while having stripped the wilderness of its native populations.

141

Moss, spruce, cedar, balsam, birch, and poplar cover the island to the water's edge; the granite outcroppings seem to erupt out of these woods. I cut across the cove, over a shallow rock garden of colored boulders that shimmer from a patch of sandy bottom. The rocks are all different—like the people one has for friends or family or work associates—yet somehow they all fit together in a magical puzzle.

The loon calls out on my left and starts swimming out of the fog toward me. At about 35 feet he calls again, perhaps disappointed there is no reply from the creature in the boat. I feebly attempt a loon call, and he turns and cocks his head sideways as if to say: What was that? *He holds his distance, paddling in a semicircle around one side of the canoe, and watches me continue down the bay, back into the fog. His species has lived as exactly the same life form for more than five million years. Compared to loons, humans are a failed modern innovation.*

19

An Accelerating Blur

At breakfast one morning in the fall of 1984, exhausted, I told Sarah, "I've got to leave the day-to-day survival stage behind."

"Talk to some people," she said. "Ask them how to go about building a mature, self-sustaining organization. While you're at it, ask for help getting an operations pro who can permanently take that load off your back, formalize work rules, computerize, and learn how to take time off. How's that for starters?"

It was a tall order, but she was right. I figured I'd start with forming a board of directors, selecting our first computer system, and learning how to take time off to rethink the big picture.

I asked five people with different kinds of career experience to serve on our board, and all agreed. On a Saturday in October we had our first meeting. It was cold, and I hadn't yet turned on the heat. Heat and electricity had been included in our monthly rent payments at the Hooper Construction building, but they weren't in the new space. The temperature inside was in the low 50s.

"Does this building come with heat?" Bob Beach joked, buttoning his blazer.

Before I could apologize, Rad Hastings chimed in: "It feels like you cut too good a deal on this joint. Maybe they sold the furnace for scrap. Can we start a bonfire?"

The rest of the directors guffawed in unison. When they saw that I wouldn't turn up the thermostat, one by one they slipped out to retrieve their winter coats. (Soon afterward I disbanded the board and reinstated them as a board of advisors to save the time and cost of legal paperwork and to minimize their liability.)

A couple of months before, in August 1984, after nearly five years of juggling part-time office work and 24/7 parenting duties, Sarah had left me an emotionally charged letter declaring her resignation from WinterSilks.

"I've had enough of your business obsession," was the gist of her letter. "I would prefer to be a better mother and wife. Working with and under you does not allow me to do so," she wrote with admirable restraint. Who could blame her? I was most likely a difficult spouse and boss a good deal of the time. In her shoes I would have done the same. Thankfully she stayed until the end of December and trained a replacement.

Sarah had been key to surviving the early stages of the startup. She often worked a full day in the winter selling season before running home to pick up Lisa from day care. The arrival of our second child, Ted, would have overloaded anyone. When I tried to talk about business, our small children were making demands on her time. When she needed to talk about parenting, I was at the office or too preoccupied to engage at home.

We bumped our way to the end of the 1984–85 season and then, one night in early January 1985, our accounting clerk rang me on the intercom.

"We did over $1 million."

I walked over and looked with wonder at the adding machine printout tape that stretched over her desk, onto the floor and nearly out her door. One million bucks. It was a giddy feeling. Memories of our basement and attic offices flashed through my head.

Giddy, yes. But we were still scrambling to keep up with the company's growth. Paperwork was everywhere; some people stayed late many nights. I needed to build a more formal organizational structure and support system, fast, or we were all headed to the nuthouse.

Before I could spend time on that, I needed to pound away on our telex every night, sending messages to as many as five different agents in three countries, seeking answers to production questions and pressing for on-time delivery.

144

Later that week the second wave of seasonal catalogs and magazine ads hit and pulled orders through the third week of February. Then, exhausted from order processing, WinterSilks' staff picked up the pieces and went out for an end-of-season party. The festivities soothed frayed nerves, thanks to an open bar, dinner, and music. For a few hours working at WinterSilks was fun. The feeling lasted through a good night's alcohol-induced sleep and into the first two hours or so of the next day at the office. Then the realities of a frenzied, understaffed business set in again.

"I loved working for this company about 12 hours ago, after the third glass of wine," I heard someone crack as she sorted through a stack of paperwork. "Now I'm not so sure."

From my point of view, the employees were lucky. When they had had enough, they could quit. I, on the other hand, had no way out—unless I shut WinterSilks down, sold her, or died.

A week after the party, the first casualty of that year knocked on my door.

"Can we talk?" Nancy's voice was the low growl of a 35-year cigarette smoker. I pushed aside a stack of phone messages and papers and pulled out a chair for her. I feared an unexpected illness might have cropped up in her family.

"This place is nuts, Frank," she said, slapping a letter onto my desk with a *thwack*. "Here's my resignation."

I paled; losing someone like Nancy was like shredding the mainsail on a three-masted schooner. It would take time to repair.

"Would it help if you got a raise today?" I asked timidly.

"It would not. I'm done here." Her brown eyes fixed on mine for a few seconds; then she headed for the office door. She stopped and turned.

"Two weeks, Frank. Then I'm gone." She made a knife motion across her throat. I nodded glumly, and felt a sinking feeling.

Seasonal demand, hard-to-get product. Inadequate systems to handle volume. A miserable combination. Who wouldn't want out?

Sure, cash flow was good in season. But we were just making it, operations-wise, week to week. Employees like Nancy saw little hope of a change for the better, an easing of the pressure—and, to be honest, I didn't either—not for operations, anyway. Where could

I find just the right person to run the people side of things? The year 1985 ended as a slice of vanished time.

"This is a year I want to forget," I told Sarah at the end of December.

"Me too," she said without hesitation. Although she was now at home full-time, she still had to listen to company troubles every night.

The year 1985 quickly receded from my mind; I had time only for the present and future. Magazine advertising usually succeeded, sometimes wildly. Orders poured in by telephone and mail, often overwhelming our staff and piecemeal order-processing systems. Revenues doubled from $1.1 million to $2.2 million.

Some employees cursed me and quit in mid-season. Some made it through February 1986 and then announced they weren't coming back, ever. Replacing them with fresh ones, and adding more to handle the expected growth the following season, wasn't good enough. We needed to build a system and team that could absorb growth comfortably. The trouble was, I kept waiting for a break from the endlessly spinning hamster-wheel of annual preparation and fulfillment in which I could set up such a system. But such a break never came; I couldn't find time to break the cycle.

Competing in the holiday-driven mail-order business required faith that we would emerge early each March with enough reserve cash to have made it all worthwhile. It took a iron-clad belief in the continued appeal of our products.

Statistics from the previous season supported such a belief and drove product and list selection for the next. These statistics gave us the confidence to order the right segments of the right mailing lists and the right products that those lists would be ordering, in the right sizes and colors—six months in advance for imported garments, and two months in advance for mailing lists. This meant coming up with circulation plans for each winter by the preceding March—so a few eye blinks after one winter season had ended, we needed to be planning the next.

I either negotiated lists directly from catalog owners or used brokers. The brokers placed orders for us, earned a commission, and didn't care who we mailed to. I could have asked the list brokers for a list of a hundred thousand hard-drinking, clubfooted, left-handed bowlers west of the Wabash River, and they would have said: *We'll get 'em . . . and send you a bill.*

Staff recorded source-code data with each order received. Mailing list advisor Mike McCarthy gave some good advice:

"That data has to be accurately input—has to be good enough for a GPS-driven smart bomb to find its way down a narrow backwoods chimney at night. Otherwise waves of catalogs will be sent off into oblivion—"

I finished for him: "With few orders coming back and too little cash flow to pay the mountain of bills caused up front by production, printing, postage, and merchandise commitments."

"You got it," Mike said. "Everyone on the team has to get it exactly right."

Fortunately, our list data was solid. Still, there were so many things to worry about. Every time I signed postal checks at a printing plant's mailing dock, I wondered: *Will this be the year the postal service lost our mailing? Will our catalog sail out to sea like an overconfident* Titanic? *Am I a delusional Don Quixote at the helm?* As a management team of one, I foolishly tried to do it all.

While I worked late hours, some employees coasted. In the heady local economy of the 1980s, I had to thank some employees for showing up.

If I didn't have the people skills I needed, at least I could get a deal on the best mail-order software—which I had finally done in May 1985. After two years of research and waiting for prices to come down and processor speed to increase, I ordered hardware and industry-specific software. Our staff watched as a team of unshaven, early-era geeks installed an icebox-sized computer in a small office next to mine. A $4,000 air conditioner was added to keep the room cool, and computer terminals sprang up around the building. Within two days, staff knew how to enter orders and were stupefied by the efficiency of it all.

The catalog-specific software, from Nashbar Associates, changed the business and our lives and prepared us for continued growth. Bar code wands were hooked up in the shipping room and credit card orders were authorized on magnetic tape reels in large batches, instead of one by one over the telephone. The new software captured sales and inventory history; customer service staff no longer had to dig through boxes of records. The computer system made us legitimate, part of a new age. This earned me points with employees. It also bought precious time.

During lunch hour one day, on a whim, I went to Middleton's grass-strip airport a half-mile away and paid $20 for a demonstration ride. The instructor let me maneuver the controls of the tiny Cessna 152 and at the end of the flight asked if I wanted to start regular lessons. I realized that for the 45 minutes of the flight my mind had been completely diverted from business. I stared wide-eyed at the calendar on the hangar wall and, against all reason, said yes. *Maybe it will help me relax and interact better with Sarah and the kids. Maybe I'll sleep better. Maybe . . . Hell, why not?* So I took the leap.

One week later . . . "Hey, you're not supposed to bounce!" my instructor yelled above the roar of the engine as I misread the height above touchdown and the airplane careened back into the air. "Just ease the power back gently and kiss the asphalt."

"OK, OK, I'll try."

Three evenings a week for the next three months I severely tested the instructor's patience. I droned around the airport pattern, a thousand feet above ground level, passing the WinterSilks building as I turned from the downwind to base leg, readying for descent to final approach. I thought I saw the poor instructor close his eyes a few times as I hammered the little airplane too fast and too hard into the pavement and felt it spring involuntarily back into the air before settling for good on the narrow, cracked asphalt runway. Each hour cost about $65 for instruction, aircraft rental, and fuel—about as much as a bale of cardboard shipping boxes in the warehouse. And sure enough, it diverted my attention, like letting air out of an overinflated balloon.

In the months and years ahead, as I moved up through commercial and instrument ratings, to pressurized and then twin, jet-prop aircraft, flying not only took my mind to a different, separate world but also taught me things about business management I could not have learned anywhere else.

The explosive selling season of fall 1985 exceeded our projections, and we had to expand staff, but finding employees was a challenge.

148

The local economy, anchored by the state capital and the 43,000-student University of Wisconsin, was booming. For several months Dane County had the lowest unemployment rate in the United States. Fortunately, the new computer system and a few all-star employees kept us above water.

But they merely bought us a little time, and now that time was running out. The following season revenues would double again—to $4,491,588—because many list segments could be profitably used in greater volumes.

As I tried to sleep at night in 1985, I prayed for a greater number of qualified employees who could get orders processed and out the door on time. I prayed for help getting out the next catalog. Some of those nights, if I could have given away WinterSilks, I would have gladly done so.

Then I could have held Lisa's and Ted's small hands in mine and walked carefree in the park across the street.

20

Rookie's Waltz

"HEEELLPPP!!!!"

The scream filled the entire east half of the building. I popped out of my office to see what was up. A terrified staffer, eight months pregnant, ran wide-eyed from a data-entry room. She was drenched, absolutely soaking wet. I bet this had not happened at her previous places of employment.

It was late winter 1986. A huge snowfall had hit that morning and immediately melted. A tiny leak near a data entry station exploded through the ceiling tiles in a torrent of water. Operations manager Bonnie Collins sprang into action.

"Don't worry. It's just the exploding ceiling again," she said in an attempt to calm the drenched victim. No dice; the victim just stared back in shocked disbelief.

Bonnie cleaned up the mess, searched for dry clothes, and then moved the victim to a dry workstation to resume order entry. Total time lost: 25 minutes. Bonnie was one amazing woman.

As for me, I climbed up to the roof. After an hour of shoveling snow, the leak below stopped. I went back to my desk, wishing I could stay outside under the peaceful simplicity of a clear blue sky. I regretted ever starting a business because, despite our financial success, the meridians of my company were out of control, like constellations gone haywire in a young capitalist's tilted night sky: too many employees, too many customers wanting our product, too many problems with trying to manufacture garments in Asia.

True, by now we had a board of advisors, a solid computing system, and actual scheduled time off for workers (paid vacation for salaried personnel, and some paid holidays). But I still felt I had to be at the company nearly 24/7 to oversee operations. I just had to find The Leader who could bring operations to a mature level of year-to-year functioning: more assured, smoother, more predictable—something I clearly had neither the time nor the expertise to accomplish.

Actually, finding such a leader would be easy. Convincing him or her to join our madhouse of an organization was the challenge.

I approached my people-and-operations-talented friend John Jeffery one day at lunch. He managed a seven-store furniture and ski equipment chain where he put in long hours, was underpaid and, I thought, underappreciated. Maybe I could convince him to join me.

Our first meeting, at my office, had an uneasy aura. I felt like an inconsequential friend of a beautiful woman who had surprised her by asking for a date. John squirmed with mild discomfort when I popped the question; he looked around our building, noncommittal. Two days later he called.

"I've got a family to support. Can't take the risk. But good luck," he mumbled. I think what he really wanted to say was, *Are you kidding?*

I retreated behind stacks of paper on my desk and went through my address book, looking for reliability and honesty. My siblings weren't businesspeople, nor were they interested. Friends from Northwestern all had hot jobs and big salaries and would laugh out loud if I offered them a job. The only option was trying to find an experienced senior operations manager in the gloomy swamps of the industry's classified ads. I started looking but again got buried with the minutiae of day-to-day survival.

And bank loans.

Even as we established a larger credit line, up until the late 1980s I never paid myself more than $30,000 annually. I cut costs and simplified operations wherever possible and scrambled to minimize debt. When I did go into debt, it was usually for a few months before peak season, when the cost of producing and mailing catalogs and paying for imported goods preceded the holidays and there was only a trickle of summer sales to offset these expenses. When our then-current banker, Sharp-Eyed Rookie, came on board, he understood—as Chicken Lips and Happy Linebacker never had—that in my search for capital I was merely loading the cannons.

By the 1985–1986 holiday season we were on a far less precarious financial footing. We often were able to pay for 20-foot container loads of silk garments out of our checking balance, avoiding a draw on the line of credit. This began to vex the bank, which had hoped I would be deeply into the line of credit all year, manage to bail myself out for the 30 days required in their lending agreement, and then beg for more credit to cover the next season—profiting them handsomely all the while.

The first year of the new loan agreement, 1983, I had upheld my part of the bargain. Sales had increased and positive cash flow easily serviced bank debt, so Sharp-Eyed Rookie extended our credit line to $850,000. But the new liquidity still came with a personal guarantee that hung ominously over my head.

The second year with United Bank was a boom season. Our credit line was paid down to zero on December 9, two months and 22 days ahead of schedule. Sharp-Eyed Rookie and United Bank were impressed and, when negotiations came around the following February, agreed to extend more credit, pending the final year-end audit. As final deliveries from Asia arrived, WinterSilks paid for them out of cash flow without touching the credit line. I asked for a doubling of the credit line, to $1,650,000. Once the final auditor's report was in, Sharp-Eyed Rookie looked at our numbers and won agreement from United Bank.

I had talked with Smiling Dan periodically since our first meeting, and when we next spoke he said, "See? I told you it would work."

I was too exhausted to answer. I would appear at home two or three hours before midnight and find that Sarah had cooked dinner for Lisa and Ted at 6:00 P.M., for herself at 7:30 P.M., and then again for me at 9:30 P.M. or later. I inhaled the dinner and went through work papers in my briefcase.

"When will I see you again?" Sarah asked one night, as if I was boarding a slow boat to China. She went to bed, wondering when she would have a normal husband and family. It was hard for anyone to understand that I was chained to WinterSilks and the bank loans that carried my personal guarantee.

That year from hell, 1986, ended with a stark awakening. When Sarah opened her two gifts from me on Christmas day, I realized I must have bought and wrapped the first, forgotten I'd done so, and made the exact same purchase again. And my choice was not a silk nightshirt, or the mystery novels that she loved so much;

not her favorite toffee candy, or poetry, or promises of a brighter future. I'd given her two identical brown duffel bags—a sign of my madness.

Fortunately, 1986 was one of the best years, revenue-wise, the catalog industry had ever seen. There were several key people who helped WinterSilks through the transition from gawky teenager to promising young adult.

Diane Belanger, a farmer during the summer months, brought cheerful, disciplined order to the warehouse and shipping room. Bonnie Collins—the operations coordinator who came to the rescue of the leak-drenched employee—moved like an organized, smiling, human whirlwind, overseeing order processing, in-bound telephone calls, customer service, and many other details. What had been a dysfunctional arena of my own making—rescued only by hard work, computers, and the cash flow from a hot product line—was starting to take on a tentative aura of confidence. Through measured repetition—doing the same tasks every month, just as had been done in the same months in the seven prior years—we had established a critical foundation.

One method I didn't repeat was wholesale selling to stores on credit. It was tempting, but I stopped short before getting into trouble. I tested wholesale on a tiny scale, always afraid of the difficulty of collecting accounts receivable. I didn't need any new sources of stress.

Over time we evolved a workable protocol for limited wholesaling: do no wholesale advertising, and ship orders only to accounts that came to us by word of mouth, from store owners who had seen our catalogs or magazine ads and had strong credit references. This made it a tiny but profitable sideline.

It took some bad experiences, though, before we reached that conclusion. Some big companies told me, after we'd shipped our product and asked repeatedly for payment, "Our standard terms are 90 days"—even though they had agreed to 30 days when they signed the purchase order. Once we had shipped the goods, there was little we could do other than send more invoices, persist—and swear never to waste time selling to them again.

I was not keen on having my wholesale customers use me as a bank.

The most common line from late-paying customers was, "We never got the invoice." Two weeks later: "I got your invoice and I passed it on to the controller, but he hasn't gotten approval yet on it."

The boring excuses from middle-size and larger companies—"It's waiting for the vice president's signature"—were much less fun than replies from mom-and-pop outfits: "It was right here last week, but I think we used it to start the wood stove."

In late February 1986, when sales from that last color catalog had wound down, I got back to my flying lessons. My instructor seemed to slump down in his chair when I walked in.

"*You* back again, huh?"

Over the next two weeks he took me through stall and recovery practice, in which we intentionally increased angle of attack skyward until the airplane dropped violently toward earth. It was satisfying to learn how to recover fast to stabilized, level flight.

By the third week, after a decent landing, I had earned the instructor's faith. Either that or he was trying to kill me. He told me to pull over to the taxi apron at the end of the runway. When I'd stopped, he quickly, jumped out, slammed the flimsy door, and walked away.

"Take it around the block!" he yelled over his shoulder. Then he walked toward the hangar office, never looking back.

My God—he wants me to solo! After a few sweaty moments to ponder this new development, during which the engine idled like a giant lawn mower without a muffler, I figured—*What the hell, it's time.* My hands shook only a little as I reviewed the pre-takeoff checklist, scanned for traffic, made a departure announcement on the radio, took the center of the runway, and moved the throttle to the firewall.

The oversized mosquito of an airplane proudly rattled its aluminum belly and then seemed to swell with new assurance. I kept my feet on the brakes as the engine built power, scanned for traffic one last time, and then released the brakes. The airplane rattled down the runway, gathering speed. A few hundred feet before the thin, cracked pavement ended, I pulled gently on the steering yoke and it shot into the air. Suddenly the farms spreading out 10 miles or more were in full, spectacular sight below, tucked into a rolling blanket of greening, early-spring Wisconsin landscape. *What a view!*

I realized later that, once again, my business worries had been instantly vacuumed from the tired innards of my brain.

After three decent takeoffs and landings I taxied to the hangar. Inside, the instructor grunted in approval and signed my logbook. I was authorized to fly alone locally, and I was hooked.

By late May the instructor and I had completed a string of long cross-country flights. My employees were no doubt happy to have me out of the building. By June, I had passed the written test and was approved for solo cross-country flights. On June 30, the local FAA examiner, Field Morey, second-generation owner of Middleton's Morey Airport, accompanied me on a final check ride, and at the end of the day signed my license. My instructor was officially done with me; he had other fresh turkeys to work with, in between charter flights in a Cessna 340.

A while later I found a particularly unattractive 1975 Cessna 182, a reliable flying mule that could be bought for under $30,000. At the closing, Sarah saw the color and wrinkled her nose.

"This is one ugly airplane, Frank."

"Maybe we could paint it."

"Good idea. Barf yellow was never my favorite color."

I flew it home to the grass tie-down area at Morey Airport, where it was restored to perfect condition.

I now had frequent windows of time to fly, because the summer sale catalogs were easy to produce. They were mailed monthly to customers who had purchased before or recently requested a catalog. We reused existing photography and separations and had no list rental expense because we already owned the names. These catalogs sold overstocks, factory seconds, and refurbished customer returns for low prices—and often at an overall profit.

The first or last sale catalog mailing of the off-season pulled the best, often over $1.00 per catalog mailed. Our in-the-mail total cost ranged from $.20 to $.45 per catalog, so when we pulled $1.00 a piece in gross revenue, we realized gross profits of $.55 to $.80 per catalog mailed in March or September, the best off-season months. For every 100,000 summer catalogs mailed, this meant $55,000 to $80,000 of gross profits to go toward fixed expenses—in a season when most apparel catalogs were losing serious money.

As our customer list reached 50,000, then 100,000, it was a meaningful cash flow producer because we could mail profitably to it every 25 to 30 days. Hence the useful portion of a house list could be reused—that is, leveraged—12.5 to 13 times a year. With 150,000 house-list recent buyer and catalog request names, to which sale catalogs were mailed seven times a year, we thus produced a gross circulation of 1,050,000—at no list rental cost. If these catalogs pulled an average of $.55 per piece mailed, then they produced $577,500 in revenue—enough, at that time, to pay summer payroll and over-head, after paying printing, postage, and residual merchandise costs. Because we survived the summer on a marginal loss basis, most of the profits and positive cash flow of the explosive four- to five-month winter selling season could thus accumulate.

In addition to allowing me family time and the escape and challenge of flying, the sale catalogs opened up enough manage-ment time for me to teach merchandise assistant Rauel Labreche to summarize merchandise statistics from the season just finished. His growing expertise allowed me additional time to deal with the per-petual deadlines of owning a business—and to fly. This remained the only activity that could free me from my business focus. But to find the senior operations pro I still so desperately needed, I'd have to roll the dice two more times.

21

The Philosophy of Numbers

"Find someone, Frank. This is getting ridiculous," Sarah called as I left for work one day. There was an edge to her voice.

If only it were so simple. On one hand, WinterSilks had survived battle after bruising battle and always emerged looking, financially speaking, like a promising young racehorse with her prime still to come. On the other hand, this season looked different: too much activity loomed on too great a scale. Who could save us?

Because John Jeffery had said no to the operations chief position, and I still hadn't found anyone else, I figured I'd break the big-position hiring task into smaller pieces. Hiring a staff CPA was achievable, and it would help chip away at our financial reporting and operations shortcomings. We had been hiring a procession of accounting clerks who each burned out within a year or so. When each quit, it took precious time to select and train a replacement. It was time to bring in bigger artillery.

Our big-name accounting firm recommended Pat Virgutz; her husband had just been hired by the firm, and now she, new in town, needed a job.

Pat showed up for her interview wearing a pressed gray flannel suit and sporting an unflappable, can-do attitude. When it came time to tour the building, I stopped at the accounting clerk's office last. Reluctantly I opened the door, knowing there would be a mess of paperwork inside. The previous accounting clerk had walked off the job a few days earlier in a fit of despair. Boxes were stacked on boxes; papers floated from shelves and filing cabinet tops as the draft from the door opening circulated through the room. I figured Pat would take one look and say, "Are you crazy? You think I want to work in a nuthouse like this?"

Instead, her sharp eyes took it all in for a few seconds. Then she turned to me with a confident look.

"I can do it," she said. Nothing more. Just the certainty of good training and experience that a CPA certificate entails.

I was stunned. "You think so?"

She nodded calmly; her ice-blue eyes glimmered with confidence.

Pat probably figured it would have taken a heck of a turkey to let a mess like this happen, and for a few seconds she looked at me with disapproving, narrowed eyes. But she humored me with a smile as we walked back to my office to finalize details.

Pat worked feverishly for the first month. A week after that, she marched triumphantly into my office with a stack of neatly stapled computer reports. She smacked them down on my wooden desk with an I-told-you-so look of satisfaction.

"Here's your income statement, profit and loss statement, and balance sheet for last month and the year to date."

I pushed back in my chair, my jaw gone slack.

"No kidding," I mumbled. It was as if I had sent her off to slay a dragon and she had calmly done so in short order, and then returned with barely a scratch on her armor and the dragon's head tucked neatly under her arm. I stared in admiration, remembering something about her high grades at the University of Wisconsin-Whitewater, home of the best accounting programs in the Midwest, along with The Ohio State University. There on my desk was the proof of what such an education could do.

Until then we had had these reports a few months after the end of the year, following a short flurry of questions by our outside accountant. Pat had cracked the logjam of our numbers sooner, better, more accurately—and for less cost.

Each month thereafter she presented updated financial reports within seven days of the previous month's close. With an assistant, added a while later, she did bimonthly payroll, handled quarterly state and federal tax filings and monthly employment tax filings, and provided financial analysis tools to identify and control costs and increase profits and cash flow. She catapulted WinterSilks into financial reporting legitimacy.

Pat's arrival helped me free up time to spawn other improvements. The next request from employees was another warehouse. Rauel Labreche told me he needed expansion for storage—a $50,000 expenditure.

"No way," I grumbled. Then I thought about it. "Tell you what. Get a ticket on the same flight as me and come to Hong Kong."

It was a buying trip to Hong Kong and China. "They operate . . . differently here," Rauel said when he saw warehouses with items stacked to the ceiling; crowded work areas; extreme heat; negligible fire codes; no ventilation; and workers laboring through six-day, sixty-hour work weeks.

The investment of $2,700 to bring him along on that trip paid off almost twentyfold. Back in Wisconsin, he rescinded his request for a new warehouse. He made better use of what we had, and he told other warehouse employees how lucky they were to be working in the good old U.S.A.—where we ventilate and sometimes even air condition our warehouses.

Rauel became enlightened by the discipline of cost control—the need to see a business as a delicate entity that must be nourished, rather than taken advantage of. He, along with Pat and a few others, now thought like a business owner. He understood that little sacrifices made every day pay off with a stronger, lasting, more durable company—one that can afford secure jobs and larger salaries for its employees.

Later that year I met a seasoned construction entrepreneur who had an ingenious way to motivate employees to contain costs.

"I got a half dozen construction guys on my payroll," he explained. "Over the years, nearly all of 'em want to work for themselves, and every year one or two of 'em quit to go try to do it. Drove me crazy.

"After a few seasons of such pain-in-the-ass turnover, I came up with a plan. I started tellin' new hires I'd groom 'em to go out on their own, in two years.

"So most new guys worked hard to learn from the boss before heading out solo. Then after a coupla years they're usually broke up the wazoo, maybe 30, 40 grand in debt. Most of 'em ask for their jobs back. They work good from then on."

"I wish I had thought of that," I marveled.

He spat out the tip of a fresh cigar. "You will. See, small biz is capitalism in its purest, most unforgivin' form." He gestured with his now-lit Havana. "Cash is king. Gotta produce enough of it before you run outta time. Most guys can't do that in a coupla years." He exhaled a triumphant cloud of thick smoke, which was promptly carried off by the afternoon breeze.

As Pat kept producing detailed financial reports, one expense line that stood out uncomfortably was taxes. Wisconsin is an extremely unkind tax state, and the taxes we coughed up to both state and federal governments staggered me. We couldn't do anything about the federal government, but maybe we could change states, free up cash flow, and survive more easily.

A little research found seven states with no income tax: Alaska, Florida, Texas, Wyoming, Washington, South Dakota and Nevada. I responded to a small classified "Move to Wyoming" ad in a business magazine and a month later found myself wined and dined on a two-day tour through Casper, in eastern Wyoming. It was one of the hardest-hit boom-and-bust regions of the United States, and just then it was in a bust mode. If we moved there I could negotiate better banking terms, requiring less collateral and personal guarantees. The city, state, and county would help guarantee part of a bank line of credit in return for new jobs. An industrial revenue bond for a new computer and warehouse could be floated much more easily in bankrupt cowboy country than in conservative, tax-abusive Wisconsin.

We could offer a few hundred bucks a month for an enormous, lavish office and warehouse building and they'd probably take it, providing we could pay a little more a year later after things got going.

Wyoming seemed like a pathway to a greener, cleaner pasture for my family, lower taxes, and better financing terms.

But little things are critical clues. Returning me to my hotel, a realtor drove past a small shopping mall. "With the oil boom," the realtor said, "just about every able-bodied hourly employee quit his job and dashed for the big paychecks. Jobs at places like Kmart went begging. Stores could barely operate."

If the oil boom came back, WinterSilks wouldn't be able to compete for the local workforce.

Sarah and I talked it over. Her ties to the farm country of west-central Illinois, six hours southwest of Madison by car, ran deep. Moving our newly installed computer system would be risky. Wisconsin cost more in state taxes but provided a predictable labor force and access to key support services, all within a 25-minute drive. Lisa and Ted loved their friends and schools. We decided to stay put, gambling that the stable economy of Dane County would be worth its price. Madison was home.

"You gotta do this, Frank," Mike McCarthy said as he plunked down a report on my desk and took a seat. "It'll cost you $6,000, but it'll pay for itself many times over."

"Six thousand?" I said.

"Peanuts, for what you get."

I had convinced Mike, a mailing list guru at the Wisconsin Cheeseman food-by-mail gift catalog, to moonlight for me. I couldn't pay much, but Mike liked the challenge.

I thumbed through the reams of data—a sample of what the Colorado Computer House of Brainy Mega-Nerds had spewed out in a demonstration project.

"This is a lot of junk," I said.

Mike stiffened. "It's a lot of *data*," he corrected. "You get this X-ray of your list, and you'll increase your mailing universe five- or tenfold. It will be easier to reach your target audience. You'll know where your customers shop, what they wear, just about the frequency of their breathing."

So I placed an order with the Mega-Nerds for a profile of our customer list. It was the first customer profiling survey I had done since the down-home one produced on our antiquated typewriter and copier—1,002 copies stuffed into outgoing customer packages in the spring and summer of 1983. Of those 1,002 outgoing surveys, produced at near-zero cost, we'd received a terrific 29.3-percent response rate. It provided a dozen or so valuable criteria such as age, gender, household income, winter hobbies, and zip codes.

WinterSilks had grown, and now Mike knew it was time to take customer profiling to the next level—a full-blown database over-lay analysis. All we had to do was dump our customer names and addresses onto magnetic reel tapes and send them to the Colorado firm. The Mega-Nerds would match our names against a national database they maintained. If they found a statistically appropriate overlay between their master database and our house list, they could proceed, with statistical confidence, with an analysis of the names that matched between the two.

Three weeks later a heavy cardboard box arrived containing two bound copies of printouts and charts, each about the size of a Chicago telephone book. Maps showed color-coded concentration of our customers, analysis of the number of theater tickets they bought each month when living in New York versus Omaha, and page after page of stuff that would quickly put anyone to sleep.

I looked through the data for about 10 minutes and then started spinning through the pages as if I were once again a budget-minded journalist trying to order pizza from the yellow pages while working late at the *Daily Eagle*. Eventually I came upon two pages buried in back.

Sure enough, the top three criteria from this fancy database analysis of our then-current customers exactly matched the criteria from our zero-cost 1982 and 1983 self-manufactured surveys: specific gender, specific age range, and threshold household income. I called Mike.

"It's all the same," I said.

"What's all the same?"

"The junk in the Colorado report."

"I told you, it's data, not junk."

"No, it's junk. It's the same criteria we got for damn-near free a few years ago.

"I knew *that* would be the same," Mike said, "because they're the same customers that crossed over from the national database to your list, so of course they profile similarly. What's new is their very existence, in statistical significance, within the Colorado shop's national mail-order database."

"I don't get it."

"Simple: Customers exactly like yours exist in volume within the Colorado guys' sliced-and-diced national database. Hundreds of thousands of them in each test panel. Now you know more about your own customers and can rent and profitably mail to these database, almost-like-your-own-customer names."

I was silent, mulling this over. I sensed Mike grinning on the other end of the phone. He knew he had earned his fee a hundred times over.

"You've instantly got a huge new universe," he continued. "Millions of criteria-qualified mail-order buyer names you can rent at a modest price. You're no longer limited to renting overpriced customer lists from other catalogers—who could stop renting to you at any time or go out of business themselves. You've just at least quintupled the potential of your business *with less risk than before*."

I looked at the phone books of data with a newfound admiration; computers really were changing the world, or at least the commerce within it. Customer profiling had just coughed up a new, low-cost source for hot names. Mike had put turbochargers on WinterSilks.

More growth would present more staffing and operations challenges, but the extra profit it would bring was hard to turn down. What I really needed before we went one step further was that senior operations pro. I promised Sarah I would start running ads in industry publications.

But an hour after I spoke with Mike, there was a soft knocking on my door.

"What's going on with the sale catalog?" a veteran telemarketing staffer asked from the doorway. "It's pretty quiet out here. Orders are slim."

I looked at my screen; sure enough, revenues from the current month's sale catalog were miserably thin.

"Did the post office lose our catalogs this time?"

"I hope not," the staffer said, shrugging her shoulders. She went back to her workstation.

I pulled up response data on my computer terminal. The only plausible explanation was that U.S. Postal Service had lost our catalogs, though we couldn't prove it. Sales had been strong in May's sales catalog, and there was no reason for them to fall off a cliff this month. I remembered that every year or so one of the industry publications did a feature article on a catalog company bankrupted by such nondelivery. If this had happened to us, we were in danger.

Audits by a catalog industry group, and by the Postal Service itself, later proved that in 1986, 14 percent of catalogs mailed through the USPS system were dumped into the trash by postal employees. The Postal Service union demanded higher wages, yet did a poorer job with third-class mail delivery. If they had been working for a real business they would have been shown the door.

Order flow stayed thin for a month. Finally orders from the next catalog kicked in and sales-per-catalog-mailed came back to April and May levels.

Bureaucratic lapses like this one vaporized at least $40,000 in sales, never to be recovered, nor did we have any legal recourse against the federal government. It was hard to forgive the post office; a private delivery company would not have lost those catalogs. For about three weeks I felt like an ant screaming that he wasn't going to forgive the truck that had run over it.

The *New York Times* later reported: "The catalog business is a lot like farming, in that you make all investments up front in printing and creative costs and mailing, and sit back and wait to reap the harvest. When there is an act of nature that intervenes, that can be a painful experience."

My only remedy was remembering something Smiling Dan had told me: "Stick to basics, keep going, and try to be unkillable. In time, everything will change."

22

Employees from Heaven—and Hell

The nice thing about statistics is that they are steady and silent. People, especially when they are your employees, are a bit different.

On a cold, rainy Saturday that fall, warehouse staff refused to come in—even for overtime pay—to count inventory in a much-needed shipment from China. So warehouse manager Nellie Ellendt worked alone and counted one-third of the contents of a huge shipment until 6:30 P.M.

"Don't work too hard," I said to Nellie as I prepared to shut down the building after dark.

"Ain't afraid of work," she replied, without looking up. "But the rest of them is."

At 60-something, Nellie outworked the 20-year-olds by a wide margin and looked on the no-shows with an uninhibited disdain. After 40 years of post-war prosperity, the scars of the 1930s still shaped her life. As a child and teenager in the Great Depression she knew that if someone had work, they'd have cash. With cash, they could eat; with more work, maybe buy a place to sleep. She had a head of white-gray hair, a full stomach, an apartment of her own, and a car with no debt on it. Life was good, as long as she continued working.

"I don't trust banks," she told me. "And there shouldn't be no Social Security," she added with the disdain of a survivor. "Just look at the classifieds. There's work."

Besides a long Monday-to-Friday week, Nellie worked most Saturdays and some Sundays, whether a new shipment arrived from China or not. Sometimes she brought her husband, Robert. He helped count incoming inventory and shelved it in computer-assigned bins. Nellie was happy to be American, on someone's payroll. What we had in common was fear. For her, fear of hunger. For me, fear of failure.

The problem was, there was only one Nellie in the world, and I had found her. The rest of the people who made up our workforce could sometimes be dangerous.

One day that season our bookkeeper/computer maintenance staff person came in for her semi-annual review, let me finish a 30-minute job performance summary, then handed in her resignation.

"I'm quitting, effective in one week," she said.

Not again. There always seemed to be some employer who would pay more.

No one else could operate the computer, through which we made credit card deposits. Without her knowledge, we couldn't make bank deposits. And with a holiday the following Monday, there were only four business days to train a replacement.

"This could kill us," I said. "I need you to give me the customary two weeks."

"I said one week. My new job starts in two weeks and I want a week off in between."

Loyalties can change quickly. I sat up straight in my chair.

"Listen," I said. "You hold a key position, and I really need you for two weeks more. And my attorney thinks you should give the customary two weeks."

She said she'd think about it.

Her notice was extended to two weeks, which gave me nine business days to find a successor and for her to provide training. The new person was hired and trained and barely saved us. This people thing was getting to me.

For nearly a month there was some normalcy. Then Bonnie, our operations coordinator, brought me terrifying news. "Something's screwed up our computer. It's frozen."

More memory had been added to the computer, something we normally did at our slowest point of the year, in June or July. The software technician was on his way home to Ohio; all that remained for the new accounting assistant/computer coordinator was to complete a file restore—loading three 15-inch reels of magnetic tape in A-B-C sequence.

For reasons unknown, the new computer coordinator had loaded tape A, tape C, then tape B. We had not done a total file backup for ten days, so when she pressed Start at the end of the file restore program, all of the data keyed in during the most recent period between file backups was overwritten and lost. With data out of sync, the system froze up. WinterSilks could not enter or ship orders or make bank deposits. We called our Ohio software technician at home and interrupted his family dinner. Even he was sobered by the news.

The next morning I found a letter from the new computer coordinator on my desk:

". . . I'm tired of being underpaid and require a doubling of my salary immediately or I will leave and turn you over to the employment harassment division of the State of Wisconsin."

This person had been at the company three and a half weeks and was making a fair, market-level salary. I called her into my office and put on my best poker face.

"Thanks for taking the time to write me a personal letter," I said. "I'd be happy to increase your salary, as you . . . requested," I said through a steel-lipped smile.

She nodded, staring at me with the deep black eyes of a devilish creature. The inhuman look scared me right down to the worn-through toes of my socks. The transparency of her blackmail was more saddening than the treachery of the act itself.

Secure with her newly doubled salary, the Employee from Hell returned to her desk.

My mind raced. Bonnie came in and closed the door.

"Every keystroke since the last accurate file save, about one week's worth of data—thankfully, low-season data—has to be manually reentered," she said.

"Can you put this back together?" I asked quietly.

Bonnie nodded. "I think so," she said.

For the next 10 days, she led the reconstruction project. Key employees stepped up to do the labor-intensive effort to reestablish our system. The Black-Eyed Devil didn't help.

While the data recovery was going on, I scurried to hire an assistant who could learn the new system. Once he was in place and knowledgeable, about two weeks later, I fired the blackmailer.

A few days later, the Wisconsin Department of Human Resources and Labor called.

"I need to see you, Mr. Farwell. Serious allegations have been made concerning your company." Our blackmailer had blown the whistle.

A most unpleasant individual from the state came out to investigate the blackmailer's complaints. He returned several times, burning with skepticism and mistrust. Eventually he ruled in the company's favor. However, the unsmiling fellow did uncover an error in our vacation payroll accounting regarding one employee. He levied a $50 fine and left.

Dealing with such employee shenanigans felt increasingly burdensome, especially after returning from factories in South Korea, Hong Kong, and China where people knew the importance of a job. American labor, by comparison, usually has it easy. Nellie knew this.

My dealing with employee demands stole time and energy away from the needs of health, sleep, family, and critical office work. Our existing managers didn't have much of a support system to back them up. More than ever, I needed someone from the outside.

I interviewed four acquaintances; all of them were skeptical. WinterSilks looked too small, too risky, and too uncertain. One of these people was, again, John Jeffery. He walked through the building, said complimentary things to placate me, but turned me down. I was too high-risk; WinterSilks was too crazy. He wasn't ready to join a wild locomotive of a small company that looked like it could jump its tracks at any moment. Couldn't justify the leap. I had heard it all before.

John had won the New York State High School cross-country running championships twice, out of thousands of runners; on one try, he'd blacked out a few hundred yards from the finish. He won a scholarship to Colgate University and competed in Madison Square Garden with Marty Liquori and the fastest runners of the era. He was a self-made *samurai*, organized, honest, humble, and tough. WinterSilks could spring his career. Unfortunately, I couldn't convince him of that. The interview process began without him.

More ads were run in direct-mail publications. A wave of resumes arrived. Some looked promising, but there was no way to tell whether they were *samurai*. Anyone else would melt down in WinterSilks' preholiday season inferno.

Promising applicants claimed to be highly experienced, able to do great things. None of them came close to John. Most, I sensed, would put themselves, not the company, first when push came to shove. I focused on the quiet ones, not the ones blabbering on about themselves. I tried to look into their eyes and see whether a champion was hiding in there, waiting for a chance to come out.

In late September the big Christmas catalog rolled off the presses and into the mail, and sales kicked in a week later. It produced the most spectacular sales per catalog in the history of the company. The economy was good, mail order was not yet a fully mature industry, and there were plenty of customers to go around for the catalogs that were seriously doing business at Christmas in our demographic zone. WinterSilks' average sales of $1.60 per catalog mailed was never reached again, even when the catalog was increased to 64 or more pages. Old-timers said the 1986 holiday season was the best they could remember.

The security of strong positive cash flow helped temper the ongoing stress of a straining, immature seasonal business. I used the extra cash to pay off the seasonal bank line of credit loan early and to pay for warehouse expansions and computer upgrades. What was left sat in a money market fund at our bank, as a negotiating tool to entice bankers to loan more for the next season so we could do the same thing on a larger scale.

Snow came early, and again the office roof leaked. Water seeped into the ceiling, and without warning the sodden tiles let go again, releasing an icy torrent onto whoever was working at the terminal below. Long-time employees bet on where the ceiling would cave in next.

A new security alarm system, whose errant security light beams would detect the slightest shift of gravity, sometimes went off in the middle of the night when a box fell over in the warehouse. I'd rush into the office at 3:00 A.M., half-expecting to see a burglar's truck backed up to our loading dock, taking hundreds of thousands of dollars worth of knitted silk garments under cover of night. I even imagined I might see the Hard-Asses from New York with nylon stockings over their heads, getting a little revenge. But once inside I'd find everything quiet—no thieves, just the rustling of nearby cornfields.

That season left us worn down but financially secure, with a large block of new cash in the bank and no draw on our credit line. We bought the building from our landlord, and I scheduled a warehouse expansion. We were sweating all the details, improving quality control and order-processing efficiency, increasing computer capacity, trying to make every sale a positive customer experience. WinterSilks was a powerful little retailing machine but still lacked a management system.

The next new hire was a catalog and advertising design manager to take over some of my last remaining roles and replace expensive freelancers. I interviewed a half-dozen candidates, culled from 30 or so resumes from an ad in a national trade publication. They were all expensive, often egotistical and more concerned about the job's benefits than what they could do for WinterSilks. Then at the bottom of the stack I found the resume of a Wendy Bale and called her in for an interview. I was familiar with the local business publication she worked for. She was making $6 an hour and reminded me of myself in my early journalism years.

When I asked her what she thought of our catalog, she looked it over closely and said, "It looks really boring. Who did it?"

"I did—with a freelancer," I answered.

Wendy wasn't embarrassed in the least. There was something special about her. Many of the other applicants had done great things in Chicago or New York or locally in Madison, and they had attitudes to go with their accomplishments. Wendy had not yet done great things, but I sensed that she could. She just needed a chance. I went with my gut; it proved to be one of my best decisions.

Wendy suggested we buy an Apple computer with QuarkXPress software and a laser printer. (In 1987, these were daring choices.) She settled into the vacant vice-president's office next to mine for two weeks before emerging with several computer-generated layouts for sale catalogs and store promotion ads. Suddenly we had not just an in-house art department, but a high-tech one.

Another Apple computer, laser scanner, and miscellaneous equipment were added a while later, along with an assistant. Wendy began sending page proofs by modem to our film separation house, making her department one of the first in the state to do so. The new setup allowed for last-minute copy and price changes and enabled us to produce a good catalog or space ad at a fraction of the cost compared to our competitors. Wendy also encouraged layout decisions that weighed customer and employee input. Improvements happened fast, at zero cost. WinterSilks became one of the most efficient catalog production sites in the industry. At this writing Wendy Bale has been with the company for more than 25 years.

Soon WinterSilks was selling and shipping more dollars per square foot of building space than most direct-mail businesses our bankers had ever seen. The company was building lift and airspeed by constantly reducing its drag coefficient.

But it still lacked the key operations employee I dreamed of every day. I didn't know how much longer I could last.

23

Stocks Crash, Workers Strike

Summer 1987. The holidays inched closer; still no operations pro from the outside. We were a skeleton crew sailing an increasingly complex ship. When the winds of late fall hit, we would have to navigate shorthanded in the midst of storm season. There could be a nasty shipwreck.

In September I finally hired a big gun: a well-organized former athlete working a mid-level position at a larger, well-run catalog company, eager for a more senior job and the pay that came with it.

"I want to run my own show," he said, full of enthusiasm, gripping my hand in a firm, macho handshake.

New Guy moved into town with great anticipation. I had at last filled all the boxes in our organization chart, and my troubles were over. Weren't they?

Reams of list response data showed new, non-database, catalog mailing list segments that we hadn't tried yet, which most likely offered room for circulation growth—as well as various lists not to repeat. I ordered a new crop for holiday mailings; they were delivered to a computer house on large reels of magnetic tape. We had eight weeks to gear up for 50 percent more business than last year. When we started mailing catalogs in October we would be flipping the switch from off-season to on-season and would morph from 13 employees to a hundred, 87 of which did not yet exist. I was confident New Guy would handle the challenge. Computerization,

I figured, would again absorb a chunk of the workload. Even so, our 80 styles of silk garments and larger mailing lists were going to produce a blizzard of new orders. Could New Guy really orchestrate processing and shipping in time for the holidays?

Dick Norgord, our most catalog-savvy board of advisors member, called. He was the number two man at a large catalog company nearby, born on its founders' kitchen table not long after World War II.

"Are you ready this year? Or do you still feel like running away?" he asked.

"Both," I replied. "The first salvo of our tenth major catalog was mailed on time, in late September. The ball's in play. No orders yet. How are you guys doing?"

"The troops are ready. Early signs are good."

"Good luck," I said. We were both heading into a virtual battle.

After a few days, orders kicked in. All looked good.

Then, October 19, the stock market crashed. The Dow Jones Industrial Average plummeted 22.6 percent in one day, from 2,639 to 1,739. American retail sales stopped dead in its tracks. WinterSilks' revenues evaporated. Monday's 24-hour order count was half or a third of what was statistically expected, considering the increased circulation.

A few days later, at the catalog industry's convention in New Orleans where I was a speaker, no one seemed concerned—except catalog owners. Top-level execs appeared removed from the realities of the marketplace compared with scared-out-of-their-mind owner-entrepreneurs like me with borrowed money, payrolls to be met, and fingers directly on the pulse of their businesses. The salaried execs ate, drank, and socialized happily. The company owners were on the phone to headquarters.

Back home, my worries carried into the night. I dreamt the bank called in my loan, demanding immediate repayment. The next day the outlet store had paltry sales; the catalog scored a scant 300 orders by mail. Our river was running dry.

It got worse. To lighten the operations load, I had placed telephone answering at services in Phoenix and Omaha. This left our Wisconsin office strangely quiet; giving better-staffed phone organizations our telephone orders had taken the pulse out of our building. Now we merely opened mail orders and waited for computer transfer of orders that non-WinterSilks people were taking far away. When orders arrived by modem, we packed and shipped them quickly. But it didn't feel right.

"It's like a ghost town," Rauel said. "You sure this is the right thing?"

I was having the same feeling.

Wall Street's meltdown continued. On Wednesday, November 4, 1987, the mail count was half of what it had been the year before, even though the circulation of the catalog had been expanded 50 percent. A more detailed sales-per-catalog projection foretold revenues off 45 percent from the previous season. Pat told me we might break even for the year, as far as accrual accounting went. But I wondered: *Will we have enough cash and credit line to make it to Christmas 1988, a year from now—the next chance for a large-scale selling season?* I cursed the stock market.

Margaret Acker, our oldest employee and chief of the returns department, came into my office the next day.

"Are we going into Chapter 11?" she asked. Margaret was something of a stand-in for my mother, being about the same age, so seeing her so worried hit me hard.

"I don't know," I said. We stared at each other for an uncomfortable few seconds.

The next day, November 5, 1987, our outside accountant called. He had made inquiries at Lands' End, which was headquartered an hour west of Madison, and reported "nothing significant" had happened to their sales yet. He was a partner with a major national accounting firm, comfortably removed from the reality of running a business. He actually believed what he was telling me.

Our list broker called from New Jersey. "Every catalog client is generally down," she said. "But we don't know how much. There isn't enough detail yet."

Ten minutes later the owner of a sports apparel and gift catalog called. Unlike my accountant and list broker, he was in the trenches of his own business, and bank loans weighed heavily on his shoulders.

"It's fallen off the table!" he said, sounding terrified. "I've mailed 28 percent more catalogs than last season—the boom days of 1986. Now, order flow has all but dried up."

I heard him breathing fast.

"I don't know how to react. I've mailed all of my catalogs and I'm still full of inventory. I'm down 20 to 25 percent in the last two days, and things are getting worse. Last year I loved the catalog business. This year . . ." His voice trailed off.

I called an industry consultant in Chicago.

"Clients are taking serious hits," he said. "Everyone is scared— *everyone*."

I put down the phone gently. The bloodletting had come at the worst possible time of the year. When President Reagan and the Pope were shot in 1981 it was spring, a dead time of year for most catalogs. As terrible as those events were, they had a limited retail selling base to injure.

Now, in the late fall of 1987, with a robust economy and eager consumers on the edge of the holiday season, the shock of the stock market crash instantaneously endangered hundreds of direct-mail businesses and the tens of thousands of jobs that went with them. Catalogs were in the mail, or newly arrived at customers' mailboxes, and sobering stacks of bills waited to be paid on catalog owners' desks. No wonder I couldn't sleep.

Next morning: "How are orders?"

"Still falling," the order processing chief told me. "Phone orders are crawling in slowly. Mail count is 200 for the day."

That was one-quarter of what it should have been relative to the day of the week, month of the year, number of pages in the year's catalog, and number of catalogs mailed relative to this time last year.

The previous Monday had seen $80,000 in sales. This collapsed to $40,000 on Tuesday, $35,000 Wednesday, and $30,000 Thursday. I wondered if we *were* headed for Chapter 11.

Monday, November 8: a hint of hope. The stock market turned up slightly. Was the slide into oblivion ending? Catalog sales held steady and increased the following day when the Federal Reserve cut the prime lending rate to 8.75 percent. Another 12 hours and the stock exchange in Tokyo rose. WinterSilks might survive the biggest economic disaster of her life. Or would she?

Three days dragged by. Fear slowly ebbed as the national economic tide turned ever so slightly for the better. Would the American public spend more closer to Christmas to make up for what they hadn't spent in late October and early November?

The next week, New Guy had lost some of the intensity in his leadership and supervision. Now he wandered around, not saying much. I didn't think too much about it. Department managers carried the load.

Orders began to accelerate, from the post office and over the phone. The pace increased throughout the week. The Monday-to-Friday total was $234,000, which should have been achieved the first two days of the week to keep pace with invoices due. But it was better than zero. It was going to take a sprint to the finish to end the season decently and proportionately pay down inventory, printing, and postage debt.

Then, another knife wound. Tammy Acker (no relation to Margaret), who was skilled at nearly every position in the company, came into my office with an uncomfortable look.

"I'm quitting," she said, as if she were finally facing up to an abusive parent. I was stunned.

"I'm going to work for Middleton Ford. It's a calmer, more normal."

So close to Christmas. Tammy was a gem. How could I keep people as good as her?

A few days later it looked like sales would be down 35 percent in the fourth quarter and we would do $1 million per month, instead of $1.5 million, in October, November, and December. This should have been our zenith year. I wondered when the bleeding would stop.

Another week, and—*daylight*. Order flow came back strong. Hope surged.

Then we hit another wall.

New Guy interrupted my closed-door, 20-minute lunch: "The shipping crew is on strike—all except Nellie. They don't like your system of wage deductions for errors they make." He looked helpless. "I'm dead in the water with these people. Can you give it a try?"

If we couldn't ship orders, we couldn't make credit card deposits. If we couldn't make deposits, we couldn't generate cash. Without fresh cash daily, we couldn't . . .

I jumped out of my chair and headed for the warehouse. I spent 20 minutes listening to complaints. I agreed to each of their demands: a different, but not necessarily higher, wage scale, self-governance, and more time off. Things calmed down and then I made a straightforward request. "Well, I guess we better get back to work. We've got customers waiting."

Two dozen people stayed right where they were. A few shuffled their feet under the dull glow of fluorescent warehouse lights. No one headed for the conveyor belt and packing line.

After a pause the ringleader said, "We'd like to talk it over."

The crowd retreated to the lunchroom. Ten minutes later they emerged with a verdict: They were still unhappy and would not return to work. New Guy and I headed back to my office.

"We met all their requests but they refuse to work. What do we do now?" I asked him. "Do we fire them all, take the hit, miss a few days, and start over?"

"That's the only choice," New Guy answered. He headed for the lunchroom, where the two dozen warehouse employees sat in an unyielding, foul mood. Then he stuck his head back through my doorway.

"Let me try something."

New Guy walked the perimeter of the warehouse, rounded up a few strays, and called for another meeting in the lunchroom.

"Because you rejected the boss's offer, which was 100 percent of your wish list, I'm going to scratch everything and start over," he told them.

They looked at each other uneasily. No one left the room.

"Each worker will start at $6 an hour [in 1987 dollars; lower than their then-current wage level] and work his or her way up to a $.50/hour higher wage every two weeks over the ensuing 12-week period, through February," he continued. "If you make less than the budgeted allowance of errors during each two-week segment, you will be rewarded by advancing to the next level."

Heads started to nod with silent approval. "Management is listening," a few murmured to each other. Only two people walked out.

On paper, New Guy's plan was worse than what I'd offered. But the warehouse crew understood it and accepted it because it was couched as a reward system—whereas my system, as they saw it, was based on penalties. It also may have been something about the way New Guy had communicated his plan and the fact that he was a fellow employee, not the owner.

New Guy shook hands with each of the remaining 22 workers and watched them go back to work. Even though they had given up a bunch of money, the new, transparent program made them happy.

With the 22 survivors back on the packing line, customer orders began to be filled. New Guy had pulled it off. It was his crowning moment at WinterSilks, and one of the most amazing hours of my business life.

"Nice going," I said to him when he reached my office. He shrugged his shoulders as if he performed miracles like that all the time.

A day later, on the brink of peak season, our phone answering service in Omaha and Phoenix called. "You'll have to find another place to take your business," the manager said. "We'll continue for four more weeks, then we're turning off your lines."

Not this. Not *now*.

We had been receiving complaints from customers, so, yes, I had badgered the phone centers incessantly. I had even traveled to Omaha and Phoenix to show management erroneous orders made by their operators. The phone centers' management seemed irked at me for pointing out their mistakes. To them, I was just a pest of a client.

We switched our 800 number back into our local phone company's trunk line and were up and running in a couple of weeks. This setup was harder to manage, but gave us better-quality operators, fewer errors, and happier customers. We switched the midnight-to-7:00 A.M. shift to an answering service in Chicago because staffing it was too difficult and order flow during that period was thin. This experience taught me never to let anyone else take care of our customers.

Meanwhile, New Guy had had a change of heart. Back in late summer he'd been delighted with his new title—director of fulfillment—and the perception of opportunity. But the rigors of day-to-day reality had reduced that perception to disappointment: as the season intensified, he couldn't move fast enough nor juggle the barrage of details. He performed like a battery running out of juice. Had I made a hiring mistake? Or was I too difficult to work with? Maybe both.

I had more at risk, considering personal guarantees on bank loans, so I was faster moving; I demanded the same from others. But New Guy, it turned out, just wanted a good paycheck, a nice title, and a comfortable workload. Despite all the claims in his resume, the truth was out: he was no *samurai*. The stress of a seasonal business and the responsibility of nearly a hundred employees was too much for him. He was overwhelmed by the complexity of so many people, so many orders, so much inventory, so many questions, so little time. He cruised the buildings half in a daze, choking on the thought of it all. I realized I had hired an introvert, just like me, and now he too was burned out.

How could I get senior managers to think like an owner? How could I motivate *all* employees? How did legends like Lands' End and L.L.Bean do it? How could I do it?

A week later, with things back to normal in the warehouse shipping area and the phone and mail-processing centers, a man with a thick Indian accent called requesting time for consulting services. He was importing finished leather products from India to a nearby office and wanted to learn the mail-order business. I was not interested in being unpaid after delivering information, so I requested payment up front.

On the appointed day the Indian fellow arrived, well dressed, with his wife and business partner in tow. He plunked down a check for $300 for two hours of my time and turned on a tape recorder. We talked and then, with a satisfied look, he asked for a tour. I proudly gave him a walk through the computer room, telemarketing center, customer service center, mail opening and batching center, data entry room, warehouse, shipping—the works. Then I showed him to the door, shook hands, and thought no more of it.

Four days later a fairly new, extremely promising employee resigned to go to work for him. I tried to convince her to stay, but she was snowed by promises of new opportunities. She left two weeks later, after a few months of mail-order training at my expense. I stopped giving tours of our operation. Losing a promising employee was a tragedy; interviewing and retraining was a time-intensive, expensive process.

By then the stress of the season had gotten to everyone, including New Guy. The day after I lost this key employee, New Guy also resigned, giving two weeks' notice. Then he went home to nurse his wounds, having negotiated another job. With three weeks of peak season still to come, I felt ambushed. I wished I could put New Guy in a box and send him to a factory in Pusan. The Koreans would have laughed at a wimp like him.

24

Our Own Saint George, and Shanghai Ed

It was too late in the season to interview and hire a replacement, so the night New Guy served notice, on a whim, I visited John Jeffery. Just before I headed out, I dashed off a one-paragraph job offer. John had turned me down twice before; I held little hope it would be different this time.

I felt the penetrating chill of a late November evening as I walked across an empty parking lot and climbed stairs to his office. It was 7:00 P.M.

Emerging from a darkened hallway into the light of his office, a little breathless from the dash up the stairs, I said, "You're in late for a guy who doesn't own the company." His desk was half-buried with paperwork that reeked of deadlines.

"Have a seat," he said, pleased but surprised.

I remained standing. "Time's tight. I'll make it quick."

He straightened and stared at up at me with curiosity and concern.

"My new guy just quit," I said.

"Oh God. I'm sorry." His eyes narrowed, revealing wrinkles of fatigue.

"Me too. Now look—this is your opportunity. I'll pay more than you're making here, and you'll be better appreciated. You can take over if I leave. This was meant for you."

I handed him the one-paragraph offer ("Operations Director, $50,000 starting salary [that's 1987 dollars] plus bonus"). He took it, perhaps hoping that if he feigned interest I would leave sooner so he could get back to work.

He read it through and looked up. "I'll talk it over with my wife." It was the perfect, cautious response of a veteran card player.

Just what I'd expected. But worth a try. I shook his hand and walked out.

Some long shots are worth taking. You never know when the planets of time, place, and circumstance might line up. You never know when you might get lucky.

Three days later John called. "I want to talk a little more."

"Uhh . . . anytime . . ." I felt full of astonishment and hope.

We met the following Sunday night and sat on a snowdrift in the park across from Sarah's and my house, to get some distance from Lisa and Ted's high-volume carousing. A street lamp partially lit the scene. It was a rather informal setting for the denouement of a three-year quest to land one of the most talented management people in Dane County.

"I wanted to tell you I'm considering it," John said.

"*Really?*" I almost fell off the edge of the snow bank.

We talked for a few minutes, covering the basics. Then John drove off into the night. At home, I told Sarah the news and started to choke up with tears.

"If John takes the job, our lives will change," I said. Sarah smiled with amazement. Maybe this time . . . We both knew John could organize and lead a permanent operations team—something I obviously had neither the time nor the skills to do. My time could be freed up to do what I do best, and to rest, be with family, and recreate in activities that got my mind off business. The depth of Sarah's blue eyes showed that she would give anything for a change. Maybe our children would have a real father around the house. Maybe WinterSilks would become a career place to work.

Two days later John called. "I accept your offer," he said.

It was like clean, cool air suddenly filling my lungs, revitalizing every cell of my body. I felt life changing already.

Two weeks before joining WinterSilks full time, John showed up in the outlet store after his own job's long hours. He worked behind the counter, bagging garments for retail shoppers. He wanted to learn WinterSilks' systems from the ground up—and set an example for his troops. My gut feeling had been right: He had the kind of goodness and desire that business schools can't teach. He had a winner's attitude, brains, focus, and work ethic. He was everything that the stacks of fancy resumes on my desk were not. He was a champion. And now he was on our turf, about to lead our team out of the swamps.

When John officially started, he immediately showed the dedication, speed, and detail ability of an owner-manager. He began to search for key people from both inside and outside the company, and he settled employees' conflicts with assurance, as if born to it. He was WinterSilks' missing link, what every business founder dreams of.

John created procedures to bring us to the top of the class in catalog systems administration. WinterSilks' operations, employee teamwork, and attitude began to equal the level of its research, marketing, importing and art production.

The leaky roof was fixed that December—ceiling tiles no longer caved in under torrents of melted ice. No one tried computer blackmail. Rules were established. John, clean-cut and always available, fielded nonstop operations questions with precision, consistency, authority, a hint of toughness, and—usually—a smile. I peered out from my office doorway at the innards of the company, happily surprised at the workforce's growing sense of order. Sure enough, our own Saint George had come to slay our dragons.

As I waited in line outside John's office one day I heard him tell a recently promoted department co-chief: "I want you to show me you can do this perfectly, and on time."

"Piece of cake, John," she replied.

When she passed me on her way out, I saw a huge smile and sensed a new aura of pride. John empowered his troops to do things they had previously thought difficult.

Mid-December 1987: the sprint was at its peak. Fourth-quarter sales rebounded to a decent level. We had gutted our way past the stock market crash and now finished 1987 with $7 million in revenue. In the midst of the rush season John began to change the lives of scores of employees. It was just as I had hoped: Sarah and I now had room to breathe.

Our rapid growth had worn down our previously inexperienced management team; everyone needed time to recover. But there was no time, because the new year came on strong. In January 1988 we hit $2 million for the month. Thankfully, John's systematic staffing and training reduced stress in data entry and telemarketing; the pressure of too many orders lasted only 10 days, through mid-January. John insisted we mail portions of each catalog salvo over a 12-day period, rather than five days, which provided a steadier, less punishing impact on inbound phones lines. Rested staff answered phones and took orders with better care and attention. Fewer quit; more said they would return the following season.

Compared with office workers in Hong Kong and South Korea—where intense, six-day work weeks in Spartan offices were then normal—WinterSilks' office finally was different. It became a quiet, ordered place as late winter 1988 came to a close. Now there was time to laugh and joke in the hallways and establish friendships. Employees enjoyed a sense of accomplishment. WinterSilks had morphed into a comfortable, permanent workplace. John focused on keeping the many good people we had and, thanks to him, we began to win that game.

I promoted Rauel Labreche from merchandise assistant to merchandise manager and then eagerly looked for others like him. We rushed to finalize orders for new inventory from overseas, and my assistant Kristine and I secured lists and computer merge-purge services from domestic sources. Instead of dealing with every employee in the building on an hourly or twice-daily basis, I now dealt with only five or six people, once or twice daily. I sensed that business might be fun again, just as it was in the beginning.

"You're home early," Sarah said one evening. It was 7:00 P.M.

I turned to focus on my health. I'd had chest pains off and on starting in 1984, depending on the day's stress level. Numerous cardiology and lab tests showed nothing wrong. "Probably a side effect of working too hard and worrying too much," my doctor speculated.

Three weeks later Sarah and I took a week off—one bonus of a management team I hadn't dared to anticipate. When we come back, Rauel was ably handling daily decisions and communications with agents in Asia. Other people handled some of my other tasks—in some cases, better than I had.

Ever since the demise of Mr. Kim in Korea, we'd had continuing problems with Tiger Lady and Hammerhead and their successors. To simplify things for Rauel and me, the company needed one or two new, straight-shooting agents. I had found one in Gentleman John—Stanford-educated, an NCAA Division I tennis athlete, and a Hong Kong resident. He expertly worked a few early orders, but WinterSilks was too small, inexperienced, and unsophisticated for his company's taste, with too many product styles and rigorous pricing demands. One day in mid-April 1986, after some polite conversation at a swank Hong Kong bar, he and his Hong Kong Chinese partner abruptly fired me. "We're not the right firm for your needs," Gentleman John said diplomatically. I slunk from the room while they sipped their drinks and pretended not to watch my exit.

I experimented with other agents, with mixed results. Then I got a good lead, via New Jersey. One of our customers was married to an employee of a Swiss trading company with offices in Zurich, New Jersey, and Hong Kong. She must have said something to her husband, because he called, then visited, and I was impressed. Soon afterward I visited their office in Hong Kong, where I found a hard-working ethic and Germanic routine. I placed a trial order and it was executed with painstaking detail over an eight-month period—an experience much different from the triple-agent chess the Silver Fox had played with us.

The man in charge of our account at the Swiss agency's offices in Hong Kong was the Entertain-Them-to-Death German. (He earned this nickname over time, as you shall see.) The first year with Entertain-Them-to-Death, quality control was good, deliveries were on time, and prices were competitive. Product return rates from customers declined, and so did the time needed from me to import goods, compared with prior seasons. The second season, reducing our dependence on Tiger Lady and Hammerhead, we imported more from Entertain-Them-to-Death, and again things went smoothly. We dropped Tiger Lady and Hammerhead altogether and imported about $3 million of finished silk garments from Entertain-Them-to-Death's offices. On my visits to Hong Kong I was respectfully entertained with modestly priced drinks and dinners.

The third season, Entertain-Them-to-Death convinced his Swiss headquarters to let him start a separate division focusing on his 10 largest customers, including WinterSilks. It was a grand promotion for him; he was now president of a new corporate division. But it seemed to disconnect him from a proper sense of cost control. One night he rented a Mercedes limousine to pick me up from my hotel and took me a few miles to a lavish dinner on Hong Kong Island.

187

His wife joined us on most outings. I enjoyed his good company, but his skills were in selling and communicating, not administration and detail. In his old office, a support staff had done that.

Quality control of our garments declined, returns from our customers rose, and communications with Entertain-Them-to-Death became difficult. His ratio of entertaining to sales dollars merely went up. Any time a quality control problem arose, we were taken out to a lavish dinner—even if it meant Entertain-Them-to-Death had to travel from Hong Kong to Wisconsin to do it. During opulent luncheons and dinners at French restaurants throughout Hong Kong, I worriedly looked at my watch. What Entertain-Them-to-Death spent on meals should have been allocated to quality control. It was a dead-end path for both of us.

Rauel and I politely complained about the quality control and late-delivery aspects of the new relationship. Entertain-Them-to-Death was stupefied. He could not believe, after those magnificent gourmet dinners and luncheons, that we could possibly have any complaints. I think that's when I again started grinding my teeth in my sleep.

We cut back on Entertain-Them-to-Death's business. He immediately flew to Wisconsin and tried to . . . take us out to dinner. I turned the situation over to John and Rauel, who prepared a 30-page summary detailing specific batches of problems. Entertain-Them-to-Death sat down at our conference table and we besieged him with well-documented questions. He began chain-smoking. His buttoned-down Swiss associate from the New Jersey office was present to review the evidence, and by the end of the afternoon he had taken our position. After two hours of punishment, Entertain-Them-to-Death went outside for a long, solitary walk. When he returned, he endured another hour's questioning and looked like a beaten animal. Alas, all of those entertainment dollars could not cover up the unfortunate truth.

Entertain-Them-to-Death never owned up to his errors nor regained his rank as WinterSilks' number one supplier. I learned that people can go through changes when they're promoted. Or perhaps a promotion unveils something previously hidden at a lower rank.

Entertain-Them-to-Death was partially replaced by Shanghai Ed, a detail-oriented American with a buying office in Shanghai, in the heart of early-1980s China. Ed chose Shanghai, with all its challenges of the era, rather than in Hong Kong, so he could be closer to factories. He was about six years older than me, in his mid-forties when we met. About six feet tall, with slicked-back dark hair, Ed wore baggy suits and hippie-style eyeglasses and had a relaxed, hang-loose approach—he feared nothing. He often traveled with a stunning female secretary and the best Cadillac that Hertz would rent. He shaved once a week and chain-smoked cigars. Shanghai Ed reminded me of a 1960s version of Al Capone.

Despite appearances, Ed came with one glittering credential: he had been selling silk knit garments and cashmere sweaters to Lands' End for two seasons. Lands' End doesn't place orders with losers, and they don't repeat with the same vendor unless things go very well indeed. So when a Lands' End senior merchandise executive, a neighbor of John's, recommended we talk with Ed, we wasted no time. WinterSilks was a pipsqueak of a company compared with Lands' End's then $500 million in revenues; John's neighbor tipped us off about Ed in a spirit of catalog industry camaraderie and out of respect for John.

Shanghai Ed was the fourteenth agent I contracted with, and our first year with him went flawlessly. We imported $1 million of goods on a trial basis, and the garments were on specification and on time, better than any shipment we had imported before. He helped bring WinterSilks' quality control and customer satisfaction to its highest level.

His top executive was a British fellow who spoke fluent Mandarin and loved doing business in 1980s China. The rest of the staff in Shanghai was mostly Chinese; many were former junior Red Guards.

Shanghai Ed's greatest find as an agent was a cashmere sweater for Lands' End. He found an underutilized producer in Inner Mongolia and in the first season was able to sell Lands' End a cashmere sweater at a landed cost (product, commissions, freight, and customs duty) of around $35. Lands' End sold the sweater for $99—at a time when normal retail for such an item would be over $200. Within days of the offering Lands' End was entirely cleaned out and badly backordered; it was a blowout. Whatever Shanghai Ed's restaurant and bar bills were, they were worth it.

An ebullient fellow, Shanghai Ed lived for the chase, for the here and now; he was the Seventh Avenue version of Marco Polo and a reminder that working for yourself can be enormously fun when you are surrounded by interesting tasks and the right people.

The last time I saw him, Shanghai Ed was lighting up a cigar in the lobby of a five-star, harborside hotel in Hong Kong. I shook his hand and thanked him for making our importing job so much easier. As I walked away I realized Ed had so much more fun than I did. He was in this game of business for the adventure and some profits along the way, strictly in that order. He trusted that the future would take care of itself.

As for me, I had a family to support. I had wanted to start a business, build it, and find the right people to manage it and enable me to take time off and live a balanced life. So I wondered: *How can I loosen the trap of ownership that keeps me pinned in its invisible, viselike jaws?*

25

The Mulberry
Tree Drought

"We regret to inform you . . ." the fax from Entertain-Them-to-Death's Hong Kong office began. It was April 1988, a few weeks after Sarah commended me for being home early.

Oh no—what *now?* I closed my eyes before I read more. I thought I had dodged the last bullet of this war.

". . . of unexpected price changes by factories in China," the first line ended. "Most items have shot up 30–50 percent. Some have doubled."

Damn! Why is this happening?

It was April 16, 1988, and the ominous letter from Entertain-Them-to-Death had come chugging out of our new fax machine while I slept. Despite being demoted, he still clung to a meaningful chunk of our business, as we couldn't risk putting all our eggs in Shanghai Ed's basket.

I dropped into my chair. How could supply prices pop out of control when we had signed a contract a few weeks before? Rauel and I called Shanghai Ed. Same story. We hopped a plane for Hong Kong.

The day after we arrived, still drugged with jet lag, we were in meetings from 8:30 in the morning until 11:30 that night. News was grim: the Chinese had taken our order to our Swiss agents for $2 million and now were trying to gouge us, and every other western buyer, for a big increase.

Deluxe, three-ply spun silk fiber, used to make heavier-weight knitted silk turtlenecks, was unavailable. Single-weight knitted silk fabric was available, but at surging prices, due to increased demand from the United States, Japan, and Europe. The Chinese were learning of their near-monopoly on knitted silk fabric production. Then, a double whammy: drought hit the Chinese countryside. Prices leapt skyward.

Precious young mulberry tree plantations were damaged by the summer's extreme heat; not enough tender young mulberry leaves were left for all the hungry silkworms. Fewer mulberry leaves, fewer silkworms; fewer silkworms, fewer cocoons from which to spin yarn; less yarn, less knitted silk fabric—and higher prices for the limited fabric that could be produced. Knitted silk garments were selling in the United States for utility and price-value reasons: light weight, warmth, softness against the skin, and affordability. In Japan, high-priced knitted silk garments were selling for snob appeal, so Japanese buyers' fashion-driven business could take the hit; our business, mathematically derived, price-sensitive, and direct mail-based, could not. WinterSilks' market would be instantly shrunk by price increases; the econometric model of our catalog's product line would be busted.

Entertain-Them-to-Death again chain-smoked feverishly when we met at his company's offices in Hong Kong. Then we worked all day at the annual Canton Trade Fair. On one side of the hallway were offices in which European, American, and other buyers were begging for allotments of knitted silk from the Chinese government's silk production and export offices. Japanese importers had their own set of buying offices. They had made a deal: they'd pay top dollar, but they wanted first option on all knitted silk fabric and garment factory production. The Chinese happily gave them first crack. So the Japanese called the shots on the Chinese, who called the shots on the rest of us.

To cover the proposed 10- to 30-percent higher costs, we would have to raise retail prices by 30, 40, 50, or 60 percent. If we did so, we couldn't expect customers to buy silk instead of new, constantly improving synthetic garments, whose prices were declining with increases in volume and developments in fiber technology. I figured higher prices would choke demand and we would be out of business within two years.

Two days, 10 hours of heated negotiations. A conflict with Entertain-Them-to-Death, who was caught between making a profit for his Swiss bosses and obtaining product for us at prices we could survive on. We tried to tell the Chinese that WinterSilks had been a customer for several years and could be a customer for a long, long time to come, albeit at lower prices. The pricier Japanese market, on the other hand, could wither away to nothing with the fickle whims of fashion. So what was it to be? A whole lot of cash for an unknown period of time, or a good amount of cash for a long, long time? By the end of the second day the Chinese softened and agreed to a 5-percent price increase over 1988–89 contract prices placed weeks before, which were higher than the previous season's. The new prices wouldn't kill us, though they would make our products less appealing. Our business model wasn't crushed, but it was dented.

I signed the new deal. As we walked out of the room, thinking we had reached a workable equilibrium with Communist government offices, the Chinese told us to expect price increases throughout the next season. I shook my head. Trying to get through to these guys was worse than dealing with Chicken Lips at my local bank. At least he understood the fundamentals of capitalism.

The news from the United States was no better. Postage and paper costs were rising and more competition was brewing from L.L. Bean, Eddie Bauer, Orvis, and Lands' End. This would also cause 1988–89 profitability, on a percentage-of-sales basis, to sag from 1987 levels—unless sales per catalog picked up from the prior year. I saw no reason sales per catalog would increase, especially because retail prices would be higher, so I figured the sum total of our work over the last nine years—all of the heartache, risk, time away from kids and family—was once again about to go up in smoke, for reasons beyond my control.

We weren't the only victims. While markets for silk fabric and finished silk garments were exploding, the very source of silk—the Chinese silk cocoon farmers—were getting squeezed. They could no longer make a worthwhile profit because their government controlled the prices that thread-reeling factories, fabric-knitting factories, and garment-finishing factories paid for silk cocoons. The farmers also faced rising costs and the lure of greater profit from raising pigs, poultry, and vegetables—some of the first categories opened for free-market selling.

Korea was no longer an option, nor was India. China held all the cards, and they knew it. But they were playing them wrong.

I walked the labyrinth of hallways in the huge building and sat on a bench, my head in my hands. If all the work of so many people over 10 years could be derailed by the Chinese in a few weeks, then this game wasn't worth playing.

Rauel and I made the long flight back to Madison, entirely demoralized. Just as things looked good in operations, the supply side had turned bleak. Unlike operations, the supply side was beyond our control.

At my fifteenth college reunion that summer, I met a classmate who had taken over her father's upscale silk necktie business in New York. "Even woven silk production is scarce," she told me. "Italian silk weavers are having trouble getting enough yarn. The Japanese are buying up most of China's production. Silk has become a speculative commodity."

Our eyes locked for a moment. I stared despondently across the college quadrangle. We exchanged cards and I wandered off.

Studying for the FAA instrument written exam and preparing for its flight test took my mind off business problems. The last part of the instrument training entailed a seven-day, eight-hour-a-day flight to the West Coast and back with another student and Field Morey, the FAA examiner and instructor and local airport owner. The other student, Bob Beckman, and I wore sight-restrictive goggles and flew instrument approaches every 45 minutes as we hopped westward. After each approach we switched pilots. On day three we took a break and landed visually on a tiny, one-way mountainside strip along Idaho's Snake River and then flew around the remnants of the cone of Mount St. Helens before heading into busy California airspace.

Two nights later, on a high-speed instrument landing into Las Vegas, with my eyesight limited by "Foggles" and able to see only the instrument panel, I heard the controller call:

"Triple One Sierra, keep the speed up, three 737s behind you."

I pushed the throttle all the way forward as our Cessna descended through the blackness of a moonless desert night. Thirty seconds later Field Morey called over the intercom, "Take the Foggles off."

I stripped the sight-limiting glasses from my face and looked up from the panel, past instruments that lit the darkened cockpit. The lights of Las Vegas exploded on the desert skyline.

"Nice, huh?" said Field. He added casually, "One other thing. You're not landing on this runway."

"*Whaaat?*" I yelled back through my headset microphone. "The runway is right here! We are way over approach speed! Where the hell else would we go?"

I shot a glance sideways. Field was smiling like a cat that had just ingested a plump canary. This was the forty-third class of two on his one-week West Coast Adventures. He pushed his students to the max; if they survived the week, after months of preparation, they were signed off with an FAA instrument license.

Field pretended to look nonchalant. The altimeter showed us descending into the inner jaws of the big runway. I thought he had gone mad. He turned slowly toward me, feigning indifference.

"Over there," he said, pointing to a tiny runway parallel to the one we were about to land on. "Ask for a side step."

I whacked the push-to-talk transmit switch.

"Las-Vegas-tower, Triple-One-Sierra-requesting-side-step-right-to-the-old-parallel-runway," I spat out, hoping I could salvage a passable landing.

The ground kept rushing up as I waited for the controller's reply. Finally a voice came through the darkness: "Triple-One Sierra, side step approved."

I chopped power, slammed the aluminum bird into an aggressive right turn, cut back to the left, hit the opposite rudder pedal, set full flaps, and nursed the yoke to control pitch. We slowed, dropped, and, a few seconds later, met the warm asphalt with a soft thud—an acceptable landing. Was this a test to see whether I could revise my thinking when circumstances changed? Whatever, it taught me that dealing with change is part of life—for one thing, it showed me China's eccentricities in a new, more acceptable light.

The next day we overflew the Grand Canyon and skirted thunderstorms and hail in Colorado, and a day later neared our home base. "Let me see your licenses," Field called out, 50 miles from his Middleton airport.

Bob and I dug them out of our wallets. Field scrawled his signature, and offered congratulations. Bob and I heaved a sigh of relief; neither of us would ever forget the intense tutorial in precision instrument and mountain flying, and the months of air work, study, and written test that had preceded it. The journey to instrument rating had taught me about more than weather and flying; I had improved the art of decision making—not just as a pilot but also in the unending minefields of operating a business.

Back at the office I was determined to get the marketing and advertising production load off my back. So on August 29 I hired Chris Vig, 28—a brainy, energetic fellow employed at a large catalog company nearby who would now serve as my marketing assistant. I had no plan for what he would do, other than begin to remove some of the daily responsibilities from my plate. I knew Chris had scored a near-record result for the Wisconsin region in an industrial psychology and IQ test.

Over the next 12 months Chris took over marketing analysis, catalog planning, print buying and production, magazine ad placement, art production supervision, list broker relations, list purchase order, merge purge, and mailing supervision—and the pressure in my life was hugely relieved. I met with him for 30 to 40 minutes a day; he did the rest. I wished I had found more people like him five years before.

Late September, the first salvo of the season: I watched one night as our main color catalog went out to be mailed. The check I signed for postage was for about $250,000—three times the cost of Sarah's and my house. Again I worried about another presidential assassination attempt, space shuttle explosion, or stock market crash, which could bring the retail world to a grinding halt just as we were reaching out to sell.

To forget my worries, some nights that fall I went to Middleton's tiny airport and did 10 to 12 landings in a row. It was dark during the last half dozen and I often doused the plane's and the runway's lights on final approach to see if I could make a perfect, sensory night landing. It was an eerie feeling, but with the right airspeed and pitch, the dark runway rose gently out of the neighboring cornfields and embraced my old Cessna's rubber tires in a big, almost soft embrace of tar, gravel, and chipped asphalt. It was reassuring; it reminded me that with preparation, risk can be handled. I loved flying for its intricacies and challenge, solitude, and life lessons.

October 1988 began with millions spent and committed on our part, but no orders yet. A week passed and finally the catalog ignited; we were hit with a wall of orders. Now I worried whether there would be enough time, personnel, and systems to ship them all before the Christmas deadline. It was a race of costs versus cash flow, and time and costs always started with a big lead. I carried this worry home with me on days when I didn't fly after work, and it still colored my life with Sarah.

By late November WinterSilks' war rooms were in full swing. Then the Sharp-Eyed Rookie and United Bank advised us their lending rate had risen from 9.5 to 10 percent; we would have to make up additional interest costs elsewhere just to stay even. Just another flesh wound.

The stock market remained stable; the Dow passed 2000. WinterSilks roared ahead, though each Monday morning brought a whiplash of new problems and the needs of over 100 employees. John handled it steadfastly; the operation ran better than ever; orders were received, processed, and placed in the waiting dark cave of a UPS semi-trailer at our loading dock within 12 hours of receipt. On a peak Monday sales hit $250,000, a 24-hour total inconceivable five years before.

The holiday season came to a memorable finish. Thanks to fast order processing and shipping, we pulled repeat orders from satisfied customers and made up for most price increases from China. When all the numbers were tallied, WinterSilks' retained earnings and book value had increased 50 percent from the previous year.

Late one night, a few days before Christmas, I stood outside in the parking lot before going home, watching the second shift through brightly lit windows. It was cold but there was no snow yet—just the promise of winter. The sky had been washed clear of clouds by a wind from the northwest; a swath of intense silver stars floated in the black universe above. I walked a while, and when I returned the late shift had shut down for the night. Just a dim glow from emergency exit lights illuminated the building's innards.

As I started the car to go home I realized there was only one more step to building an established organization: changing to a larger bank, if I could get a simpler, less risky deal.

26

Running on Fumes

A week later John stopped by, smiling and momentarily relaxed.

"We broke $10 million for '88," he said. "Estimated pretax profits will be about two-and-a-half million bucks."

B-i-n-g-o! For a few seconds we stared at each other, savoring the moment. He was proud to have straightened out operations; I was proud to have survived. The $2.5 million in accompanying positive cash flow would cover the advance costs of next season's growth and make it easier to borrow more.

An hour after John's visit a shy new employee stepped into my office. "The bank won't cash our paychecks," she said.

"*Whaaat?*"

"My payroll check bounced. So did some others. The bank says there's no money in the account."

United Bank had recently been acquired by a large regional bank system, which had also just bought a string of suburban Madison banks. The inevitable bureaucracy of a large organization had set in. The day before, I had dashed into our local branch of the newly expanded bank to cash a personal check. The teller didn't recognize me, and the bank computer system was down. She searched a few files and then told me she wouldn't cash my check. As I fumed, I caught a glimpse of the bank's annual report on the counter near her. It had pictures of two local entrepreneurs on the cover. I showed her the cover. She looked at it, then at me, and cashed the check.

Now my employees' paychecks were being spat back at them, and I was being made to look like a turkey. WinterSilks had been doing business with the bank for about five years, and just then had $800,000 in its checking account.

After calling the bank to straighten things out, I called the victimized employees back in.

"Let me know if you have more trouble cashing checks," I said.

They retreated, whispering. I don't know whether they believed my story or not, but all future paychecks were cashed without incident.

I took precious time to write a letter to the president of the bank system, pointing out we had been a good customer over the years and sure would appreciate it if he would allow WinterSilks employees to cash their paychecks, particularly in view of the $800,000 we had in our checking account. Typical of the late 1980s, he never wrote back, although he eventually sent a few stiff-suited officers from headquarters to check out the problem, a month too late.

Because their bank had been bought out by this larger organization, Sharp-Eyed Rookie and Uncle Bob could no longer offer their signature, personalized customer service. Regrettably, it was time to find a new banker.

On the mezzanine floor of the Big Glass Bank, a huge, all-glass building overlooking Madison's tree-shaded Capitol Square—a well-appointed, risk-averse banker picked up the phone and took my call. I had pitched his bank for a loan over the years, without success. This year, he took my call, earning himself the name Now's-the-Time.

In previous years his associate, Officer "No," had told me politely, "The situation is not bankable just now," as if he was snuffing out an unsavory, still-ignited cigar butt on the polished marble floor with his fine leather shoe and was anxious to move on.

One subsequent year, Now's-the-Time had actually come out to WinterSilks and toured our warehouses and offices, then sent a polite rejection letter on fancy stationery, saying basically the same thing.

Just as Smiling Dan had warned me, WinterSilks had had to grow using our own raw wits and the less-than-we-needed resources at hand. Over time our financial statements showed steady growth toward a well-defined goal, predictably and consistent. But when we needed help, bankers still wouldn't lend. Smiling Dan had told me that would happen—but in future years, when we finally needed help less, they'd be eager to offer it.

Bankers like Now's-the-Time had seen catalog companies grow fast and then go bankrupt when industry costs rose and sales per catalog mailed shrank. Stockholders of catalog companies, and their bankers, ended up with nothing to show for years of effort. WinterSilks might have ended up similarly if we had concentrated on raw growth rather than growth of profits and positive cash flow.

The secret had been repeating everything year after year, getting a little better each time, and staying out of unmanageable debt. Following this path, WinterSilks had become a healthy property—a plain vanilla outfit that grew less than it could have. Once it reached that stage—thanks to the financial faith of the Sharp-Eyed Rookie and Uncle Bob—it became the kind of borrower bankers were looking for: high margins, strong cash flow, little debt, a focused market, and prudent management. Even a Chicago bank or two called to bid on our business.

So when Now's-the-Time took my call that winter day in 1989, he had a new and different tone. Yes, he had seen our recent financial statements. Yes, he'd like to discuss a loan. Could he come out for a chat, say . . . tomorrow? My throat went dry with disbelief.

Now's-the-Time appeared at my office door with a most accommodating smile, endured a facility tour, flattered me in a suspiciously patronizing way, and invited me to his golf club for lunch later that week.

Credit analysts at the Big Glass Bank had taken WinterSilks' audited financials and dissected our earnings and balance sheet statistics like a forensic team at a police crime lab. Large, rumbling computers in the bowels of the Big Glass Bank, spat out reams of tedious financial ratios. Reading the report, Now's-the-Time was ready to do business. The Big Glass Bank was ready to open its floodgates for us, eight years after Chicken Lips' repeated denials.

Now's-the-Time made a good offer, undercutting every competing bank. Five million bucks—mine for a year.

"What about personal guarantees?" I asked suspiciously.

"Not necessary. We just need a limited guarantee of $1 million from the company."

I felt like dancing on the table.

So it was that Now's-the-Time and the Big Glass Bank took over WinterSilks' banking business. They provided the $5 million annual revolving credit line I asked for to cover the 1989–1990 season, plus a computer loan of $250,000, with only a limited guarantee from the company and a lien on assets.

I signed the paperwork that Now's-the-Time brought to the office a week later and then stood shaking my head as he drove out of our parking lot, dust and gravel spewing from his tires. Where the hell had he been when we were writhing in financial agony back in the dark, cash-void days of pleading with Chicken Lips and Happy Linebacker?

He'd simply been biding his time, waiting to see whether we'd succeed. And that we did, sooner than Now's-the-Time had imagined.

I took the rest of the day off, nearly floating with delight.

Our steadily rising revenue and profits financed the hiring or promotion of new aides—more Chris Vigs. With their fresh energy, and John running operations, routines that I'd developed over the previous ten years while doing every task myself were passed to individuals whose sole responsibility was a single defined area. As each of the new staffers performed their assigned tasks, I had time to stay away from the office for a few hours, a day, several days, and sometimes a week. The time away was restorative and gave me valuable new perspective to the blur of daily challenges. I realized that I, or any manager, needed to do this regularly.

A week later Sarah and Lisa drove to west-central Illinois to visit Sarah's grandmother, and I flew Ted, now nearly six, in my Cessna north to Sault Saint Marie, Ontario. There we boarded a 1957 De Havilland Beaver floatplane and flew to interior Ontario to spend a week camping on a remote lake with a friend and his two kids. Ted sat on my lap on the ride in and fell asleep. He awoke to sky, forest, and water as we landed on a crystal blue lake. When the plane cut its engine and drifted to a sandy beach, the quiet enveloped us in peace and pristine beauty.

Back at the office nine days later, it took one-fifth the time to clear off my desk that it would have in a pre-management-team year. But headaches from the U.S. Postal Service continued. A new third-class rate hike had gone into effect in April 1988; the fall catalog took it in stride, thanks to a strong national economy and better marketing efforts. Higher postal costs meant any downturn in the economy would hurt us sooner; every cost increase pushed breakeven points to a harder-to-achieve level. This forced us to reach for continually higher volume and efficiency to maintain profitability. It felt like swimming upstream, with the postal unions controlling the water and rate of current.

After the rate hike came another surprise in July 1989.

"This month's sale catalog has bombed," Chris Vig said. "It's pulling 50 percent less than last year at this time. We're gonna take a hit of $200,000 or so, and I can't figure out why."

We considered all the possibilities: nondelivery of the catalogs by the postal service, a flattened demand for silk, saturated market. Then I spotted the reason.

"It was me—I priced the two cover items a dollar or two too high and that killed demand for the entire catalog," I said.

Chris nodded his head politely. I wondered what he was really thinking.

That $200,000 in lost revenue would have paid for three creative directors and the retirement of all computer debt, or the construction of a deluxe new warehouse, or a certificate of deposit for a fifth of a million bucks, or . . .

I priced the next sale catalog more aggressively and customer response climbed back to normal. We recaptured some of the lost sales from the first issue, but the lesson burned in my mind: as volume grows, the ramifications of errors are magnified.

By early November sales projections exceeded the previous year's by exactly the percentage of increased circulation. Across the phone center room, calls came through silently through individual headsets, and a new automatic call-distributing computer system allocated calls to the most-rested operators. WinterSilks was calm and focused, a true retailing machine, a Land of Steady Paychecks. All the stars of a retailer's universe were properly aligned: computerization, a superior product, fast delivery, accurate sizing and fit, rare backorder situations, and dedication to winning every customer for life.

Now customer complaints just trickled in. In both 1983 and 1989 there were three full-time customer service employees, yet sales were $250,000 in 1983 and $14,300,000 in 1989. In other words, by 1989 we were 5,720 percent better at satisfying our customers. This spurred reorders from happy customers, at zero marketing cost.

I was still subject to health scares, a lingering effect of too many desperate, do-it-all-myself years. One afternoon, while inspecting the returns handling department and talking with Margaret Acker, I had yet another vertigo blackout. My vision went blank, the room spun, and I fell violently to the floor in front of her desk. In a minute,

I staggered back to my feet, reassuring her. I held onto her desk and then wobbled back to my office, closed the door, and lay down on a couch in a flood of nausea. In 40 minutes or so my inner ears returned to normal and the nausea passed.

The message was clear: I couldn't stay stuck in this game forever. I had to make a new, healthier life for myself.

PART 4

The Dance of Divesture

I have a confession to make: From the beginning I hoped, like many entrepreneurs, to sell the business after 10 years and walk away— if I could survive the process and build something of value. I figured my family and I would be tired from intense work on one subject area for such a long time. So from 1985 on—five and a half years into the business—I lived a double life, taking a few minutes a month to read and research the selling-out process while simultaneously threading the precarious needle of starting and building a business. Until December 1987, when John signed on, the only people who knew this were Sarah, my parents, and a few friends. Here follows the parallel timeline of WinterSilks' and my double life from 1985 to 1990. It was a nerve-wracking process of dealing with a cast of characters from the investment world and an endgame I'll never forget. In some ways, closing a deal was more difficult than starting and building a business.

27

The Plain Truth About Overfed Cowboy

At breakfast one Sunday morning in 1985, Lisa piped up across the kitchen table: "Daddy stay home today?"

There was an uncomfortable silence. I *had* to telex agents in Hong Kong and Korea, nearly 24 hours ahead of us.

Sarah broke the silence. "You could stay home if you sold the business," she said evenly. "Or are you going to wait until it kills you?"

I was caught in the middle, between the demands of family and my all-consuming venture. And I wondered how much longer I could last. I needed an exit. What was the best way to find one?

I had read how-to books that described building a catalog business, selling it, and then working at an interesting job 30 to 35 hours a week with time for recreation and health. I had missed out on many family, recreational, and social activities; they were starting to seem more valuable than an enlarged net worth.

So during the year of Lisa's breakfast-table comment, I began the selling-out process. I figured the business was worth between $2 and $3 million, and the selling-out process would take a year.

Wrong.

I quickly found that potential buyers didn't move fast. They didn't need another business in order to function day-to-day, the way they needed a house, clothing, food, or car. Hence they were unlikely to rush into the purchase of any small company; my selling-out process was going to take time and encounter obstacles. I called Smiling Dan for advice.

"Buying a business, even a small or very profitable one, is a big risk for any buyer to take on. Payrolls must be met, debt serviced, employees kept happy, customers taken care of, and product quality sustained," he told me. "Business buyers have many choices, so they usually take their time and call the shots. But you can do it if you're careful."

"Thanks," I said in a tired voice to a dead phone line. Dan had hurried to take another call.

Year One of the divesting process was the year the Sharp-Eyed Rookie doubled our credit line to $850,000. Annual revenues were a little over $2 million, with about 15-percent pretax profits—$300,000. I naively hoped for a sale price of $3 million—10 times pretax earnings—to net $2 million after taxes. Profits were above the industry average, percentage-wise, because our core products had, at that time, limited competition and strong pricing power.

After the rush of the Christmas season I called a well-known mail order consultant in a western state who had recently started a mergers and acquisition division. We shall discreetly refer to this fellow as Overfed Cowboy. Overfed had a capable lieutenant in his mergers and acquisitions division—Fast-Talking Cowboy.

Fast-Talking Cowboy spoke with me during a mail-order conference in Chicago in the spring of 1985 and described in glowing terms how much my company was worth—without having seen it, other than a few unaudited financial statements. After an hour or so he had me half convinced that a frenzied crowd of bidders would drive the price to unrealistic heights, far in excess of the $2 or $3 million I planned to ask for, or the $2 million it probably was worth. I was temporarily entranced.

But if this guy was such a fantastic consultant, why wasn't he in the catalog mail-order business himself, making really big money? Quite simply, it was easier and more profitable to soak naive consulting clients than to go through the rigors of operating a mail-order business, with demanding importing, marketing, merchandise acquisition, personnel, and fulfillment requirements. The real mission of Overfed and Fast-Talking Cowboy was to sell me an inflated evaluation of my business, which of course their organization would be pleased to provide for that week's special price of $40,000.

I did a little checking and found that any of the decent accounting firms in Madison could provide the same product for $4,000 to $5,000. In Milwaukee it would be $5,000 to $6,000. When I grilled Overfed and Fast-Talking Cowboy over the phone a few days later and discovered they hadn't actually closed any deals, I realized they were business broker pretenders—just business evaluators in disguise. They knew where the easy money was.

We communicated for six or eight weeks. By then, getting out the next catalog and praying that merchandise from China would arrive on time took up all my time. I was ensnared by the office until 10:00 or 11:00 P.M. most nights, the hour best for typing coded telexes to various agents in Hong Kong, Canada, and Korea. If I was going to hire a business broker, they had to be worth the time.

When I mentioned Overfed to an acquaintance in Chicago, I heard an interesting story: At a recent direct marketing conference of Fortune 500 division heads, private catalog company owners, and public catalog company CEOs, Overfed had been a featured speaker. He had become well known for his periodic assessments and statistical summaries of the industry and his adeptness at selling his services to Fortune 500 corporations—most of which had no hands-on mail-order experience. His success at selling his services to the people who actually owned and operated mail order businesses was considerably less.

In the middle of his presentation about catalog statistics and trends, Overfed used a particular company as an example. He gave sales and profit figures, as if he knew the company intimately. A hand went up in the audience, and Overfed took the question.

"I have reason to believe the numbers on the company you just mentioned are inaccurate," said the doubter.

Overfed stood his ground. "Our researchers have spent months on this, and I am 100-percent positive we're accurate. You are obviously misinformed," he said.

Overfed then went on speaking; the fellow remained standing and again politely contested the statistics and figures. Pretty soon, Overfed's presentation came to a halt while the two exchanged rounds. The fellow in the audience politely stuck to his guns. So did Overfed, who was becoming angry that his rehearsed speech to such a large crowd of potential new customers was being derailed.

Then another attendee stood up and called out to Overfed, "Aw, shut up—he's the owner of the company!" The audience roared with laughter. Overfed reddened noticeably, his triple chins quivering. He stumbled through the rest of his speech and got a trickle of marginally polite applause.

When I heard this, I was pretty sure that if either Cowboy ever called again I would unplug my phone. I shut down selling efforts for the year; it was time to mail the fall catalog, and preparing for another selling season absorbed all available time. Project Sellout, Round One, ended with a score of Rookie Midwest Seller 1, Overfed Cowboy 0.

28

The Pantyhose King and Wall Street Con Man

"Hey Frank, you into pantyhose?" a caller asked me one afternoon the following February.

"*Whaa . . . ?*"

"Just answer the question. You into pantyhose or not?"

"Who the hell is this?"

"It's Mike, and I said pantyhose. You like it?" he repeated. (Mike McCarthy was that mailing list guru I introduced in Chapter 19; he worked at one of the huge food gifts-by-mail catalogs in Wisconsin and occasionally freelanced for me.)

I went stone quiet. Then I ventured, "Uh . . . hadn't thought about it. Why do you ask?"

"Because one of the largest privately-owned hosiery catalogs in the U.S. wants to buy you. Or at least take a serious look. Shall I tell them to call?"

A few days later Mike walked in with Eddie Smith, a gentleman in his seventies who had been orphaned early in life, barely completed high school, and built a $50,000,000 empire of mail-order catalogs. His best-selling niche product was pantyhose, in all imaginable sizes, colors, and styles.

It was now March, the end of our second holiday selling season in the new Middleton building. The Pantyhose King was a pilot and had flown in on his corporate jet with several associates. He arrived at our offices while I was walking through the warehouse. I found the Pantyhose King and his entourage with their feet up on my desk, telling flying stories.

"Frank, meet Eddie Smith," Mike said as I closed the door.

Eddie swept his feet off my desk and stood, as did three senior executives from his North Carolina headquarters. Eddie was about 5'10 and wore a crisp white shirt with patterned silk tie. His sparse white hair didn't come close to covering his shining bald head. Here was a 73-year-old guy who looked like he had gotten a great big bang out of life so far and planned on getting a whale of a lot more fun out of the trip before it ended. He looked me over, connecting my telephone voice with my in-person, harried persona. Then he extended his hand.

"We come up to see what ya got here," Eddie said in a soothing southern drawl. I gave a tour of the building and returned to my office for shop talk about the catalog business.

Two hours later Eddie rose to go. "We like what we seen. We'll get back to you real soon."

Two weeks later, a preliminary offer came via Izzy, their accountant in New York, also in his seventies. I was invited down to North Carolina to see their operation and continue discussions. Their senior marketing officer flew me down in their company Cessna Citation.

Once we got settled at his favorite luncheon club, the Pantyhose King asked me, "You like grits?"

"What are grits?" I responded.

A deep hush fell on the room. I might as well have said, "What is NASCAR?" or "Who was Robert E. Lee?" Finally an aide cleared his throat.

"Grits are a little different from Milwaukee bratwurst—real different, actually," he said, as the rest of the group tried to muffle their laughter at my culinary ignorance. The bone-headed visiting Yankee was getting off on the wrong foot.

Fortunately my *faux pas* blew over. For the rest of the day the Pantyhose King showed me his offices, warehouses, and shipping facility. His mail-order operation was the cleanest and best equipped I had ever visited. Many of his employees had been there 10 or 15 years. One of them told me that the Pantyhose King spent about half of his time at the company and the other half as a local volunteer for children's charities.

Eddie had three aircraft in the company hangar, three pilots under contract, and legions of employees who respected and loved him dearly. Most Monday mornings he and a senior executive cooked biscuits and breakfast for their 250-plus workforce.

The deal they offered me was the classic "Your price, our terms." It included a handsome salary and bonus, and earn-out provisions— which would require me to stay on for several years to realize my full price. Because I was so tired and burned out, I wasn't interested in staying on. I wasn't sure I'd be alive in a few years if I didn't sell.

"Tell Eddie I can't do it. I need to get out," I told Izzy over the phone a week later. And so the Pantyhose King faded from my life; I focused on preparing for the next selling season.

I learned four things from Eddie and Izzy that changed my life: (1) employees need to be truly happy if they are going to do good work and help build a solid organization; (2) hire appropriate people to help carry the management load, and then live life fully while running the business; (3) try to laugh when things go wrong, as well as when they go right; and (4) understand how difficult buying or selling a business can be. It was the last lesson that made me sit up straight.

I did the best I could juggling selling-out calls when time permitted, and two months later I signed a Chicago consultant. He brought me a potential buyer, an auto parts catalog owner/CEO from downstate Illinois. The fellow spent half the day grilling me. He made the beginnings of an offer a few days later, but the deal fizzled within a few weeks. Perhaps WinterSilks wasn't big enough to keep his attention.

I heard of a business broker in New York City who specialized in selling family and closely held businesses. The fellow had sold more businesses than any of the other brokers I knew, some of which were much larger. He had also been a world champion squash rackets player and brought a competitive desire to his merger and acquisition business. I talked with his partner and chief operating officer by phone and was impressed. His partner understood the long selling process, did not make wild claims the way Overfed had, and did not receive a commission until a deal was closed. Unfortunately, their commission was 7 percent. A typical investment banking firm would use the Lehman formula of 5 percent for the first million, 4 percent for the second million, 3 percent for the third million, 2 percent for the fourth million, 1 percent for the fifth million and each million thereafter up to $10 million, and declining percentages for anything beyond that. The difference was substantial. I decided 7 percent was too steep and opted out.

The next suitor was a Fortune 500 direct-mail division chief who had gone out on his own. He had bank contacts and had bought a craft catalog in central Wisconsin in a leveraged buyout; now he was looking for another acquisition. There was something about silk that struck his fancy. The Chicago Hotshot spent many hours with me, looking slightly out of place in the cramped quarters of my budget-oriented accountant's office on the outskirts of Madison. He liked WinterSilks' profits and growth prospects, but he couldn't always follow my outside accountant's compiled financial reports.

"Can one of you guys explain these numbers to me?" he asked, pointing to one line in particular. No one moved. I very slowly eased my head a few degrees to the left to look at my accountant. He sat frozen in place. His client had been too cheap to pay for anything but a bare-bones compilation.

Year-end accounting reports can be compiled, reviewed, or audited. Audited are the most detailed—and expensive. I had never had an audit or a big-name accounting firm. We were too under-staffed to do one between seasons, so we used compilations—the lowest rung offered by the accounting profession. But if a person needs to borrow beyond his collateral level from a bank or to file with the Securities and Exchange Commission, an audit from a well-known firm is required.

So when the Chicago Hotshot went away shaking his head over our compiled financial reports, another deal went up in smoke. I got the message. Our year-end financial reporting was switched to the Madison office of one of the most prestigious national accounting firms; a year after the Chicago Hotshot walked out, we had audited financials. The accounting firm's name on the cover of our statements added credibility to a future sale.

Meanwhile, the mail-order seasons went by, like a string of make-or-break battles in an ongoing war. By the time we were picking up the pieces of our last catalog mail drop in February of 1986, we had racked up sales of over $4 million for 1985, having doubled in 12 months. WinterSilks' value was more than the $2 million net I hoped for, but I still hadn't sold, and the stress of growth and management was driving me into a corner. I worked late nearly every night and then couldn't sleep, worrying about dozens of details that constantly needed attention.

No buyers. No sleep. Just what would it take to hand off the baton?

I budgeted four or five hours a week during the off-season for the selling-out process. Each year's trial-and-error experience added value, and after four or five years I knew how the dance went and the type of buyer and deal needed: full payment at closing, allowing me to walk out and never look back after no more than six months. I didn't want to be at the mercy of a new boss or to watch him goof up my company. But how to find such a buyer?

A few weeks after the Chicago Hotshot walked away, a business acquaintance recommended a Madison business broker. This fellow, Short and Smiley, actually had closed numerous deals over the last ten years and made a respectable living from it. He was a fulltime broker/mergers and acquisitions specialist, which was a lot more than I could say for guys like the Overfed and Fast-Talking Cowboys.

Short and Smiley looked over WinterSilks' financial statements and soon brought in two potential buyers. I also passed on to him one other who had contacted me directly. Short and Smiley put all three on his desk the summer I hired New Guy and went to work.

One potential buyer bowed out after a few weeks of communications, claiming the price was too high. Then I got a call out of the blue from Silver Tongue, a smooth-talking CEO of a New York Stock Exchange–traded company with $250 million in revenues from catalogs and stores it had purchased with its own stock. I turned him over to Short and Smiley.

Silver Tongue arrived impeccably dressed in East Coast pinstripes, with well groomed, slightly graying hair. He seemed to enjoy negotiating the acquisition of small, growing companies. The acquired companies were linked to headquarters, sometimes forever, by means of a unique compensation structure.

Silver Tongue paid sellers one or one-and-a-half times book value at the time of the sale (usually a pittance for companies with a negligible net worth but a promising future), and then put all of the company's after-tax earnings into an escrow fund for a period of five years, with interest. Silver Tongue's conglomerate arranged for credit lines and long-term debt for his companies, and at the end of five years the seller/president could either take the earnings and run or stay on for another five-year stint. The seller got his own earnings, and the buyer got assets and goodwill, as well as use of available cash. Silver Tongue's extended family of companies had a good track record of continuance with their sellers after the five-year earn out. His buyout recipe was a novel formula for cash-starved, growing businesses that had no other options. It was particularly good for Silver Tongue because he could build his sales and asset base at little cost and then impress investment banking analysts who would in turn talk up the stock on the New York Stock Exchange.

While other buyers might take six to twelve months of intensive background and fact checking by their staff and outside attorneys and accountants, Silver Tongue merely examined financial statements by mail, spent a day or two with the seller, and then, if he liked the seller and felt the target company was a clean operation, pulled out an informal sales agreement from his suit pocket. If there were financial bugs under the seller's rug, they would come out of the annual audited earnings of the company over the next five years—which would come out of the owner's own pocket via the escrowed five-year profit pool. This structure not only avoided the time and costs of due diligence but also put the onus of performance back on the seller, whose main compensation would come after his five-year nest egg of retained profits was released. If the seller slacked off in the interim, he would pay for it dearly at the end of the rainbow. Smart and simple—at least for the buyer.

Silver Tongue flew the same model of aircraft that I did, and we got along well. Over a two-year period of off-and-on discussions he made two offers, both with five-year earn-outs. I felt like an odd duck in his scenario because (1) WinterSilks was profitable and throwing off lots of cash flow, despite its limited history; and (2) I wanted to leave. The more I thought about it, Silver Tongue's deal was a step backward. So I said no thanks.

I don't think many people had turned Silver Tongue down before, because he was a bit disgruntled that a promising young catalog company would not want to join his high-profile family of mail-order companies and be part of a publicly traded firm (with a ridiculously fancy annual report that pictured Silver Tongue as some kind of god in a scenic corporate heaven). He went away miffed.

By early March 1988 we had our second consecutive audit. Sales for 1987 were over $7 million with over 20-percent pretax profits.

I sent a copy of the audit to Silver Tongue's office, just for kicks, and pretty soon we had a dialogue going again. I wanted to remind him that he had missed an opportunity to buy the company at 50 percent off.

One of his lieutenants negotiated for a few weeks, but eventually we both let it drop. They had decided to go after bigger companies and knew I was able to hold out for the deal I wanted.

A few years later I invested $140,000 in the stock of Silver Tongue's company. After a year or so communication from his firm slowed and then, ominously, stopped just as Silver Tongue's New York Stock Exchange-traded share price plummeted from $40 to $3, then disappeared from the radar screen entirely. I had to do a little homework to learn that the company had gone bankrupt and been delisted from the New York Stock Exchange.

How had such an apocalypse come to pass? In an effort to maximize his financial energies, Silver Tongue had sold most of his acquired companies so he could focus on his management team's time on the three largest holdings. Two of the three then ran into trouble, and the third drastically slowed down. Silver Tongue's financial sand castle dissolved. Every investor was burned.

Silver Tongue made deals better than he oversaw his own companies. A likeable, pinstriped, smooth-talking, high-end hustler, he unwittingly destroyed many of the businesses he acquired, along with thousands of jobs that went bust with them. For a while, though, he sure fooled Short and Smiley and me.

29

Gray Flannel Godzilla

If Short and Smiley in Madison couldn't get the job done, maybe a big city investment bank could. I called a few contacts in Chicago, and not long afterward two partners from one firm flew up to meet with me. That in itself was a bad sign. Madison is three hours from Chicago by car, and as a bare-bones entrepreneur I bet I could drive from Madison to the Chicago Loop in less time than it took them to fly from O'Hare to Madison, with a cab ride between congested downtown Chicago and O'Hare Airport and a cab ride from Madison's airport to our offices in Middleton. Anyone who insisted on flying from Chicago to Madison had way too much leeway in his or her expense account and probably no idea in hell what sacrifice and cost control were.

They did, however, bring several parties to look at WinterSilks over the next few months. One was a Fortune 500 food company's mail-order division. The division CEO arrived with a half-dozen senior people, and another day of my life was taken up with facility tours and innumerable questions. (Employees were told that these people were potential investors.) For several weeks this company seemed anxious to buy WinterSilks. Then a higher-up at corporate headquarters insisted they grow internally rather than via acquisition. So much for clean decision making.

For another few weeks the Chicago Pinstripes tried to broker WinterSilks to a European buyer, to no avail. When it came to selling someone else's company, the Chicago Pinstripes didn't seem to have hunger. They had eight or ten other revenue centers back at headquarters. A business broker, such as Short and Smiley, had only one. I learned another lesson: when selling, choose someone whose livelihood depends entirely on a consummated sale.

Of course, the Chicago Pinstripes were not exactly a bunch of dummies. Their elite ranks back on La Salle Street were stuffed to the gills with Ph.D.s, MBAs, lawyers, Rhodes scholars, and other luminaries, and they were not about to let their time spent on me go to waste. So when all of their prospective buyers fizzled, they reached into their own hip pocket and made me an inside offer: they proposed that I take over a losing mail-order company that their venture capital department had invested in, turn it around, physically combine it with my own operation, and use the tax loss of their loser against my winner and thereby bail them out of a bad investment, as well as subsidize the (not unreasonable) price I was asking. And oh yes: they would pay one half of their one-sided offer in cash, the other half in notes, to be paid over several years.

I was learning firsthand that investment bankers put themselves first, their company second, and customers third. If they couldn't make money on a stock, bond, underwriting, or brokerage deal themselves, some of them wouldn't hesitate to unload it on their customers. In this case, the Chicago Pinstripes' venture capital division had put some of their own capital into the Early Winters catalog, which had flirted with bankruptcy (and entered it, later). Now they wanted to acquire WinterSilks and have John and me turn around Early Winters and run both. The offer was $8 million cash at closing, $2.5 million three years later, and 15 percent of the new company's equity. But there was no clear-cut exit.

Despite excitement about the challenge, potential growth prospects, and profitability increases, I didn't bite. I had been having recurring chest pains and vertigo blackouts. *I needed to sell and walk away.* The Chicago Pinstripes didn't understand this, nor did they take the time to listen.

Why won't this guy take the bait? they seemed to mumble to themselves on the way out our door, irked that my decision did not serve their interests. How could such a ragtag company turn down their offer? It took until 2003 for my generation to understand the habits of the financial services world; that was when the media focused on crooked analysts who touted hot stocks for the public to buy while their own firms were frantically trying to unload positions in the same firms. A handful of the less discreet or unlucky investment bankers went to prison; the majority erased their e-mails and laid low for a while until things blew over. When media coverage wound down and the smoke cleared, the games of Wall Street went on as before, with barely a hiccup on the timeline of greed. We all know what happened in 2007–2008.

So I went back to square one. I had talked with enough accountants, business brokers, and cashed-out entrepreneurs to know that the price range for WinterSilks should be between a low of 5.0 and a high of 6.5 times audited pretax profits from the previous year. This was a lot less than a valuation in the public marketplace, where an initial public offering for a similar business at that time would be, roughly, 15 to 25 times after-tax earnings (or approximately 12 to 20 times pretax earnings). But a public offering has one big catch: its purpose is not to cash out an entrepreneur. An IPO is there to provide capital for the entrepreneur and the management team to continue to grow a company's sales and profits, preferably at a faster rate. A private sale, on the other hand, can buy an entrepreneur's entire stake and possibly allow a timely exit to the exhausted or aging founder.

Our next tire-kicker was a large-scale local entrepreneur who, with his wife, had purchased and brilliantly rebuilt the Rayovac battery company in Madison into a $350 million-in-sales manufacturing dynamo, and then sold it for a huge profit. Then a Boston venture capital firm showed interest if I would stay for five years and go public with money they would invest. I turned the Boston deal down, and the Rayovac inquiry fizzled on its own.

I considered financing the deal myself, selling to WinterSilks' employees under an Employee Stock Ownership Plan. But that would still leave me worrying about the company's operations while I waited to be paid over time.

More venture capital characters visited. They usually arrived in the senior person's Mercedes or other luxury car and spent part of lunch hour at our conference table talking about other deals they had invested in and why those had gone sour. They were trying for easy home runs by investing in other people's businesses, using mostly other people's money, taking annual fees they were only too happy to extract.

Later that year our new accounting firm hooked me up with a well-known executive from the Chicago area who for a time was the highest paid CEO in Illinois. He visited and eventually made an offer, but it had no ready exit for me. He couldn't understand how a fellow in his late thirties could be so interested in getting out. I looked normal on the outside, but on the inside I was about to break into bits. To get to the exit door I knew I had to stay focused on the Dance of Divesture while keeping tabs on the company. Even with John's expertise, I wondered if I could do both much longer.

Then a highly qualified local buyer came into the picture. He was Gray Flannel Godzilla.

I called a friend at a large consumer products company in Madison. "What kind of a guy is [Gray Flannel Godzilla]?"

My friend thought for a moment and answered in a slightly muffled, low voice: "There's just one thing you need to know."

He paused. I sensed he was looking around to see if anyone near him was listening.

"And that is . . . ?" I asked.

I heard him swallow. "Gray Flannel Godzilla eats small children for breakfast."

"*He what?*"

"*He. Eats. Small. Children. For. Breakfast.*"

I looked at the phone as if I expected it to correct what I had just heard.

"Be careful," he concluded. "I gotta go now."

The line went dead.

"Ah, thanks . . ." I muttered into space, placing my phone back into its cradle. It was as if I had blithely asked a Frenchman of the 1940s, "So, what do you think of Hitler?"

Gray Flannel Godzilla was recently retired from the Giant Meatpacking and Really Unhealthy Processed Food Company, but his shadow at headquarters still loomed large. Now he was CEO of a private investment boutique on Madison's capitol square and was interested in maybe buying WinterSilks. Because I did not want my two small children to be eaten for breakfast by anyone, I was concerned. Who *was* this guy? I stared off into space and then made a few calls. The story began to take shape.

Gray Flannel Godzilla grew up in rural Iowa and worked his way from the bottom to the top of one of the world's larger food companies, which happened to be based in Madison and which had been acquired by one of the world's really, really giant food companies a few years before. Fifteen thousand employees had reported to CEO Gray Flannel Godzilla; most of them would acknowledge he was the best CEO in the business. All of them would concur he was also the toughest.

My friend on the telephone was a hard-working New Englander, well spoken, highly educated, married to a sophisticated European woman, also an M.B.A. And he was incapable of uttering many profanities. So I had not been prepared to hear what he said about Gray Flannel Godzilla, because Gray Flannel Godzilla was stopping by at 9:00 A.M. the next morning. I figured it was a good thing Lisa and Ted would be at school.

I also put out feelers regarding Gray Flannel Godzilla's business partner, the Just-Say-No CPA—a highly regarded accountant and business consultant. Just-Say-No was an expert in business valuations, a delightful person, and a paragon of business ethics and self-restraint. Asking a guy like Just-Say-No to invest in stocks, venture capital, or anything that remotely resembled risk was like suggesting he jump out of an airplane with a half-secured parachute, just for the fun of it. He was not the adventuring type. But if you coupled Just-Say-No with Gray Flannel Godzilla, you really had something.

The next morning Gray Flannel Godzilla and Just-Say-No, along with another likable, experienced partner who looked like a slightly aging Hollywood movie star, came to call. Gray Flannel Godzilla, a thick-boned 5'10, looked like a rough-and-ready football linebacker dressed in an incongruous pinstriped suit. His group had reviewed WinterSilks' financial statements and were ready for the game to start. They took seats at our $99 glass conference table—which I, as always, feared would break at any moment—and looked around at the Spartan furnishings. The dance of divesture began again.

"Where do you keep the cash?" Gray Flannel Godzilla asked with a grin, craning his neck around the room from our rickety chairs and table. I watched his eyes as he surveyed the $5 door laid over two filing cabinets, the worn-out carpet underfoot. I saw him smile.

After a tour of the facility, they gave each other a look that seemed to say: *We've seen the financials, now we've seen the facility.*

This kid is salting away cash, and he doesn't like to spend it. Maybe he's our kind of guy.

After one more meeting there, I journeyed to Gray Flannel Godzilla's downtown executive suite, overlooking the state capitol. I stepped into the elevator at that glass building on the Wisconsin state capitol square—where Now's-the-Time was scheduling the next luncheon at his golf club—and felt an upward rush. From Gray Flannel Godzilla's office there was a view of the entire tree-lined park across the street; it was the office of a commanding officer.

Gray Flannel Godzilla, Just-Say-No, Aging Hollywood, and another partner sat around the conference table sizing me up. They threw out small talk for a short time, then vague business discussion for three minutes, then specific business for a few eye blinks. I could tell that Just-Say-No was getting a little sweaty. He looked like a 15-year-old preparing to ask a pretty girl out on a first date.

I knew what was coming. The other three partners were probably tempted to make a decent offer, but Just-Say-No had thought of 200 or 300 reasons why things could go wrong: nuclear attack on Madison, knitted silk garments linked to cancer, China's silkworms shriveling up and dying mysteriously, and so on. You can't blame him; CPAs are born to worry.

He also may have suspected that something was screwy with WinterSilks and me, because most sellers ask for too much, yet I had confused the situation by asking an acceptable price: just six times pretax earnings, based on recently completed calendar year 1988 audited financials.

So I figured the group had reached an internal compromise: offer the WinterSilks guy his asking price, but construe it in a way that left the buyers protected—another case of "Your price, our terms." So as not to alienate me, I guessed they'd smile politely and say, "The asking price is not unreasonable. We have just a few structuring details that need to be fine-tuned . . ."

Sure enough, Just-Say-No ran off on a soliloquy explaining why WinterSilks was a swell business but they had to be careful taking on financial risk. I shifted in my chair and sensed the partners wanted to kick Just-Say-No under the table to get him going with the offer.

Gray Flannel Godzilla was probably thinking to himself, *Let's start with a borderline offer and work up from there. Let's see if this guy is dumb. He's built a little gold mine of a business, but now he wants out. If he accepts our offer it's good for us but proves he's an idiot.*

I steeled myself. Finally Just-Say-No pushed the two-page offer across the table toward me.

"We're willing to pay your asking price of $12,000,000, or six times pretax earnings," he said. "But with $6,000,000 at closing and the other $6,000,000 over time, providing a few conditions are met." Just-Say-No smiled and looked to me for a reply.

At that moment, WinterSilks had $2,000,000 of cash sitting in Now's-the-Time's bank from the previous year's earnings, after all taxes and debts were paid, and a bit more from the season before that. If I took their offer, I was taking half of what the company was worth (as payment of deferred money is never a sure thing), I'd have new bosses to look over my shoulder, and I'd be letting them use my hard-earned $2 million to buy me out. I also would have to stay for three to five years—doing the same job I was trying to end by selling out. Thin cash, delayed exit. Didn't sound like freedom to me.

I finished reading, put the offer down, and looked around. Just-Say-No looked proud of himself. He had waltzed his way through a long, carefully orchestrated process that basically said, *You look like a decent enough guy we could put up with for a while, we like your company a whole lot, and now we'd like to try to steal it from you.*

They stared at me in frosty silence for about 10 seconds.

"Can I think about this over the weekend?"

"Of course," Just-Say-No said with a tinge of disappointment. I had not jumped at their offer; thus I had disqualified myself as the idiot they hoped for in any seller. The room's energy sagged with the weight of a failed deal.

Unless it was all, or nearly all, cash—plus a ready exit—I wasn't going to jump for anybody. But I couldn't blame Gray Flannel Godzilla and his buddies for trying.

The meeting was over. I'd had my sliver of time with the local investment gods. They had dozens of other deals to look at.

Follow-up discussions wandered back and forth by mail and telephone until I got busy with the fall selling season, then the discussions came to a halt. By the end of the year, WinterSilks exceeded the projections on which Gray Flannel Godzilla and Just-Say-No had based their offer. This inspired them to return to the hunt the following spring; they brought in a guy from a New York bank's venture capital department. Still, they wanted me to stick around and wouldn't pay up if I left. The deal fizzled with barely a whimper. Gray Flannel Godzilla's partners were busy looking after the firms the big guy did buy. And when the big guy called from his glass ramparts office, partners, employees—and even former employees—jumped a foot and a half.

Me? I felt stuck. All I needed was one deal that would hold together to closing, but I couldn't pin one down. It was like trying to steer a tomato seed across a salad plate with a greasy thumb. It drove me crazy.

30

Wheeler-Dealer, Big Hitter, and the Beady-Eyed M.B.A.

It was 1988, nearly a year since John Jeffery started and about the time we demoted Entertain-Them-to-Death. I kept searching for a deal that would pay six times the previous year's pretax earnings and let me leave soon afterward. My asking price met with little resistance, but it was hard to find a buyer who would let me walk away. I had to find just the right partner and then keep him or her in synchronized step so we could waltz together to the end of the dance.

As sales from the 1988 holiday catalogs took off, I juggled running my portion of the business and trying to find just that buyer. It was a difficult balancing act; I needed to step back, get my mind off the process, and get some fresh, trusted advice.

One Friday afternoon in early December I flew my Cessna to the Lake Michigan shoreline and then south to Chicago, where I had dinner with Dan, a close friend.

"Stick to fundamentals and just run the business," he told me. "Don't listen to investment bankers; they have no idea in hell how to run a business for the good of the business. Find your own path to divesture. Something good will happen."

The holiday and winter season of 1988–1989 was strong: $10 million in annual sales and $3 million in after-tax cash at Now's-the-Time's bank, with only $30,000 of long-term debt. These numbers were of a scale to be more readily noticed by institutional buyers. If just one would fall in love with the company, then a deal, and subsequent closing, could be simple—because just one skinny, pale, tired-looking guy held all the stock.

Two new potential buyers materialized in April. They visited with great interest and flurries of questions. But their interest dissolved. More of my time was wasted.

What about local banks? Would they provide a loan to senior managers at WinterSilks to buy me out? Yes, but any bank wanted me to hang around until their loan to WinterSilks' was paid off; I would give up control without being paid. I was always the sticking point of the deal; buyers thought they needed me at the helm.

I asked John for advice. He dropped into a chair in my office like a tired coach after a game.

"You get out of here; I'll cover for you," he said. "Several times a month, go for a rest. The buyers need to learn they gotta deal with me."

"Can you give them the answers they need?" My tone was unsure. John's eyes went steel cold, like they must have before a major race. After a pause: "I won't blow this."

Another pause. Then: "The key is demonstrating to lenders and buyers that you are dispensable. We need to cross that bridge sometime. Might as well do it now."

So I did it—I disappeared. But first, to stimulate a deal, I offered John a bonus plan, contingent on a sale closing. It was a one-page letter backed by a handshake. We were probably the only two Americans who concluded a sizeable agreement that day without subsidizing a lawyer.

Potential buyers, finding I was not available to return their phone calls, had no option but to turn to John. They soon realized he had become as knowledgeable as me about the inner workings of WinterSilks. Pretty soon they didn't need to talk with me at all.

But those buyers also fizzled out, so I kept hoping for a new buyer with a special connection to the company—someone who understood they were dealing with a home-grown, Ma-and-Pa, scrubbed-behind-the-ears little enterprise.

"Selling out is a real pain," I complained over the phone to Izzy, a CPA who also worked for Eddie Smith. "Deals take up my time and keep aborting. You got any leads?"

"Harry in Los Angeles," Izzy replied without hesitation in his thick Brooklyn accent. "He'll fix you up."

I called Harry an hour later.

"Send me the numbers," he said. "If they look good like Izzy says, we'll come out." He sent a representative, WinterSilks passed muster, and soon a new inquiry materialized from one of his catalog-acquisition clients in New York, a real wheeler-dealer.

"Sounds like a nice little outfit," Wheeler-Dealer said patronizingly. "Plenty of cash, little debt, nice growth potential. I'll be there Thursday morning."

A few days after Wheeler-Dealer's visit, a formal, 12-page Letter of Intent to Purchase arrived by fax. Page after page of legalese spilled onto the floor. I stooped to collect them like a famished cat cornering a most promising meal.

The money was fair, at $15.1 million, and there was an exit within a year, but it was a leveraged deal: they would borrow to pay me and use WinterSilks' assets and earning power as collateral. The thought was unsettling; I didn't want my company leveraged. I wanted to pass the baton of ownership off to someone with fresh energy who could take it to the next level, keeping it clean and simple in the process.

Keep dreaming. Wheeler-Dealer's deal said: *Here's a virgin little company from the Midwest just waiting to be cherry-picked and L-E-V-E-R-A-G-E-D.* In the acquisition world, this is nothing more than a polite term for financial rape.

While most of the Wall Street world seemed to be one big legitimized den of thieves, WinterSilks was, financially speaking, about as dewy-eyed and clean-cut as Little Red Riding Hood on the way to Grandma's. But buyers as clean-cut as WinterSilks were going to be hard to find.

Wheeler-Dealer and I negotiated a few details for a day or so, and I was about to sign. Then a letter arrived in that afternoon's mail. I opened it and saw it was from a mergers and acquisitions investor in San Francisco, looking to buy a small company—mine. He wanted to know more. I held off on signing Wheeler-Dealer's letter of intent and picked up the phone.

The deep, slightly contrived voice of a very smart fellow who probably regretted being the shortest guy in his high school class resonated huskily over the line. He said he'd express reference documents to arrive the following morning. I was about to hang up when I thought to ask:

"How did you hear about WinterSilks?"

"My wife is one of your customers," he said. "She told me I should buy the company."

The next day his resume and references arrived. Sure enough, he was a very big hitter: the top mergers and acquisition executive with a Fortune 500 corporation in the 1960s and '70s. He had retired, purchased small companies, and then brought them public as a group. A decade later, he sold that firm to a large private investor for a jaw-dropping sum, traveled the world, earned a Ph.D. at Stanford, and married a young foreign woman. Now he was starting over again, just for kicks, and perhaps for ego sustainment. He had recently purchased a furniture manufacturer in California, and WinterSilks, if he closed a deal, would be the second acquisition of his third career.

A long phone conversation ensued. Then an eager, bright, beady-eyed M.B.A.—the big hitter's right-hand man—came out and scouted us. Most of the time was spent sitting at our conference table, where he peppered me with questions. I imagined his checklist:

Is the owner a crook?
Forced to sell by some exterior circumstance?
Any skeletons in the closet?
Any new technology that has made the business obsolete?
Is the industry about to collapse?
Is the main source of supply suddenly not available?
What's the real reason he wants out?

The Beady-Eyed M.B.A. queried me all day like a tireless prosecutor, keeping a quick pace, and then he flew back to San Francisco. His report must have been favorable, because Big Hitter called the next day and finalized negotiations. After that, the Beady-Eyed M.B.A. became a regular visitor.

I soon learned that Beady-Eyed was not a sentimental fellow. He was bright as blazes, all right—handpicked by Big Hitter from hundreds of resumes that must have flooded his desk—but also cold-blooded and cagey. He was a quantitative analysis jock who knew numbers and spreadsheets and how to execute the sometimes-complex deals Big Hitter approved. But I guessed he had little appreciation for what it took to grow a fair-and-square, made-from-scratch business.

Beady-Eyed knew I was looking for a deal that would let me walk away at closing or shortly thereafter. What he didn't know was that in the interim of fizzled deals I had become a stabilized entrepreneur. Now I had a good company to sell, with good management; I could pick and choose among proposals. Over the past year the lead partner in the Dance of Divesture had changed from the buyers—who still thought they were rescuing an exhausted and desperate, in-over-his-head entrepreneur—to the seller: a more confident, slightly more rested me.

"Which one do I take?" I asked Sarah one night as she juggled a flurry of baths, teeth brushing, and bedtime stories for Lisa and Ted. She paused for a few seconds, tired of the business. After 10 years her voice sometimes took on a hard edge.

"Take the one that will *close*," she said, looking hard at me. Few business school professors had enough real-life experience to give such good advice.

I held off on signing Wheeler-Dealer's offer and gave a deadline of April 1 for final, updated offers from both Wheeler-Dealer and Big Hitter. Soon a formal revised offer came from Big Hitter. I negotiated until it was entirely fair to me; then I left on April 12 for Hong Kong and China, with a stop at Big Hitter's San Francisco office.

Big Hitter had offered $12 million at closing and a note for $3 million to be escrowed for one year, for a total of $15 million. In addition, he would pay me a meaningful salary for four and a half months and then let me slip away. I said I would sign.

When I called to tell Wheeler-Dealer, he increased his offer. Tempting, but it was more complex. I stuck with Big Hitter's, knowing that having another offer would encourage the first one to close and give me a viable option if the first offer fell apart.

At Big Hitter's handsomely appointed offices I thought he looked like an aging, softened Napoleon in pinstripes. I felt self-conscious about my ill-fitting blue suit, which looked hung from an overworked human scarecrow. I was pale and felt a case of the flu coming on.

We spent the next two hours in his corporate nest overlooking San Francisco's skyline, and then dined with his wife, an experienced marketing pro. My flu symptoms worsened and I barely avoided vomiting.

The letter of intent was signed; Beady-Eyed set out to round up financing. The wheels of closing started turning. I set a deadline of June 30. If Big Hitter's deal wasn't closed then, I had an option to bow out and take Wheeler-Dealer's offer.

Beady-Eyed raced for the finish. He commuted between WinterSilks and San Francisco and hired New York accountants who tore into our records, loan documents, bank statements, and deposit confirmations, and talked with employees. They seemed surprised that our hole-in-the-wall outfit truly had a ton of hard-earned cash socked away in a money market account and steady sales in the off-season—just as John and I had said. After a week or so of skeptical probing, the senior accountant from a big-name firm in Manhattan stopped talking down to us and became less biased against the Midwest. He seemed surprised that people here did what they said they were going to do and were decently polite. We showed him more than just the guts of a good little company.

Beady-Eyed talked up banks and financial institutions, trying to come up with cheap capital to finance the deal. Why use Big Hitter's money when they could borrow someone else's and deduct the interest? Their game was simple: put in as little of their dough as possible, borrow as much as possible, and strip all available cash from the company along the way. WinterSilks' scant debt and relatively large cash reserves made it a sweet target.

In the end, Beady-Eyed and Big Hitter ended up with a financing package from an asset management group in Los Angeles that had a private equity office in Manhattan. The financiers from the New York office sent out yet another accounting firm to audit our financials. Then the commercial bank from Chicago that would be providing operating credit facilities for WinterSilks (replacing Now's-the-Time's bank), as opposed to investment equity dollars, sent out its own team of auditors. It felt like we were giving a pint of blood to every accountant in the yellow pages.

I also sensed that the company's critical simplicity was slipping away as WinterSilks entered a one-way track to the Land of Leverage. But no other divesture trains were running just then—at least none that I could find. Sales of companies for cash and stock were out of vogue.

Beady-Eyed knew how to do all the things a quantitative analysis jock is supposed to do, and I had no doubt he was smart. I was also sure he did not appreciate the real, total process of running a business. To him, a business was a characterless entity that could be analyzed on spreadsheets and financial statements and then twisted and tweaked to his advantage. The way he saw it, businesses existed to be leveraged. Especially squeaky-clean, homegrown, straightforward businesses like WinterSilks.

To me and most other company founder-owners, a business is something to be nourished and developed, like rearing a child or planting a garden. How could I risk financially leveraging WinterSilks? But if I was going to sell, it was inevitable that some brainy but heartless white-gloved financial surgeon like Beady-Eyed would vacuum up the easy pickings on WinterSilks' balance sheet and put the company back on the shelf with a ton of debt, like a hapless patient operated on for his body parts and left with mechanical replacements. Beady-Eyed was like a professional financial assassin: he did his heinous job, banked his paycheck, and felt no remorse.

Sarah and I had borne the WinterSilks child, and John, Chris, and I had raised it into a sturdy young adult. Now we were getting ready to release our child to new, unknown guardians. I sensed that life for the company might never be the same again.

And there was one other thing: China was about to erupt.

31

Marathon Poker

Our accountants said Big Hitter's offer was fair: $12 million cash, $3 million in a revised, three-year escrow. The escrow would be held by Now's-the-Time's bank and was bankable, as John would be running WinterSilks and responsible for paying the notes.

The $15 million offer from Big Hitter was $100,000 less than Wheeler-Dealer's, but Big Hitter's deal was simpler, allowed me to leave after four and a half or five months, and was more likely to close. In taking it I could hold Wheeler-Dealer's higher offer like a sword on a string, silently pressuring Big Hitter to close without beating me up on terms or price. If, on the other hand, I accepted the higher offer from Wheeler-Dealer, Big Hitter's offer might go away and Wheeler-Dealer would have room to negotiate down. I stayed with Big Hitter, hoping the deal would close in three months. John shepherded due diligence; I took some precious time off. Beady-Eyed hustled to beat the June 30 deadline while Big Hitter looked over his shoulder from afar.

Meanwhile, WinterSilks' revenues remained on target. Summer sale catalogs sold obsolete inventory and overstocks, providing a limited but steady stream of income as we readied operations and holiday catalogs. It was smooth sailing that late spring of 1989 for both the divesture process and the company. A few nearly carefree weeks passed.

Then the words *Tiananmen Square* flashed across every TV set in the world. Student protesters in Beijing were fired on and, in one case, driven over by the Chinese military. Some Chinese troops fired into crowds. The killing of students was shocking and horrendous enough. For importers from China, there were also practical, economic ramifications: export shipments were now in question. Bank interest in financing Big Hitter and Beady Eyed's acquisition dried up. So here we were, three weeks from closing, and now the deal was dead—and our supply line was endangered. I was demoralized and exhausted.

I went to Vernon County for a couple of days and took my 67-year-old mother bicycling on the Elroy-Sparta trail and fishing on a stream near Richland Center. While she pursued brown trout one afternoon, I fell asleep in a field. When I awoke I sensed a large life force above me. I had slumbered by an open gate in a fenced pasture, and through that gate had wandered a herd of Holstein cows, one of which now stood over me, quite curious. I gingerly crawled away from beneath its hulk and went looking for my mother.

By July 5 I figured we would go through another Christmas season before a sale of the company could take place. I would again take all the risk and get little reward for it—a salary of $50,000 that year, a paper gain on the value of the company, and plenty of headaches. Ten years of long hours, worry, and limited sleep had taken their toll, even with recent time off. I wanted the relief of a clean-cut sale; I wanted out. But it looked like that glimmering prospect had evaporated again.

On August 3 a loan officer from the third-largest bank in New York called, representing potential debt financing for Big Hitter and Beady-Eyed. The banker figured Big Hitter would put up 10 percent of the deal and borrow the rest. But he was cautious.

"Some of my investment friends have been burned by mail-order deals," he told me. "And I'm scared of China, post-Tiananmen. I want to take time with this deal."

I sagged in my chair, then rose and walked to John's office.

"Shoot me now and get it over with."

"Not so fast," John said. "If China normalizes, the deal with [Big Hitter] could come back to life. China needs its business link with the world, and the cash it brings. They can't afford to shut us or anyone out."

On September 15 came an explosion of sunlight and hope. A small stack of export cartons from China arrived at U.S. Customs in Chicago. It was just a trickle of goods, but the WinterSilks name was on them; it was the front end of our season's supply from Shanghai Ed— on time. The hard-liners in Beijing had been overruled. International commerce, and the precious cash flow it produced, had come to be king in China, same as everywhere else. China had recommitted to the Open Door policy, and was in the quasi-capitalist game to stay.

Another week or so, and Shanghai Ed, Entertain-Them-to-Death, and American President Lines verified that all scheduled deliveries were on board ships on the Pacific, en route to us, on schedule for Christmas. The Chinese government wanted to teach the unfortunate dissidents a lesson but didn't want to sever its growing stream of hard currency. Silk was a steady earner for China. Our franchise was safe.

Export agents in China continued to be optimistic. But the financiers for Big Hitter's deal were on another wavelength. "We'll have to wait this out," the New York banker told Beady-Eyed.

The original letter of intent had expired when Big Hitter did not close by June 30. This left the door open for Wheeler-Dealer to come back in. I gave him the on-time shipping news, and he made a new offer: $10 million in cash, $5 million in notes. I asked him to change this to $10 million in cash and $8 million in notes because their last offer, several months before, was based on the prior year's earnings—about $2.5 million before taxes. When that deal fizzled because of Tiananmen Square, time passed and we marched into a new season in which pretax profits were expected to be $3 million. Therefore a six-time multiple on the difference of $500,000 would be $3 million, and the new, same-benchmark total should be $18 million.

Wheeler-Dealer was reluctant. He wanted last year's price for this year's profits. I stood firm. WinterSilks had sailed through the Tiananmen debacle undamaged and would be bigger, stronger, and more cash-rich at the end of the season, just three months away. We were mailing more catalogs as a result of the prior year's response analysis and had increasing operational ability to ship orders faster, thus ensuring more repeat orders. The U.S. economy was in good shape, the holiday season looked promising, and bankers' confidence was firming up. Why should I bite on Wheeler-Dealer's same-deal-as-last-season's offer?

Big Hitter and Beady-Eyed heard from John that Wheeler-Dealer had put his chips back on the table. To set the tone, I stopped taking calls from them. A slight panic set in.

"What will it take to get the deal?" they asked John.

"I don't know," John replied, ratcheting up the poker game tension.

"Where is he?"

"I don't know. Biking out to the Mississippi, I think."

"How do we reach him?"

"There's no phone on his bike."

Big Hitter and Beady-Eyed festered in angst; WinterSilks became more valuable every day. Holiday catalogs with high-probability lists were about to be launched into the postal stream. Good management was giving me bits of time away to rest and renew and to properly pace the selling of the company. For the first time, I didn't have to accept if offers were low. It was a secure new feeling. I felt a strengthening confidence that the company would grow year after year by doing the same thing, at the same time, in the same way it had done for the past nine years, divesture or not.

My absence caused Big Hitter and Wheeler-Dealer to think I was spending time talking to the other suitor, making a new deal. Actually, I was hiking up to my upper pasture in Vernon County, counting wild turkeys. I had recently purchased 171 acres with a house, 1911 round barn, and cold-water pond for a song. It was deep in Amish hill country, 60 miles east of the Mississippi, marked by oak-studded ridges that towered over small valleys with rich, black earth and pure, spring-fed creeks.

Big Hitter and Beady-Eyed told John they'd prepare a revised Letter of Intent. So did Wheeler-Dealer. When I reemerged at the office, I cleared paperwork from my desk and then ducked out early for dinner at home. Then I went back to our farm. The Dance of Divesture was on again, and this time I held the cards.

Two days later Beady-Eyed somehow got my number at the farm. I spoke briefly, then ended the call and flew my Cessna north for two hours with my friend Bruce Allison. We disappeared to my parents' cabin on the south shore of Lake Superior and forgot about our respective businesses. For three days we took long hikes through the woods of the forested Upper Peninsula, paddled canoes on inland lakes, and discussed literature with the former chairman of the English department at Rutgers University. The professor spoke of early American writers while standing under a forest of 200- and 300-year-old hemlocks.

My absence produced results. Big Hitter and Wheeler-Dealer made revised offers of $17.0 and $17.5 million—up $2.0 and $2.5 million, respectively, since Tiananmen Square.

Two days later I called Beady Eyed. "I'll go with your offer if you put money up front and close by December 31st," I said. "Otherwise, I'll go with the other group. They're willing to pay $500,000 more and close sooner."

Big Hitter and Beady-Eyed's offer was again less, and still simpler. It offered me a departure five months after closing. But could they borrow enough to make the deal happen? And when would they close? I called Wheeler-Dealer.

"We'll close sooner," Wheeler-Dealer promised, "but we need you to stay around for at least a year."

No thanks. Back on the phone to Beady-Eyed and Big Hitter.

"I need money up front to prove the seriousness of your offer. Your letter of intent is half a million bucks less than another offer."

Big Hitter must have thought I was blowing smoke. I sensed an energy change as he put on his best poker face.

"We can't do that," he purred, slow as oozing molasses. "You go ahead with the other party. We'll be your backup."

Big Hitter sounded confident. Actually, he had played into what had become a trap. The only way out was for him to ask for the deal back on any reasonable terms I wanted. But that card could wait.

I thanked him politely for his past interest and got back on the phone to Wheeler-Dealer. I signed with him the following day for the additional $500,000.

I had asked him for references from other catalog companies he had purchased. An hour later a batch of names came coughing out of our fax machine. One, a former owner and now a salaried president of a company in Wheeler-Dealer's conglomerate, painted a stark picture.

"They're really leveraged. And living in a leveraged, debt-ridden, cash-starved environment is not fun. Think twice before you do it."

There was a pause. "I'll tell you one other thing," he added. "These guys always have trouble getting financing. That's what happens when you are leveraged to the hilt."

So if I went with Wheeler-Dealer, one piece of bad luck and my company could be toast. I put the phone down slowly. Was signing with Wheeler-Dealer a mistake? Would he really be able to close? Would he be able to get larger and larger lines of credit as WinterSilks grew, or would he siphon off excess cash? Big Hitter and Beady-Eyed might be a better choice. At least I knew them.

Big Hitter smoldered on the other end of the line when I called to tell him I'd signed with the other party. But no money had changed hands yet, so technically there was no commitment; both parties had seesawed toward a vague finish line. Big Hitter had focused on WinterSilks for much of nine months of his life, and he was damned if he was going to be outflanked by some rookie entrepreneur from a third-tier city in the Midwest.

But he had no choice. He needed to cough up a revised, higher offer or lose the deal. He wanted WinterSilks so he could end the year with a two-company, $65-million retailing group. I also knew Big Hitter planned to buy a computerized auto parts salvage business in two months, which would give him total sales of $100 million from all three companies—and, he hoped, enough free cash flow to service all associated debt plus the acquisition of a fourth company. Then he planned to take the group public. Now I was screwing up his plans.

Big Hitter liked control, but he had lost that when he'd delayed (wanting to see how our Christmas catalog would do with higher silk prices from China and resultant higher retail prices). Now he realized the delay had been a mistake.

Twelve hours later he cracked and faxed his revised offer. It resolved my few remaining sticking points.

Wheeler-Dealer's offer was still higher, but had no money up front. However, signing it had put me in a gray area. I called an attorney.

"The deal may not be binding, since there was no down payment. You can walk away."

I called Big Hitter. "Close by December 31 and we have a deal."

Big Hitter grunted approval.

By early October the first of five salvos of WinterSilks' 1989 holiday catalog had been mailed, arrived at a million homes, and begun to stir waiting bodies in the call center room. Our refrigerator-sized computer and its dedicated hulk of a printer spat out fulfillment tickets for each order. Pickers and packers scurried around the warehouse. UPS left an empty half-length semi-trailer at our loading dock for us to fill. John and I had one eye on the business, where another four million catalogs were teed up for sequenced mailing, and the other on the deal. I sure as hell didn't want another year of running the business while juggling the selling-out process. I cleared off my

240

desk and headed home. Lisa and Ted's joyous greeting was always a salve for my funk.

WinterSilks ran like a well-oiled Swiss watch; department managers handled training and staffing. Unbeknownst to them, the Dance of Divesture went on in the background. Attorneys for Big Hitter delivered a draft of a formalized purchase agreement, and a small army of lawyers representing his bankers pored over it like crows over fresh roadkill.

Then, in mid-November, catalog sales hit a flat spot; revenues fell below target. I felt a panic. The finish line of selling out seemed to keep moving further away, thanks to softening revenues and a modest winter. By contrast, payroll had grown to $45,000 every two weeks in anticipation of the holiday rush. But just then the rush wasn't happening. And hearing of this, Big Hitter was cooling off. He said he wasn't ready to close. It was November 20.

32

Fight to the Finish

W hen I arrived at the office in the morning, sleep deprived, I stuck my head into John's office. He read my quizzical expression.

"Things are finally looking up," he said. "Four hundred orders in the mail so far, still counting. Phones are a little soft. Might pick up later today."

WinterSilks' eleventh season was a nail-biter like all the rest.

In the fourth week of November, catalog sales finally crept ahead of the previous year's. It was like cheering on a determined old race horse that had fallen behind but now was slowly, steadily catching the field.

I stopped in at Chris Vig's office and learned that circulation was up 40 percent from the prior year.

"Relatively speaking," he said, "we're coming on target. Adjusted sales per catalog mailed are holding steady. Average magazine ad order is almost 65 bucks, up a little from last year. Most lists are pulling good, some like gangbusters. Product-wise, 001's, 002's, 023's are blowin' the doors off. 035's, 018's, 019's steady as usual. Returns nominal, so far. We keep this up, we're gonna kick ass."

I breathed a sigh of relief. Chris had picked up part of John's administrative load since Beady-Eyed pestered John with phone calls all day. John fed sales data to Beady-Eyed over the phone; Beady-Eyed plugged it into his laptop in San Francisco and then built spreadsheets of his own. The numbers on Beady-Eyed's laptop must have said good things, because a few days later Big Hitter came out of his chill and urged the deal on.

In early December the holiday sprint took off. Most days 90 to 95 percent of all orders were promptly shipped. Employees were happy, even though we were in the always-grueling home stretch.

I perched at the office every day, meeting with five managers for 20 or 30 minutes each. Trying to stay out of John's way, often unsuccessfully, I inspected the inner workings of what was still my company. I wandered hallways, talked with department managers, and reviewed timeliness of shipped orders and customer service communication. It was a strange feeling having other people sweat the details. Still, I was anxious to shed the responsibility of ownership.

With 10 days to go before Christmas, northern Midwest temperatures hovered around −10°F at nine o'clock one morning, the third day in a row of frigid weather. Our phone lines exploded with last-minute Christmas shoppers. The final Monday before Christmas we did $250,000 in a 24-hour period. Day-to-day sales were nearly three times those of the same day the prior year. Consumers were buying closer to Christmas, marketing analyses were better, the economy was stronger, and cold weather had people scared. It would be a rocket finish, if we could keep up with orders.

Walking the hallways, I wondered: *Could a human staff possibly fill all these orders in time? Or would they self-destruct?*

The team held together to the finish line. December 1989 ended with this powerful, confident sprint. The expanded computer network and shipping systems handled the 40-percent sales increase—from $10 to $14 million—more calmly than the jump from $1 million to $2 million, or $2 million to $4 million a few years before. Goods arrived on time from China. Magazine ads, and catalogs mailed to carefully tested lists, pulled enough orders to return a solid profit. The postal service did not go on strike or throw out our catalogs. Computers did not crash, nor did the roof leak. Employees showed up; UPS did not go out on strike. Sales topped $3,000,000 for the month and $14.3 million for the year, with $3 million pretax profit. Enough to finance another, larger year in the catalog game if the deal fell apart.

On December 19, the final purchase agreement arrived from various lawyers. Big Hitter had seen that sales were on target and became confident 1989 would be the season we hoped for. He still wanted the deal.

For me, the negotiation process had been like a crowd of sweating, shirtless people wrestling ropes around a bucking wild horse that refuses to be tamed, let alone ridden. I prayed the deal would close. I just wanted out.

Then, two days of silence from Big Hitter and Beady-Eyed. Finally, on December 21, with 10 days to the scheduled closing, Beady-Eyed called.

"We're backing off," he said, giving no details. Something had again spooked him. Maybe he lost his financing. I gave a ferocious kick to the wastebasket beside my desk.

John tried to console me. "There's [Wheeler-Dealer] and plenty of other parties who will want to buy the company, especially now."

I grimaced. Closing a deal with a new group, even if it was Wheeler-Dealer, would take time. The prospect of another year of uncertainty was unthinkable. I slept for three hours and awoke with a killer headache.

Two days passed. Then, out of the blue, Beady-Eyed called.

"We can complete the deal now," he said, giving no explanation. My pulse returned to normal.

Big Hitter's lawyers and bankers finished with my part of the deal and then began to slice each other up. It was capitalism at its highbrow worst. Big Hitter and Beady-Eyed immersed themselves in teleconferences and asked for an extension. My Chicago lawyer, David Genelly, and I consented to give them until January 2. If they missed that, we would assess a penalty of $6,000 a day until the closing took place. Big Hitter agreed.

From what I heard, Big Hitter and his San Francisco staff and their financial partners in New York fought viciously over the details. Christmas came and went. At home, it was a quiet holiday with Lisa, Ted, and Sarah. I sat tight, waiting for a seismic change.

Then, the day after Christmas, a senior partner from the Humongous Trust Company—the New York investment company that had teamed up with Big Hitter to provide capital for the buyout—called me at home.

"How about if you and I deal directly?" he said.

"What about the San Francisco guys?"

"We don't need them now."

Steal the deal from Big Hitter? It didn't feel right. It must mean I was selling too cheap. I guessed the New York guy was thinking: *If I'm going to take the time and trouble to invest in this deal, I might as well take the whole thing, rather than share with Big Hitter and Beady-Eyed.* Never mind that Big Hitter and Beady-Eyed had labored for nine months to put the deal together. It saddened me that this fellow could dream up something so self-serving and easily profitable, and feel no guilt.

"No thanks," I said. "I want to stick with the original deal." I didn't like the mess that going direct would make, nor the lawsuits that could potentially follow.

The fellow expertly changed the subject, backing off with the smoothness of a society page cocktail party veteran. He had the mercenary, velvet tongue that prospers on Wall Street, as well as the mind-set that skims the easy money from the comings and goings of capitalism.

The closing was still targeted for January 2, seven days away. I heard from Beady-Eyed that the fight between buyers and their bankers had intensified, steaming phone lines between New York and San Francisco.

By December 31 little issues had been beaten to death and a close was imminent. Sarah and the kids would not be returning home as soon as planned, due to weather, so I ate alone and then drove through unseasonal fog and drizzle to the office. Might as well pay real estate taxes and deal with paperwork—and say goodbye.

As I turned the familiar corner, the outlet store's sign glowed through the mist. The parking lot was empty. I felt suspended in an eerie time-freeze, gazing through drizzle at our homely metal buildings. Over the years, WinterSilks' staff had built something from the ground up, and now a bunch of heartless spreadsheet jocks was about to buy the place. The tender care of the company, which made it solid and profitable, would be over. I feel guilty not to have sold to the employees, but it wasn't possible to strike such a deal with banks that would let me leave. Every offer received was, in its own way, a leveraged buyout, just like Big Hitter's.

I punched in the alarm code and walked the empty building slowly, my steps echoing on the smooth cement floors. I wandered every room. I had come of age here. After half an hour, I said my thanks in silence and turned off the lights.

Halfway to the car I stopped and turned. Memories came gushing back. Before WinterSilks, I had said to challenges: "I can't do it. I am too ordinary, fragile, and scared." And so my prior life had been partially empty, rarely lived with abandon—until I jumped into the dangerous currents of starting a business. Then my dream became a fixation, and running the WinterSilks gauntlet scared the fear right out of my bones. I'd learned to welcome fear and, in a way, relish it.

At 11:00 P.M. I stood in the light rain, not sure how to say good-bye to something as intangible as a business. I would own the place for another two days, but the purchase agreement and its hundreds of documents had already put an invisible wall between the company and me. It was over. I drove away, and then, ridiculously, began to sob.

I headed for neighboring Morey Airport and walked the length of Runway 27, an east-west, 2-700-foot-long grass strip. Fine drizzle saturated the darkened earth; my shoes became soaked. At the end of the runway I breathed deeply, absorbing the wet silence of a traffic-still night. Planes were landing at Madison, across the lake, thanks to ground-based instrument landing systems. But at this tiny airport there was a deep quiet. I drove home in a netherworld of silence, feeling an unaccustomed peace coming on.

33

Yawning on
Park Avenue

On the evening of January 1, 1990, John and I walked a hotel's nondescript hallway on lower Madison Avenue, juggling brief-cases and duffel bags. We shared a room to keep costs down. The closing would take place the next day at the Citibank building, 54th Street and Park Avenue—the office of the Humongous Trust Company's lawyers.

We showed up the next morning, thinking we'd be done in a few hours. By noon I had signed all necessary documents, but the bank-ers, buyers, buyers' lawyers, and bankers' lawyers were just getting warmed up.

Waiting for them to sort things out became tedious theater. My eyes wandered and I noticed a stack of documents with a sheet of paper askew. It showed the total $89,232 investment Sarah and I had made, part of it borrowed. No additional investment had been needed; the value of the company grew 190.8 times in 10 years. We had been efficient with capital; I doubted the people closing the deal could do that.

"What's taking so long?" I mumbled, looking around.

My lawyer, Genelly, was tied up back in Chicago; he had sent his associate, Hip-and-Handsome, a bright young fellow with designer black-rimmed glasses and a full head of slicked-down, matching jet-black hair. He seemed amused at the question.

"*Half the guys in the room are lawyers,*" he whispered. John smirked.

The three of us sat at one end of a huge conference table in a room with a partial view of Central Park and the west side of Manhattan. At the other end were a phalanx of fourteen investors, bankers, and lawyers, representing the buyers. Different factions occasionally squirreled themselves away in offices up and down the hallway and discussed strategy—basically, how to get the other party to pay for the costs in question. Hours passed. Documents began filling three four-inch-thick binders. By the end of the first day there was a heap of outdated legal paper, lunch wrappings, and other refuse piled under the table. We disposed of our refuse properly; the 14 attorneys and investment bankers did not. No doubt they thought such menial courtesies beneath them. By dusk, the mess under their end of the table looked like the beginnings of a landfill.

To kill time, I strolled around the office. Walking with me, the buyers' senior lawyer told of much bigger deals he had recently closed and about trout fishing in Montana. I pictured this Park Avenue egomaniac in tailored khaki fishing clothes on a pristine river bank, ordering fish out of the stream and into his net.

The closing took 25 hours. I was paid $6,000 as a late fee. At 5:00 P.M. on the third day, January 4, 1990, it was over. Money was wired to my account at Now's-the-Time's bank. A buyers' attorney handed me a phone. "The funds are here," a cheerful Wisconsin voice said. I felt no emotion.

Eventually Hip-and-Handsome, John, and I piled into a taxi and headed for La Guardia. I managed a brief whoop-like yell as I got out of the cab; John whacked me on the back in congratulations. Passersby stopped to look for a few milliseconds. Then life roared on in a gray New York blur. The Dance was over.

I paid the cab driver and looked around slowly, as if being at an airport was a bizarre new experience. For a few seconds I felt like a clean-shaven, freshly washed and released prisoner, standing at a terminal with good cash money in hand, uncertain where to go.

A harried traveler bumped into me. I came to my senses and joined the maelstrom. When we stopped at Detroit three hours later, I gave a check for $20,000 to Hip-and-Handsome to take back to Genelly's office. My legal fees for nine months of work, including the review of thousands of pages of legal documents, totaled $50,000.

The buyers, on the other hand, had run up more than $700,000 in fees to various law and accounting firms in New York, Los Angeles, and Madison. They weren't as concerned about keeping costs down because, in time-honored Wall Street tradition, they merely dumped the costs on the defenseless little company they had just purchased.

As we left Detroit for Madison, the investment bankers who provided the deal's financing went out to dinner in New York. Like true corporate carrion eaters, they charged their pricey, post-closing dinner to the now-leveraged carcass of my former company. John and I had a sandwich at the airport.

On the way home I gave John a personal check for $200,000 to make good on our handshake agreement. Later I added another $100,000. He complained, with a good-natured smile of surprise, that it was three times what we'd agreed on. I also wrote a slew of checks to key employees and our board of advisors.

We drove west to Madison from the Milwaukee airport in two hours of comfortable silence, and my mind tried to reframe the past 11 years. Growing WinterSilks had been exhilarating. Selling her had been absolutely draining, the most complex exercise I'd ever been through.

John arranged a staff party the next day at the West Side Businessmen's Association hall, where he announced to employees what had transpired. They were full of questions.

"Will we still have our jobs?" one old-timer asked.

"Who's in charge?"

"What about the 401(k)?"

"How do we know the new people won't move the company somewhere else?"

John tried to calm them. "Nothing will change for the foreseeable future," he said. There was an uncomfortable murmur, as if a long-time single parent had just told his numerous children he was bringing home a new live-in girlfriend. Questions ran for an hour; eventually employees relaxed, drank beer and wine, and went home happy.

In the morning, Nellie appeared in my office doorway.

"We're doin' reconciliation counts. You got the bill of lading and packing list for the 61-carton shipment? Or should I ask Rauel? Or John?"

"I had it and gave it to Rauel. But you should ask John," I replied.

Nellie cocked her white-haired head and stared at up at me. Her eyes narrowed.

"I know you don't own the place no more," she said in a husky, low voice, as if she had an opponent cornered. "So tell me. Who's in charge now?"

"John's the boss when I leave in four months. Might as well start early and ask him now."

Nellie shook her head and walked toward John's office.

"Why change what was working good?" she mumbled. Nellie probably had no idea that Warren Buffett had amassed one of the world's largest fortunes by acquiring well-run companies with niche products and applying exactly this strategy.

Big Hitter, Beady-Eyed, and their financial partners at the Humongous Trust Company said they wanted everything to stay the same when I left, with management just moved up a notch. Most of my mail was diverted to John, so I didn't have much to do. Because I would be leaving soon, it would be counterproductive to take on new projects, so I kept my hands off things I had done every day for 11 years and merely replied to the dwindling mail and communications that crossed my desk. I still held the title of president, but it had waning authority.

Just beyond my office door, WinterSilks ran flawlessly under the management team it had taken so long to build, and with the easier demands of the off-season. It was still winter: too early for spring, too late for the holidays, a time between seasons for WinterSilks—and for me. I tried to bring a quiet calm to my mind but did not succeed.

Three weeks later, the 1989–90 holiday catalog was selected as cowinner of the American Catalog Awards' gold medal in the apparel division (along with Spiegel). Our models, photography, layouts, and copy were finally equal to the best in the nation. Even with the catalog's sophistication there was still an occasional inquiry from friends who wondered what had happened to Miss Wisconsin and the Mt. Horeb Honey. They had become legends.

I thought back to the attic light table, scissors, glue pot, and 20-cent razor, and felt a twinge of nostalgia. There is no feeling in the world like a start-up.

In late January, Lisa, now eight, and I parked in a dirt lot near Stokely Creek Lodge in Goulais River, Ontario, and walked a half-kilometer trail to the lodge. At dawn it was −25°F. Each morning for the next week we cross-country skied side by side, holding hands. In the afternoons, while she did her homework, I skied trails within the Algoma Highlands. I saw her acquire a new self-confidence. After dinner each night we craned our necks to see an ocean of stars, then slept deeply.

At the end of the week we were hit with a monster snowstorm, and our departure was delayed. Finally, on the ninth day, we flew back along the south shore of Lake Superior and then down the east shore of Lake Michigan, to Madison. Lisa drew with crayons and then slept in the back seat while I ghosted the little plane over a broken cloud layer, mindful of my precious cargo in this, one of the best weeks of my life.

When I returned to the office, unbeknownst to me a dark new virus was festering. The company checking account's daily summary had been a key element of my daily analysis, and there were few changes to the procedure through the first three months of 1990. Then, on April 2, I noted that our opening checking balance, as reported by our accounting manager's summary sheet, was $70,123—about what I expected. But the buyers now had told our staff accountant to write a $225,187 check to me, for interest on a note they owed, and to pay one of their legal bills for $150,000. And one for $393,917 to themselves. For "acquisition interest."

To balance against this outgoing tidal wave of cash, we had low-season mail-order checks, received in that day's mail, for $7,743, and checks from other sources for $49. The day's credit card charges totaled $5,134 and charge card credits (for refunds on returned items) of $280. Store sales were $542. Hence, total net revenue for the day was $13,188. This was a long way from the $250,000 on our peak day the previous December, but good for that specific day of April, an off-season month.

Normally the bank balance would have been the aforementioned $70,123 plus the day's net sales of $13,188, for a total of $83,311, to be saved as dry powder for surviving the summer.

Under the new regime it was another story. Our hard-earned balance of $70,123—plus about $3 million of cash that was sitting at Now's-the-Time's bank—was blindsided. At the end of the day, April 2, 1990, WinterSilks' checking account showed a deficit: ($685,791.92). The new buyers calmly dipped into the $3 million cash reserves to cover the deficit. They had little idea what it had taken to earn those reserves over 11 years and thought nothing of their financial plundering.

And they didn't seem to realize they were shooting themselves in the foot.

I looked at the ending balance and felt like I had fallen down an elevator shaft. I'd expected some leverage to creep into the company, but not to this extent, or so soon. I didn't think Big Hitter would have allowed it. But he wasn't in control any more. The majority owners from Wall Street were.

If I had still owned WinterSilks, the cataclysmic change in the bank balance would have meant that someone had robbed me. Actually, that was about right. The new owners had robbed not me, but their own company. They just didn't see it that way, nor did they care.

They had chosen to butcher the cash cow, rather than nurture and feed it so it could breed and generate more revenue and positive cash flow over a longer period of time. Perhaps the new owners considered themselves on a higher level than people who merely worked at normal, non–investment banking jobs.

To John, Chris, key employees, and me, a business was a stage on which to seek perfection—in manufacturing, transport, warehousing, marketing, advertising, delivery, statistics analysis, customer service, technology—everything. How else could a good, enduring company be built?

So we were saddened to witness the dark side of Wall Street—the condescending side that views the pick-and-shovel route to success as too tedious, something that only fools would tolerate. Seeing this attitude up close sent a chill down my spine. What else could Wall Street ruin?

But how could I gripe? I had a payout and new life. I didn't own the company any more nor did I have any say. I had been paid fair and square and couldn't take issue with the people who owned her. If they were willing to burn off WinterSilks' cash reserves and saddle her and her managers with new debt, that was, unfortunately, their right. Even so, seeing the seismic shift in the checking balance showed me why LBOs are a monstrously terrible idea.

That dark, nearly bottomless pit of a checking account summary stared helplessly back at me, as if to ask, "What have you done?" I felt guilt, as if I had sold a beautiful daughter into prostitution. I wished I had had the physical strength to stay put.

Dream on.

34

The Chinese Limo

A week later a paycheck materialized on my desk, courtesy of the new owners. It was a giddy sensation, but I felt uneasy taking the money. I also felt uneasy searching the classifieds for office space; the thought of moving to a solo perch was unsettling, when for years I had made it clear to suitors that I wanted a complete, clean exit. Now the anxiety of leaving WinterSilks was so unsettling it manifested in my back: sciatica pain shot down my right leg in excruciating stabs.

Two days later, en route to China and Hong Kong for the last time, I stayed in San Francisco with an old high school friend. He was chief financial officer of a promising young toy company. The pain had worsened, so I spent two days lying on his floor with ice on my spine and missed my flight to Shanghai. On the third day I hobbled onto a shuttle to the San Francisco airport, feeling sharp pain at every bump in the road as loose nerve endings on my spinal cord were pinched by vertebrae. At the airport I made a rare splurge and upgraded to a first-class seat on a shorter flight to Tokyo, hoping the fully reclining seat would lessen the pressure on my spine. The gamble worked; for 14 hours, with the seat tilted flat, the pain subsided as the big 747 lumbered through the night high above the dark Pacific.

On to China the next day. I had hoped my last trip there would be one of cultural and social enjoyment, as there was no longer financial pressure. Instead, I was traumatized by intense, nauseating pain whenever I sat upright in a chair or vehicle.

As the plane left Japan, Japanese model efficiency was replaced by 1980s Chinese sloppiness. The plane from Tokyo was a Chinese regional airliner, a new, clean Boeing. It was 40-percent full, yet staffed with twice as many flight attendants as a proper Western airline with financial responsibilities to stockholders and creditors would have provided. The shiny new Boeing seemed strangely out of place.

The Chinese flight attendants served lunch and then retreated to their stations to chatter among themselves, perhaps enjoying their good fortune to have such cushy jobs. Meanwhile their customers were left to juggle empty plates and leftover food trays under their seats or on their laps. The attendants showed no concept of responsibility. Even before we reached the border, 32 thousand feet in the air, a netherworld free-for-all had begun.

At the Shanghai airport it felt like perpetual chaos: there were no runway perimeter or taxiway lights that I could see, and the customs clearance operation next to baggage claim was a ramshackle, ineffective affair. I grabbed a taxi and tried to lean back to ease the pain. At dinner in the hotel, another American garment buyer told me he had had sciatica for years and I should expect to learn to live with the pain. I cringed, shuffled back to my room, and fell into a deep sleep, awaking at 4:30 A.M.

In the morning I found Rauel and John; they had flown in two days earlier with Beady-Eyed, who had been sent to look after Big Hitter's investment. We hopped into hired cars with Shanghai Ed and his employees to visit the Chinese provincial government's Knitted Silk Garment Factory #7. I sat in the right front seat of a small vehicle and tilted the chair back. The pain moderated to a tolerable throb.

There were no seat belts or air bags; the driver accelerated to 30, 40, and then 50 miles per hour on a 15-foot-wide bumpy road filled with oxcarts, bicyclists, pedestrians, and an occasional vehicle coming straight at us. After a while I tied my handkerchief over my eyes; better to try to relax and not see what was ahead.

Tony, our Chinese driver, was in his late twenties, and had had a license for perhaps a year. He was expressing his masculinity by chainsmoking and driving as fast as he could as we tore through the fast-disappearing Chinese countryside. He was smiling with satisfaction.

Life is good, I imagined him thinking to himself. *I will drive like hell and show these pale-faced Americans I am a man.*

I figured our odds of getting out of the tin can of a car alive were about 50-50.

The gods who defend the innocent against testosterone-induced stupidity were with us. After two and a half hours we arrived at Knitted Silk Garment Factory #7. The wobbly little vehicle seemed to beg for rest. Tony, beaming, unwashed, and unshaven, lit another cigarette to celebrate his successful escapade. He smiled proudly as we disembarked. I was pale with pain, and we all reeked of his smoke.

Knitted Silk Garment Factory #7 was a 100,000-square-foot, multi-floor, 1920s-era concrete monstrosity with austere windows and, because parts of it were long, deserted hallways, the quiet of a mausoleum. The windows served as air-conditioning. Restrooms were basic, often without doors or privacy.

By western profit-and-loss standards, three or four times more people than necessary worked at the factory. Employees with the most seniority, or who had provided the most payoffs or favors to party officials, seemed to be running the automated circular silk knitting machines, or performing other easy jobs, which required five minutes of attention per hour. Young women with no ties to party officials, or who were perhaps unwilling to provide favors, labored at the bottom of the workforce in a huge, marginally lit room, soaking silk cocoons in tanks of hot water and unreeling the resultant silk threads. Still, this was an easy job by Chinese standards of the 1980s and early 1990s.

In one of the finishing rooms, Beady-Eyed's girlfriend, an American doctor, took a photo of him holding one of his company's garments. I froze. I saw John looking the other way.

After the factory tour, we had slightly cooked eel for lunch, with rice. I went long on the rice. We ended the visit in a cool, stone-quiet conference room for an hour of tea and meaningless discussion—meaningless because Shanghai Ed and his buying agents talked to the factory several times every day by telephone, telex, and fax, and met every other week in person. After a dozen party officials and factory managers spent an hour staring at these exotic foreigners from another land, with little for Shanghai Ed's staff to translate, we packed into a van and the small car for the long ride back into Shanghai.

I took two painkillers, got in the front seat, tilted it back slightly, and put the handkerchief back over my eyes. Tony drove faster. I sometimes heard the wheels squealing as he executed near miss after near miss with oncoming large mammals, overloaded bicycles, pedestrians, and an occasional slow-moving, wobbling truck. If we had a head-on with just one of the many oxen we passed, our poor, flimsy excuse of an automobile would have come down to earth in the next province in a shower of shrapnel.

That evening we walked across a once opulent section of Shanghai to the Garden Hotel for dinner with agents from Shanghai Ed's office. Afterward, we took a stroll along a suburban street where bicycles passed in the black stillness of a quiet spring night. No street lights, no lights on the bicycles, no traffic signals at intersections, no policemen in sight. This was an upscale part of the city.

A cool evening; at a street corner we felt a fresh, light breeze from the ocean estuary nearby. The air was breathable—one of the few times I can recall it being so during my seven years of visits to China. A block later, halfway back to our hotel, we passed a dimly lit building.

"What's in there?" Beady-Eyed's girlfriend asked our interpreter, pointing through the darkness.

"Hospital," the interpreter said with a hint of pride.

"Can we go inside?"

"No problem."

She led, and we were in. The examination room, about 16 × 16 feet, was piled high with papers and empty boxes. Across a shabby hallway was a recovery room, 20 × 35 feet, with six or seven patients on old beds with lumpy mattresses, and IV bottles trickling fluid into their veins. Relatives or friends sat at bedsides. We could probably have gone right into the operating room, but it was closed.

Medicine seemed primitive, even there in a modernized part of Shanghai; yet the average life span in China—according to a World Health Organization report that appeared on the front page of the *South China Morning Post* a week later—was within three years of that of the United States (71 for males in China versus 74 for males in the United States). Perhaps Western advanced medicines, surgery, and detection analysis were only an attempt to offset our unhealthy lifestyles. China's usually calmer, simpler lifestyles, on the other hand, were perhaps offset by less advanced medicine—or was it the widespread chain-smoking and horrifically polluted air? Whatever the causes, health was nearly a zero-sum game when comparing the two otherwise very different countries.

The reopening of most of China to foreign trade had made Hong Kong a less essential door to the People's Republic, and a burst of international trade had sprung up on China's eastern edge, especially in Shanghai. The gleaming giant was a vortex of humanity and commerce. Although the trappings of capitalism were steadily seeping into China like a never-ebbing tide, the Chinese of the late 1980s and early 1990s was mostly still relaxed and friendly, not yet stressed by the pace of the new Western lifestyles. In Hong Kong, people were in a hurry, accustomed to stepping on one another in the process. Shanghai of 1990, on the other hand, was still hanging on to a bit of the old world ways.

On Sunday we went to church with our buying agents' translator, at an Episcopalian house of worship left over from the early part of the century. A dozen or so expatriates sang from the hymn book in English, keeping time with a few hundred Chinese Christians who pounded out Easter hymns in Mandarin. Cool outside air filtered through unscreened doors and windows; a few struggling trees near the front steps offered rare, sweet-smelling blossoms.

In mid-afternoon we boarded another regional Chinese airliner and flew to Guangzhou for the Canton Fair and meetings with Entertain-Them-to-Death, who was still irked that he had been demoted to number two agent. The streets of Guangzhou were jammed with traffic, but some of the hillsides in the affluent, westernized residential areas had tiny patches of trees and greenery, providing precious, though vulnerable, islands of oxygen and fresh air.

Back in Hong Kong we visited existing and potential sweater factories, then arose early and traveled by hovercraft up the Pearl River to Shekou. The Chinese customs agent at Shekou wouldn't take our Chinese foreign-exchange currency to pay the visa entry fee; they would take only their domestic currency. This required another conversion of currency, with its resultant commissions. Beady-Eyed turned to us from the agent's desk and exploded in laughter.

"They won't take their own money!" he said, thinking he had found a pocket of bureaucratic incompetence.

John, Rauel, Beady-Eyed's girlfriend, Entertain-Them-to-Death, his assistant, and I gathered around the agent's desk and smirked or joined in the laughter. The agent turned away coolly and went into a back room, presumably to enjoy a bowl of noodle soup or a game of *mahjong*. After 25 minutes he reemerged.

"Are you prepared now?" he asked.

With humbled, straight faces we nodded politely, realizing the Chinese were masters of their game, attracting foreign capital and tourist revenue for investment in new manufacturing facilities and generating currency conversion profits. The system was like an invisible electromagnet. For all the chaos, diversity, distance, confusion, and unreliability of the era, China somehow worked. Behind the chaos was supreme, intelligent, calculated organization. In real terms, the chaos was an illusion.

Hong Kong was no longer a major manufacturing location; by the late 1980s it was no longer possible to manufacture garments other than machine-knitted sweaters at decent prices there. The city's garment factories had morphed into sales offices for facilities across the border in China at far lower labor costs. We commuted between the two worlds.

Fog seeped in from the harbor the next day, and our group held a merchandise meeting in Beady-Eyed's hotel room. It overlooked the harbor and Hong Kong Island; he hadn't opted for a lower-priced, street-facing room as the rest of us from WinterSilks had.

For the previous 11 years I had figured out what to buy using my own tried-and-true, decimalized, inventory sales tracking system, and handled communications directly with buying agents in Korea, Hong Kong, China, and the United States. In the last two years Rauel had skillfully taken much of that load off my shoulders. Our system absorbed a potentially complex merchandise-planning situation and made it simple. Each stock-keeping unit's total sales the previous year was divided by the catalog circulation for that period. The resulting number—usually something like .00012345—was the multiplier for the coming season's circulation. If the total circulation of the two main in-season catalogs for the coming holiday and winter season was 10,000,000, then .00012345 times 10,000,000 = 1,234.50 units, in this case—the amount of inventory needed to fill the following year's demand for that specific product in a specific slot of catalog space. Each style number was also broken down into its own subindex of individual sizes and colors, thus allowing accurate purchasing and inventorying.

To go easy on cash flow and warehouse space, John, Rauel, and I staggered deliveries so that shipments were in our warehouse three weeks before demand arose. We ordered what we needed, tried to sell to forecast, and if we ended up with too much we had an escape valve in the summer clearance catalogs. It was a system Sarah and I had started with pencil and green ledger sheets in our attic office in New York back in the cookbook days and improved on over the years through four subsequent offices.

Now Beady-Eyed was questioning the system that had made the company so profitable. I stared blankly at the new merchandise plan for the upcoming season, with its columns of product numbers, sizes, fabrics, and vendor codes. Beady-Eyed broke the tense silence.

"How many 003's you figuring on?" he called to Rauel.

"Take a look," Rauel said, handing over a carefully constructed spreadsheet.

"Still only one color?" Beady-Eyed asked.

"We don't have enough credit line to add more," John answered from the other side of the bed.

"Got to have more colors."

Rauel's jaws closed like a vise on his pencil. Beady-Eyed barely knew how to drive on our racetrack, but he had the keys to his sugar daddy's car.

Two minutes passed; each of us stared at pages of statistics. A lump grew in my throat. I stood up slowly. "I'm going to get something from my room," I said quietly.

The others made a few grunts, but they didn't look up from Beady-Eyed's newly concocted spreadsheet. I walked down the hall toward my room, realizing there was no reason to go back. I packed my belongings and slipped a note under Rauel's door; 10 minutes later I was in a cab headed for the airport.

Inventory planning fascinated me for 11 years; this was one reason I regretted leaving, even though for so long I had yearned for nothing else. But the company had new caretakers who were, in fact, a committee, and none of the committee had been present at the company's birth. I was obsolete. Was this the price of my freedom?

Getting what I wished for was a rude shock, like tons of shipping containers breaking loose on an ocean freighter's storm-tossed deck.

I flew to Bangkok, and for a couple of days commuted by river taxi to the Wat Po monastery for $4 one-hour massages on my leg and back, administered in an open-air clinic within the monastery's compound. It was an urban peacefulness I'd never felt before. That weekend I found a quiet hotel on one of Thailand's southern islands and watched native youth play soccer at low tide. A spectacular ocean sunset lit the horizon behind them. The trip behind me dissipated into a confused memory.

I resurfaced in Madison a week later, a refugee from crowds at the Bangkok airport. The pain in my back and leg was gone. Ten days later, in early May, I walked away from my business for the last time. It felt like the final yards of gradually sliding off the top of a cliff.

John became president, appointed by WinterSilks' new board of directors from the Humongous Trust Company. My communications with him gradually declined—from the previous 20 times a day to once a week, once a month, and then once every few months.

For three months I was dying to go back. I felt an intense need to see how things were going and where mistakes were being made, to try to make things as perfect as possible. I craved the identity, continuity, sense of place, and mission. I drove near the building nearly every day. I didn't understand why I couldn't take back my little kingdom—the one I had tried so hard to sell and leave behind. These feelings were a deep surprise. I couldn't shake the sensation of irreplaceable loss.

After four months, finally, I could drive by WinterSilks' neighborhood and feel no urge to go in; by the fifth month I had lost interest. The craving and sense of confusion passed, like the passion for an unobtainable lover.

A year later, in April 1991, our accountant called. "Even with your quarterly estimates counted, you still owe about three million bucks," he said.

I felt like puking. Government bureaucracies are inefficient and wasteful. Entrepreneurs are ingeniously efficient. But entrepreneurs are at the bottom of capitalism's food chain, despite creating most of the new jobs, and must subsidize the inefficiency of bureaucracies. I gritted my teeth and paid up.

My total winnings were small potatoes compared with the Big Kahunas of business. Even so, I was proud of what our saved, borrowed, and inherited start-up capital of $89,232 had achieved; that sum was half a percent of the final sales proceeds. Borrowed money, used properly, had carried the company from year to year and provided a bounty at the end of the rainbow, just as Smiling Dan had predicted. WinterSilks had grown the old-fashioned way—carefully, organically—and had proved to be unstoppable.

I set up a workspace in a suburban office building near home and enjoyed time with Lisa and Ted. For a couple of years I treaded water, doing occasional catalog consulting, financial oversight, charitable giving, and helped with the kids. Then I noticed an article in the August 11, 1993 issue of the *Wall Street Journal*: "Entrepreneurs Find Past Glory Hard to Repeat." Most entrepreneurs who go back into business, the article said, were less successful the second time around and frequently failed. Many found it hard to piece their lives back together after their company's successful sale.

On September 26, 1993, a *New York Times* article mentioned the founder of Victoria's Secret, who had committed suicide by jumping off San Francisco's Golden Gate Bridge. His first business had been a great success, and he had sold it to a Fortune 500 company. The new corporate owner took the concept nationwide through a string of lavishly provocative retail stores and expanded the Victoria's Secret catalog. The cashed-out founder's second business venture was somewhat of a disappointment, and so was his third; perhaps this was part of the reason for the jump.

I realized that by selling out I had cut sociological ties and entered minimally charted waters.

At home, Sarah encouraged me. "We have a new life, and the company will be fine. John knows the system and is better with people than you ever were."

She was right, but I had one other worry.

"Things will be OK as long as John and Chris are left in charge," I said. "If the new owners mess with our formula, then all bets are off."

Sarah was walking across the kitchen. She stopped abruptly and turned toward me, thinking of Lisa and Ted and upcoming college tuitions. Her voice took on a more serious tone.

"How much of the deal hasn't been paid yet?"

PART 5

Epilogue

*A*t the tip of the island I stand in the shallows and fill water bottles in the lake's chill, clear waters. My portable compass has a mirror panel for emergency signaling, and leaning forward I get a glimpse of myself. If someone who looked like that showed up for an interview, I would call the police.

Out in the foggy strait a leftover swell rolls in from the open lake. It feels like a living, liquid force that has gone on forever and carries me effortlessly along. Another 20 minutes of paddling, and the dull outline of the north shore is dimly visible; then midday heat dissolves the fog and visibility opens to a quarter mile. The framework of an old trapper's cabin appears around a bend in the shoreline. As if to mark the passage of time, two families of beaver have built huge lodges right outside the cabin. Nature has the last laugh.

At nightfall stars shine brightly in a clear quadrant of sky visible from my campsite. While I'm brushing my teeth, a beaver glides by in the moonlight, leaving a V-wake like a small battleship. Some fish rise out of the water, dining on surface bugs. A skunk meanders through my campsite, irritated to find me on his turf. A shooting star zooms high overhead, igniting and burning out in four seconds. A satellite hurtles through space. A blue heron flies by in the dark, its wings flapping 20 feet above the shoreline. A white-throated sparrow sings its song until about 9:00 P.M., and then packs it in for the night. Footsteps splash on the opposite shore—probably a moose or caribou. A loon calls once, then stops. I hear another moose browsing on the weeds on the near shoreline and feel the earth shake as it climbs up the bank *and nears my campsite. From inside my tent its ponderous breathing sounds like lungs the size of a 55-gallon fuel drum.*

By morning it is blowing hard from the west; the floatplane cannot land for my scheduled pickup. That evening, the sun goes down in a spectacular chorus of red and orange. Toward 11:00 P.M. the wind builds and gusts to 30 mph, ripping through the trees. They bend and creak as if talking to each other. By midnight, with the moon obscured, the wind gusts to 40, then 45, shrieking around me as I drift off to sleep.

35

The Darkest
Two Years

Transitions are tricky; one wrong move and you can fall from the summit it has taken so long to climb. WinterSilks was now at risk in a new, unfamiliar way. I watched from a distance and saw that the company's evolution into middle age was—like mine—just as complex as infancy and adolescence. I realized that businesses and organizations progress just like people: they get older, wiser, more careful—usually as a result of dumb mistakes made along the way. Sometimes a really bonehead mistake blows up decades of hard work. Businesses, like people, continually gyrate between good and bad choices.

With China's modernization and increasing business sophistication in the 1990's, the supply side of WinterSilks became vastly easier. Some large, state-owned Chinese companies even went public on Hong Kong's Hang Seng exchange or on the New York Stock Exchange. Getting product out of China in the early and mid-1980s had been like pulling teeth; a few years later, shipments arrived almost like clockwork. I was lucky to have had a glimpse of transitional China before the most astounding large-scale economic resurrection in history. *Forbes* said it best in its April 7, 2008 issue, referring to Chrysler's Beijing Jeep factory in 1984: "Those were the good old days, when Chinese workers hung their washing to dry over the assembly line." Dealing with China now, Westerners can hardly believe this really happened.

With the supply side finally secure, the remaining question was whether WinterSilks would stand the test of time—or disappear like bone-dry campfire ashes carried up and away to oblivion by a strong, gusty wind.

After I faded from the scene in spring 1990, WinterSilks ran smoothly; product and marketing stayed focused, thanks to John, Chris, and the rest of the team. The company operated in the top 5 to 10 percent of the catalog industry, as it had my last three years. But third class mailing rates kept going up. Simultaneously, too many businesses bombarded an overwhelmed public with too many catalogs. Result: lower customer response, in addition to higher postage costs. Traditional catalog selling became a marginal industry; a gathering shadow of bankruptcies began to thin the industry. Surviving catalog owners held on tight, hoping this new thing called the Internet might someday provide salvation.

With these macro forces at work, along with new competition from existing catalogs that added a few knitted silk garments to their pages, WinterSilks' mailing responses and profits declined, percentage-wise, from 1980s levels. And new management—which had no personal guarantees at the bank—seemed to be less tight-fisted than I had been with the company checkbook.

Even with thinner profits and more competition, WinterSilks remained a happy and comfortable place to work. John made sure staffing was in place for seasonal peaks. He also pursued new growth avenues. In Hong Kong, he and Beady-Eyed met with the Asian-born president of a recently bankrupted woven silk garment catalog. The president had started at about the same time as me and built a ladies' woven-silk apparel catalog that rocketed to $50 million sales in its first decade. Its executives loved publicity but devoted too little time to keeping the business profitable. In 1989 it declared bankruptcy, loaded with $11 million of debt.

WinterSilks' annual sales at that time were one-third of the bankrupt company's at its peak. Because WinterSilks grew slowly, continually lifted by a river of positive cash flow, it could pay for new computers and building additions and some inventory, and bootstrap finance the company's way while incurring minimal debt. The woven silk catalog, on the other hand, was always desperate for cash. So I wasn't surprised when the hare came to the tortoise for a bailout. John and Chris negotiated a bargain price for the 250,000-name mailing list. It was more fuel for WinterSilks' glowing fire.

John also kept a close watch on customer service. I left the company in May 1990; 10 months later he sent a copy of the following letter, perhaps to prove he had maintained our tradition of service. It was addressed to me only because my name was still on the catalog for continuity purposes:

September 18, 1990

Dear Mr. Farwell:

I recently experienced a level of customer service and concern that I perceive to be almost unique in American commerce today. The circumstances were associated with my recent purchase from your company of a silk bathrobe, a surprise-party gift for my former mother-in-law celebrating her 90th birthday in Vermont.

None of the three best department stores in Los Angeles were able to serve my needs. Although a past customer of your firm, I did not have my catalog at hand, and I was leaving for Canada on business, then directly to Vermont two days later. I called your sales desk (800-line) and explained my predicament to your representative, Dana. She was very helpful, but I had difficulty envisioning the item, despite her good description. So she faxed me a picture (her suggestion) immediately. Within minutes, I was able to complete my order (she volunteered to honor an older, lower price shown on the faxed photo) and arrange for its delivery to me at my motel in Canada by Federal Express so I could deliver the gift personally on Saturday, three days hence.

On returning to my hotel in Toronto very late Friday afternoon, I found the package had not been delivered. I called your company only to find that the customer service department was closed. However, the lady who answered my call said she would help if she could. I did not have a confirmation number, but she was able through her knowledge of the sales function (where she had previously worked), to locate my order and confirm it had been shipped the previous day as promised. She did not have a FedEx bill number however, so she contacted your fulfillment manager who was aware of the shipment because there had been some conversation with Canadian Customs that day about it. He didn't have a bill number either but, taking an extra step, called your traffic manager at home (it was after hours), determined where the bill number was located, found it, and called me back in Toronto with the information. I was able to claim the package at the FedEx office at the airport just minutes before it closed.

The robe was the most popular of the many gifts bestowed on the venerable lady the next day!

As a management consultant, I recognize both the importance of superior service, and how difficult it is to achieve and sustain. My recent experience with WinterSilks is so outstanding that I'm sure that it is not exceptional for your company to perform routinely to these high standards. I commend you and all your staff on your service accomplishments.

As an exceptionally satisfied customer and appreciative beneficiary of your service, I ask you to accept my sincerest thanks and, in my behalf, to extend them again personally to each of those individuals on your team whose care and extra efforts made this one happen.

Very truly yours,

P. B. Noonan, Los Angeles, CA

Tornado Jones would have given a rare thumbs-up. She would have reminded staff that because we were straightforward when we screwed up, customers like Mrs. Hollingsworth had stayed with us for the long haul. Tornado Jones would also have been impressed that in 1995, five years after my departure and with most of the same staff in place, WinterSilks won the catalog industry's national customer service award. The runners-up? L.L.Bean and Lands' End.

John, Chris, director of operations John Reindl, warehouse manager Nellie Ellendt, accounting manager John Pitzen, customer service chief Jean Phillips, and the rest of the all-star staff could be very proud indeed. But I wondered whether there was a similar sense of *financial* urgency. The offices were beginning to look almost deluxe.

The new board of directors was peopled by Big Hitter, Beady-Eyed, and two appointees from the Humongous Trust Company (which provided acquisition capital to Big Hitter and Beady-Eyed and owned the vast majority of WinterSilks' stock, with Big Hitter holding a minority share, and key employees holding a sliver). The board quickly recognized the gem they had in John and left him alone to operate WinterSilks as he saw fit. The board showed up for quarterly meetings to view reports and offer respectful guidance. John loved the job and performed it well. But he made one small change that set off a chain reaction—and raised a red flag for me.

When we moved into the west-side building in August 1984, the entire front portion of the building featured ugly brown carpeting. To boost morale, I eventually replaced it in the central part of the building with a better-quality carpet. But I left the old brown carpet in my office.

Soon the traffic of many feet and my scooting around in my desk chair wore through it, right down to the cement slab foundation underneath. When employees asked for more budget for a project, they couldn't help but catch a glimpse of the patches of worn-out carpet and underlying bare cement. That old brown carpet seemed to communicate Smiling Dan's wise message: *You already have the resources you need—just use them more efficiently.*

The combination of Smiling Dan's advice and the old brown carpet helped WinterSilks stockpile $3 million of excess cash, after paying taxes, following the 1989–1990 selling season, and $2 million and $1 million the two seasons before that. In all, $6 million of after-tax surplus cash in the three years just before I sold the company, derived from a start-up investment of $89,232 in 1979–1981.

Leave me just the way I am, the ratty-looking carpet seemed to growl. *And get back to work. You bums don't need a new carpet.*

So when word came through the grapevine in mid-1990 that the old brown carpet had been replaced and new furniture added, I worried. Then I heard of a veritable spending spree. The company built a $220,000 warehouse next to the original 7,800-square-foot building, with its additions of 1,100 and 4,000 square feet. Now the buildings' footprint covered about 20,000 square feet, although sales hadn't increased as much as in previous years. I shook my head; the old warehouse would have sufficed for two more years or so, and the unsightly brown carpet darn near forever.

A while later the company experimented with fashion in a separate catalog and leased 40,000 additional square feet of warehouse space in a town 30 minutes away. True, sales by then had more than doubled since my time, because management was mailing more catalogs, but profits and free cash flow as a percentage of sales were much lower than in prior years, and hundreds of thousands of dollars of extra—perhaps unnecessary—costs had crept into the income statement, bleeding what cash flow there was. New management, sometimes nudged by Big Hitter and Beady-Eyed, seemed to lack the elemental financial fear that had driven me.

So I wondered: Without the humility-inducing old brown carpet, and with the new expenses and inconveniences of decentralized warehousing, might the little fortress become vulnerable?

During this period John and Chris tested a few seasons of a summer, fashion-based catalog and found it hard to make a profit. They throttled back; their knuckles had been skinned, just like mine. The company faltered but kept moving forward; it went back to basics and quickly regained its footing.

Then a new executive from the Humongous Trust Company took over as WinterSilks' board chairman. Insensitive to the wisdom of the company's tried-and-true product line, he strong-armed John and Chris into carrying full-blown ladies' fashion apparel. He thought this would produce some magic.

John and Chris protested, but the Man from Humongous didn't budge. He ordered them into an all-out foray into blouses, skirts, and dresses in an attempt to make up for soft sales during a time of mild winters, rising postal expenses, and declining profits.

John told the Man from Humongous such a move away from basics would kill WinterSilks and explained how the recent experiment with fashion had often been a loss. The Man from Humongous would hear none of this.

In defending WinterSilks, a company he had come to love, John almost came to fisticuffs, but to no avail. The Man from Humongous did not grasp the value of a profitable, going concern—albeit slowed by a series of warm winters. Nor did he appreciate or respect the merchandise performance statistics WinterSilks had built up over nearly two decades. He was sure this bold move would recapture the growth his investors had counted on; he spurned the hard-earned knowledge of WinterSilks staff.

You nitwits in the Midwest don't know anything about fashion. That's a polite version of what he said to some employees. *My friends here in the city do. I'm giving them control of merchandising.*

He designated his tennis partner's wife (who had run a small retail store) and her friend to take over purchasing and product planning—from expensive office space in Manhattan, no less. They took generous salaries, ran up expenses that made the accounting department in Middleton gag, and bought multitudes of new silk garment styles—knowing nothing of the mail-order business's fulfillment and inventory management requirements. The new styles and decentralized decision making also caused per-catalog production costs (all production prior to printing, list rental, and mailing) to skyrocket. This didn't faze the Man from Humongous.

We'll grow this company to $50 million quickly and then go public is a kind summary of what he told a former employee. *You should have done this a long time ago. God, it's amazing how ignorant you people are in the Midwest.*

John stood up for the company and continued to argue for reason, but got nowhere. As he painfully recalled nine years later, "I didn't fight hard enough."

So WinterSilks was thrown into the Fashion Folly. Each new garment had multiple sizes and colors, thus overcomplicating merchandise statistics and vastly reducing the statistical probability of mail-order catalog success. The new chairman of the board simply bet the farm, ignoring WinterSilks' bedrock of inventory statistics—the very numbers that had made the company an attractive investment.

To understand catalog inventory planning, consider the 035 Aviator Scarf—a product that exists in all its mundane glory in one size and color and appears on the computer screen as one stock keeping unit (SKU), simply 035, like a movie or rock star with no last name.

The 035 was a simple, enduring, can't-miss success story. With one color and one size there was no chance it would not fit, little chance the color would disappoint (ivory/off-white, as a neutral color, goes with almost everything), and hence scarce chance it would be returned for a refund (it had the lowest statistical return history of any early-era WinterSilks product). The 035 was one of the mules of our merchandising plan, providing predictable profits and positive cash flow, year after year. Mega-capitalists like Warren Buffet would no doubt understand and salute its wise simplicity. (The current corporate owners' merchandise team has brazenly renumbered the Aviator Scarf as #2500, and added three colors—black, oat, and red.)

Now consider a blouse in sizes 4–16 in three colors. It takes up an array of 21 SKUs—and those for one or two finicky seasons only—whereas the 035, with its one SKU, has proven it can be sold for damn near forever and thus is always kept in stock. The blouses were sure to have at least a few of their SKUs sold out and backordered every season, with no possibility of restocking in time for Christmas. They were a risky departure.

WinterSilks' product line was conceived by me, Sarah, Bonnie, Ann Everson, Rauel, John, and others to maximize its success *in the catalog business.* We wanted products as simple as possible to make; as light as possible to ship, both from Asia and to our customers in the United States; and as easy to fit as possible. (Many WinterSilks items were unisex—such as glove liners, some sweaters, and all scarves, socks, and kimono robes—and most were made from knitted, as opposed to woven, silk, and were thus more likely to fit and less likely to be returned.) We had years of data that said: *This item will sell .0000628735 times the units of circulation in a similar catalog mailed at the same time of year, plus or minus a small variance depending on the coldness of the winter and the strength of the economy.*

Knowing this, I could pull the trigger and order the stuff year after year. Mountains of it, because our bankers let us borrow more and more to import these purchases. They knew the repetition-based strength of our inventory sales-tracking numbers.

When someone urged us to add a color or size, we deliberated long and hard. We had finite bank credit, and every borrowed dollar had to pull its weight. In the 1989–90 season, for example, $5 million of manufactured goods had to produce $15 million-plus in sales and inventory buildup and $3 million in pretax profit and positive cash flow. If any product failed, the rest would have to shoulder a larger fixed- and variable-cost load.

Each style of our easy-to-make, easy-to-fit, easy-to-ship, and unlikely-to-be-returned garments' historically proven sales coefficient needed only to be multiplied against the upcoming season's planned mailing list circulation.

Our intentional simplicity paid off: The job of merchandising was accomplished more quickly, with fewer people. Our theme of focused simplicity also allowed Chris Vig to take over mailing list analysis and procurement, and catalog print and production planning, and allowed Wendy Bale to produce the entire catalog in-house, with one assistant. Each person knew that excellence in consumer products usually resulted from keeping things less complicated.

We also knew that the most challenging inventory scenario for a catalog was women's fashion—an arena in which sales are nearly impossible to forecast. Sure, I had experimented with a few mini-forays into fashion over the years, trying to find new sources of revenue, but each had failed. Sales might look good for the first few weeks after mailing, but then returns as high as 40 percent would arrive, and net per-product sales would take a beating. Once returns were counted, fashion garments might have sold wildly, or spited their purveyors by languishing mockingly in tall stacks on warehouse shelves. Our core, proven garments were like faithful Labrador Retrievers; the new fashion items were like disdainful cats.

Through trial and error, we'd learned that it was always better to try a new color for an established product, like a knitted silk turtleneck that could be sold virtually forever, than to gamble on an untested fashion garment that might sell well for a season or two—or not at all. At least my fashion forays were done on a small scale—the company's income statement and my ego were bruised just a little.

Unfortunately, such accumulated wisdom was of no interest to the Man from Humongous. It was 1992, and he wanted WinterSilks in fashion, and fast.

John faced a terrible dilemma. He needed to support his college-bound family by keeping his job, and he didn't want to appear disloyal to the board of directors who controlled his employment. But he wanted to fight for what was right—sticking to tried-and-true basics and waiting for the weather to turn. He chose to fight but was outranked. So he had to watch the Man from Humongous steer WinterSilks into a one-way tunnel. Not being able to thwart the looming disaster was gut-wrenching. John quit, ending up with neither a healthy WinterSilks nor a job.

With John departed, the Man from Humongous moved Chris up to president. Chris reluctantly put out fashion catalogs, still trying to convince the boss they would not work. These catalogs also failed, and then another warm winter, in 1997–1998, removed what support the core WinterSilks' line could give to the Fashion Folly. Losses mounted; disaster seemed unavoidable. Finally the Man from Humongous realized that John and Chris were right. Perhaps he also discovered that good, established companies, so hard to build, can be toppled by one bad decision.

The treacherous shoals of women's fashion claimed another victim. The company and its new investors were shipwrecked. Carefully selected timbers that had gone one by one into WinterSilks' hull had been torn loose, and the ship began to flood. The official apocalypse was memorialized on page one of Madison's *Capital Times* business section. WinterSilks had filed for Chapter 11 bankruptcy on July 31, 1998. My company—or rather, John's and Chris's and the Humongous Trust Company's company—was toast.

With the apocalypse, John lost $400,000 ($300,000 of which was borrowed) that he had invested in the new enterprise. He was soon hired as vice president of the catalog division at Barnes & Noble, in New Jersey.

The Man from Humongous ended up selling WinterSilks for close to nothing, plus assumption of the debts he had caused to be run up. He lost about $20 million for his employers and investors at the Humongous Trust Company—the money they had paid me, plus another salvo of dollars pumped into buildings, equipment, and unnecessary new staff positions.

So it was that the Humongous Trust Company's investment was sabotaged. The hard work of 18 years, and the 300 jobs (in 1994's peak holiday season, including seasonal help) created by that work, evaporated into nothing. (Big Hitter and Beady-Eyed had long since given up on the new direction of the company, taken their minority position fees, and disappeared.) The Man from Humongous walked away, and no one heard from him again. Chris was left holding the bag.

There was opportunity amid the ashes. How many company founders have sold out for a fortune, seen their companies ruined by new owners, and then bought their firms back, turned them around, and sold out again for an even greater fortune? I heard that Charles Schwab had done it several times, for ever-greater amounts, and there were many more like him.

So I thought about buying WinterSilks back, and in 1998 I met with Chris. But just being in the old building evoked the old stress: how hard it was to have employees and financial responsibility—and how nice it was now to have time for kids, recreation, health maintenance, and work of my choice. So I restrained myself and wished Chris luck in his very difficult journey.

Chris talked to a myriad of potential investors and found a few individuals who would put up capital, albeit on unfavorable terms. He dug into the job as president, and the turnaround task that loomed ahead of him.

As the August 19, 1999 issue of the *Wisconsin State Journal* reported: "It marked the start of the darkest two years of his life, with sleepless nights spent furiously painting bright, abstract, aboriginal designs and writing screenplays to escape."

Chris endured a two-year hell that may well have been worse than the 11-year stretch of birthing pains that I survived. He faced a struggle for financial survival every day. No money in the bank, erratic sales, and a huge backlog of unpayable bills. He hustled for his company's life, fending off creditors and trying to scrape together enough cash to get out yet another catalog.

He also made the decision that counted most: he steered the company back to what had worked before—knitted silk garments for winter warmth, many in unisex styles. He even convinced Chinese manufacturers to continue to ship goods, even though WinterSilks had no money, or bank credit, to pay for them. "That stunned everybody," he told the *State Journal.*

Fighting temporary investors who tried to take control of the company, Chris somehow found a way for WinterSilks to survive, hour by hour, day by day, week by week. He knew that terminating the Fashion Folly and returning WinterSilks to its quintessential roots could turn the tide. Sure enough, he overcame the staggering odds and brought the company back from its ashes. Tried-and-true core products like the 035 took the company, dollar by dollar, out of insolvency, into positive cash flow, and back to profits. Chris stayed the course, and before the end of three years the company became $1 million cash-flow positive.

On February 27, 1999, the *Wisconsin State Journal* reported that Chris had merged WinterSilks with Venus Swimwear—a strong niche company in Jacksonville, Florida, with a seasonal peak during WinterSilks' off-season. WinterSilks' west-side operations center in

Middleton was shut down. Chris moved his 14-person merchandise, art production, and marketing staff to an old building in downtown Madison. He oversaw list analysis and procurement, merchandising and importing, advertising production, and media placement. Art director Wendy Bale continued to expertly oversee the design of each catalog.

In 2003, when WinterSilks opened a small retail store below its offices on the square, local media warmed to the story, sensing that a local business darling had come back to life. Far to the south, Venus Swimwear's 325-plus employees received, processed, and shipped orders for "The Ultimate Winter Warmth" from their Florida headquarters.

WinterSilks' 40,000-square-foot warehouse in DeForest, north of Madison, has long since been vacated. The series of buildings in Middleton that served as headquarters sat empty for many years, with a *For Sale* sign swaying lazily in the breeze.

By 2005, Chris's resurrection of WinterSilks bore unimaginable fruit. Some industry insiders speculated the company had grown to annual sales of $65 million, and that $100 million between the two companies was soon likely.

When I called during the winter of 2004–2005, Chris did not ring back, but did reply to an e-mail saying he would not grant an interview to me, or anyone, on the subject of the Chapter 11 turnaround. He wanted to keep the inside story for a screenplay he was writing. The tone of the exchange suggested he had become a hardened man in the 15 years since I worked with him; I sensed WinterSilks had deeply colored his life, as it had mine. It was hard for me to accept that the brilliant, smiling, happy-go-lucky 28-year-old I had hired in 1988 had become a steel-jawed, take-no-prisoners, post-bankruptcy pro. Sure, he had pulled off an against-all-odds comeback and was on his way to banking a fortune. But I wondered if he would ever let down his guard again and return to the marvelous old self of his picturesque youth in small-town Viroqua, Wisconsin.

In 2007 Chris and his Florida partner sold the resuscitated and expanded WinterSilks for an undisclosed sum to a catalog conglomerate based in San Francisco. Chris kept details close to his chest, and newspaper reports were vague.

Whatever the details may be, it's a well-deserved payoff. Chris Vig is an amazing person and incredible hero. Several hundred employees in Florida, and a dozen-plus in Wisconsin, have him to thank for their jobs.

After a few years in New Jersey overseeing the Barnes & Noble catalog, John grew tired of corporate bureaucracy; he quit and moved back to Madison. Several job offers materialized around the country, but he turned them all down. Madison was home; he wanted a job there, or at least nearby.

On his third attempt, a friend in a 2,500-employee, $1-billion-in-sales school-supplies company outside Milwaukee persuaded John to take over their $165-million catalog division, with operations in Wisconsin, Texas, and Alabama. John commuted to Milwaukee weekday mornings and flew to the company's various locations several times a month. He was paid a salary three to four times what Sarah and I paid for our house in Middleton. One of the three companies under his supervision went from an $8.5 million loss to a $7 million profit in one year, during which John reduced the number of inventory SKUs from 14,000 to 5,000.

After a few years of performance like that, he was offered an executive vice-president's position at headquarters. But he turned it down, saying he preferred hands-on management with the individual companies in his division. Privately he admitted he wanted to work in Madison and buy and run an $8 to $15 million in sales retail company.

"I love small companies because you can get your hands around everything," he told me one afternoon in January 2005. He added: "The best job I ever had was WinterSilks [in 1990–1994]." Those were the years between my departure and the arrival of the Man from Humongous. It was a golden age for John and for WinterSilks. Like sweet spots in the stock market, it would not come again for a long time.

As WinterSilks recovered from its run-in with Wall Street's rape-the-innocent mindset, and then bankruptcy, the media increased coverage of buyout firms' self-interested behavior—behavior that not only was disastrous to the underlying companies, which steadfastly provided jobs and tax revenues to local and national economies, but also warped expectations for other buyout firms. Now it is no longer enough for buyout firms to apply their financial resources and experience at target companies and hope to watch profits grow over time, as Big Hitter and the Humongous Trust Company had hoped in 1990. Now the real money is in looting acquired companies the minute a deal is closed. The *raison d'être* for many buyout firms has evolved from nurturing growth to stripping a company's cash, selling its parts, and leaving its surviving, ransacked shell to fend for itself. Financial-services firms' investment divisions have become used to plumbing this new, heinous depth—a black economic netherworld in which the fundamentals that drive a company's profits and cash flow are considered peripheral, inconsequential intricacies. The global financial system's near-implosion in 2007–2008, triggered by none other than the over-leveraged whims of investment bankers, was the last word in me-first capitalism.

Smiling Dan is no longer with us. I bet that, six feet under, he's grinding his teeth in disgust—and seeing plenty of opportunity for those who keep things simple and play the game fair and square.

By 1990, the venture capital investors I had spoken with in the early and mid-1980s experienced a bit of remorse. The Milwaukee fellow told a mutual friend that not investing in WinterSilks was a big mistake. His proposed outlay of $220,000 in the spring of 1984, for 25 percent of WinterSilks, would have paid out $4,250,000 less than six years later. The Chicago VC's more flinty $190,000, also for 25 percent of the company, would have been worth the same amount.

I'm glad that no VCs anted up. Without venture capital, and with Smiling Dan's Spartan advice to borrow from banks, deal with the pain and fear, and run a tight ship, WinterSilks was built without the decision-making conflict typical of VC investment. My energy went vertically, toward growing, and operating efficiently, rather than horizontally—dealing with partners and their inevitably differing opinions. That made all the difference.

36

Transitions

One cool evening in June 1994, while my old company WinterSilks was starved for summer orders, I savored my time at Bessbrook Farm in the hill country of Vernon County in southwestern Wisconsin. The game of the moment was Sardines (the reverse version of hide-and-seek) at our darkened house with Lisa and two other 12-year olds. Finally, at midnight, the girls grew drowsy and went to bed. Just before my eyes closed I could hear the night wind talking in the trees up on the ridges.

Earlier that year, four years after selling WinterSilks, I had been sorely tempted to fall off the workaholic wagon. I actually wound up sitting at a conference table at Now's-the-Time's bank with three lawyers, the seller of a recycled paper greeting card mail-order business, and my would-be new business partner—Dick Norgord, a highly regarded veteran catalog executive and trusted WinterSilks board of advisors member.

The seller was bankrupt. The bank wanted us to buy the business for a low price and turn it around, so the bank wouldn't have to shut it down and take a loss on a loan that couldn't be repaid. After five months of due diligence and consideration, Dick and I were ready to close. We would buy the assets for a song, apply our experience, and, we hoped, make a good profit by resuscitating the business and selling excess inventory. It would be an enjoyable project and help convert consumption from forest-devastating virgin paper products to products using recycled paper.

The room had no windows, just the ubiquitous whirr of air conditioning and the scent of chemically cleansed synthetic carpet. After

45 minutes of listening to lawyers, without conscious intent I conjured up the scent of grasses and hardwoods at Bessbrook Farm.

"I've got to talk to you for a moment," I said to my attorney. It was as if someone who was looking out for me was speaking on my behalf. We walked into the hallway, with the eyes of the anxious seller and bank officers boring into my back. Dick followed, puzzled. His kids were grown and he had retired a few years early. He was looking for a new venture to sink his teeth into. My kids, on the other hand, were young and still at home, and I had not fully recovered my health.

Fidgeting with my suit buttons, I looked from my attorney to Dick and blurted out: "I can't do this."

Dick said nothing for a moment, then his eyes widened in quiet shock. "You can't . . . ?" His voice trailed off in disbelief. Our lawyer didn't care one way or the other; he got paid whether we closed or not. Dick, as my business partner, had more grounds for disappointment; he was planning on this for a twilight career and didn't want all the risk himself.

He accepted my decision as a bad stroke of fate, a choice that a friend with a suddenly loose screw might make. He said nothing, but mentally crossed me off his list of business luncheon friends. It happened in less than five minutes; then I was out the door. The seller filed for bankruptcy the next day, and a California company bought the warehoused assets of the defunct business a few months later, at an even lower price. I paid most of my partner's legal bills and my own: the price of freedom.

With the recaptured time, I headed back to the hills of Vernon County, still unencumbered by employees, debt, or payroll. I had two small children to help raise; I had time, money, and flexibility. There was no way in hell I was trading any of these.

Later that fall, with fog in the valleys of Bessbrook Farm rising to blend with the dark, wet overcast of the evening sky above the forested ridgelines, I walked through my own woods again, soaked, but holistically happy in a way I had not known since childhood. I was still a workaholic trying to go straight, and I'd been tempted, but this place had helped me make the right choice.

In Good Company

WinterSilks was just one of numerous catalog successes in Madison, many of them far larger. One lay a few hundred yards west of our old building: Pleasant Company, the giant catalogue retailer of the American Girl collection—high-quality, historical-motif dolls. Starting in the mid-1980s, Pleasant Rowland's hard work and niche marketing savvy rapidly built her company from an idea to $350 million or so in sales (as of a few years ago) by focusing on high-quality American dolls with accompanying books and doll fashion items. She eventually sold her company to Mattel for about $700 million.

Her husband, Jerome Frautschi—who had loaned her start-up money and thus owned a good portion of the equity when Pleasant Company was sold—used his part of the sale proceeds to fund the Overture Center for the Performing Arts in downtown Madison. When his first gift of $50 million was made, it was heralded on the front page of the *New York Times* as the largest gift to the arts ever made in the United States. He enjoyed the process so much he gave more, eventually totaling $205 million. The Overture Center opened in 2004.

Pleasant Rowland also funded the Madison Children's Museum and gave extremely generously to numerous charities throughout Madison and the United States, including her alma mater, Wells College, in upstate New York. She is a Wisconsin entrepreneurial legend; next to her financial accomplishments, the rest of us are minor leaguers indeed.

37

Offshore

After dinner I wash dishes under the northern lights and then lean against a rough stump near the campfire, in the shelter of a huge black spruce, as I watch the stars. Thinking back to the early days at WinterSilks, I have to laugh . . . We were so embarrassingly green. Sarah and I knew nothing about gross margin contributions, catalog square inch analysis, inventory turnover ratios, individual and category profit contribution, or index-based SKU inventory forecasting. We just sold until we ran out and then frantically called suppliers to send more. So much to do, so little time. Surviving week to week, physically and emotionally, let alone financially, was a victory in itself. It was complex, overwhelming—but we were young, strong, energetic, still in the heady beginnings of a new marriage . . .

A little before noon on the ninth day of my trip, I hear the sound of an old piston aircraft engine in the distance. Soon a restored 1954 DeHavilland Beaver appears overhead. The sky stays partially clear, and Gary, a 26-year-old bush pilot, makes a perfect landing, taxis gingerly to an abandoned dock, loads my gear and straps the canoe to a pontoon. Thirty minutes later the Beaver climbs into the wind and then turns east. To the south, the sun glistens over the precious fresh-water sea.

For an hour we fly just above the treetops. Off the left wing, waterfall after waterfall foams down between granite slopes. It is the view of a lifetime: a slow-motion semi-blur of green and gold forest, blue-green rivers, and deep-blue lake, all going by at a leisurely 105 mph, 500 feet below. It is like having a front-row seat in an IMAX theater, except the scent of the pines below and the hammering of the big piston engine up front is real. To me, it is the greatest show on earth.

On the long drive home I detour through the town of White River, which claims the coldest recorded temperature in Canada: −71°F. I wonder how many of them are on WinterSilks' mailing list.

The trip reminds me of the impact our catalogs' paper had on forests and waters, and when I get back I pledge $250,000 to start the Lake Superior Project at the National Wildlife Federation, and I donate lesser sums to other leading conservation groups. I vow to use post-consumer recycled paper for the rest of my life.

This time alone on the north coast also reminds me that people without free time—especially employees—are like birds denied migration. It's not good for them or their employers. Companies that understand this will simmer a sweeter workplace stew—and stand a better chance to go the distance.

WinterSilks runs smoothly now, three decades and one million satisfied customers later. Technology has made it a painless task to call the company (1-800-718-3687; or 1-814-726-6896) or go online (www.wintersilks.com) and buy a knitted silk turtleneck, silk/wool sweater, knitted silk long johns, or any of dozens of other styles. The Internet makes selling and order fulfillment so simple now; it's hard to recall just how difficult it was in the early days.

Two or three times a year I make the long drive to see old friends in Madison. I sometimes visit the original, mostly vacant WinterSilks buildings to reboot my brain's hard drive with a dose of memories. Each person who cashed a WinterSilks paycheck helped build a solid little ship of an enterprise, resilient enough to emerge from financial disaster when an insensitive outsider steered her too close to a dangerous shoreline. With Chris Vig at the helm, the injured little ship returned to the roots of her core product line, came off the rocks with a tide of her own making, and sailed defiantly out to sea again, providing jobs and paychecks anew. A good product line, and business built from it, is a life form unlike any other. It is not human, nor part of nature, yet it is so precious and hard to replace.

Leaving the office late on the last night of 1989, I sobbed like a heartbroken five-year-old kid. Good thing it was dark and no one saw me.

Now, more than 20 years later, I look at the forlorn buildings, vacant for several years, and smile, remembering the early days when we were never sure what would happen next.

The old place still has good life to give and yearns to see action again. I trust that time will heal those bereft old buildings with their tin siding and leaky roofs, just as time healed me. Eventually some brave entrepreneur will see opportunity amid the cobwebs, snap them up, and bring them roaring back to life. There are plenty of capable dreamers out there, especially in a great place like Madison. All that's needed is just one of them willing to take the leap, and then the old buildings will soon be humming with prosperity again. I can feel it in my bones. Sure as cold weather and Christmas eggnog, it's going to happen.

Acknowledgments

After selling WinterSilks in 1990, I dictated my journals, notes, and memories into a tape recorder and had them transcribed. This resulted in a hell of a mess: 1,500 unorganized pages that overflowed two cardboard file boxes—such an overwhelming sight that I left the file boxes in my office closet, untouched, for eight years. Every now and then I would peek inside only to recoil in near-horror. The magnitude of the organizational task was sobering. No way was I taking that project on.

When I met my life's soul mate—Laura Kellogg, M.B.A., Ph.D.—in 1998, she instinctively knew I needed to go back into the word business and share my adventure. I dug in my heels as best I could, but—in between volunteer medical transport flights for Air Lifeline and environmental sorties for LightHawk—I soon found myself freelancing for aviation magazines, hoping to sharpen lost skills. Magazine work was finite and fun, but crafting a book from the accumulation in those boxes? *Forget it*. I pretended to work on it for a few hours a month. Eventually, however, Laura saw to it that I faced up to the boxes.

This book is the result, and it was made immeasurably better by an invisible and talented team behind it. Laura read three drafts of the manuscript and encouraged me to continue when most other sane persons would have suggested I burn it. Bob Curry—Madison neighbor, athlete extraordinaire, and writing instructor—swam through two drafts and coached me on in-scene narration. Beth Lieberman read an early version and introduced me to reference texts on dialogue. Laurie Rosen read part of a later draft and taught me about sequence and structure. Peter Gelfan reviewed two drafts, sent me back for yet more rewrites, and then helped me craft a proper proposal. Nick Wallwork, publisher of John Wiley & Sons (Asia), read that proposal, immediately understood the book, and thereafter stood behind it. Wiley's laser-sharp word *samurai*, Kristi Hein, expertly copyedited the final manuscript. Joel Balbin at Wiley maneuvered it through production with good spirit and veteran planning. Ethan Friedman, my agent at LevelFiveMedia, helped guide the process. Any warts that remain can be blamed on me alone.

In addition to these wordsmiths, folks from WinterSilks' early years have my everlasting respect. Working with them made me understand why, through thick and thin, our capitalist-based world ticks resolutely on.

For a chapter-by-chapter discussion and tutorial, e-mail the author at ffarwell@sbcglobal.net and ask for a copy of "Lessons Learned."

Index